# 500 POPU

# TROPICAL PLANTS

PERIPLUS

This edition published in Asia in 1999
by Periplus Editions (HK) Ltd

All rights reserved. No part of this book may be
reproduced, stored in a retrieval system or transmitted
in any form or by any means, electronic, mechanical,
photocopying, recording or otherwise, without the
prior written permission of the publisher.

First published in Australia in 1999
by Random House Australia Pty Ltd

© text Random House Australia Pty Ltd 1999
© photographs Random House Australia Pty Ltd 1999

ISBN 962-593-454-5

Distributed by:
Berkeley Books Pte Ltd
5 Little Road  #08-01
Singapore 536983

Printed in Hong Kong

# CONTENTS

# Botanica

- **A must for all gardeners**
- **An invaluable and enduring reference**
- **Over 10,000 plants**
- **Fully illustrated in color throughout**

**Botanica** is the world's most authoritative, comprehensive and up-to-date single volume guide to plants for all gardeners and garden lovers that's lavishly illustrated throughout. Unrivalled in scope, **Botanica** features over 10,000 plants for you to choose from in its easy A to Z format that's fully illustrated in color throughout—from annuals, perennials, bulbs and roses, to trees and shrubs, ferns and palms, fruit and nut trees, orchids, cacti and succulents, lawns and ground covers, vegetables and herbs. Plus all the really practical information you need on care and cultivation from planting and propagating, to pest and diseases is at your fingertips. **Botanica** has been written in a fresh, easy-to-read style by a team of specialist plant experts and gardening writers.

### 1008 pages • 300 mm x 230 mm

## A TO Z OF GARDEN PLANTS

**PLANT HEADINGS**
*To make it easy to find the plant you are looking for, page headings on each spread indicate the first genus described on the left-hand page and the last genus on the right-hand page.*

**PHOTOGRAPHS**
*Photographs in* **Botanica** *illustrate colour, growth habits and other ornamental features of the plants.*

**CAPTIONS**
*Each photograph is captioned identifying the plant with its full botanical name.*

**MARGIN MARKERS**
*For ready reference,* **Botanica** *has been printed with colored alphabet tabs in the margin that move down the page to help you find the plant you are looking for.*

**GENUS ENTRIES**
In the A to Z section, plants are arranged in alphabetical order by genus. Entries include plant descriptions, geographical origin, cultivation, pests and diseases, height and spread and hardiness rating by zone.

# Introduction

# Hardiness Zone Map

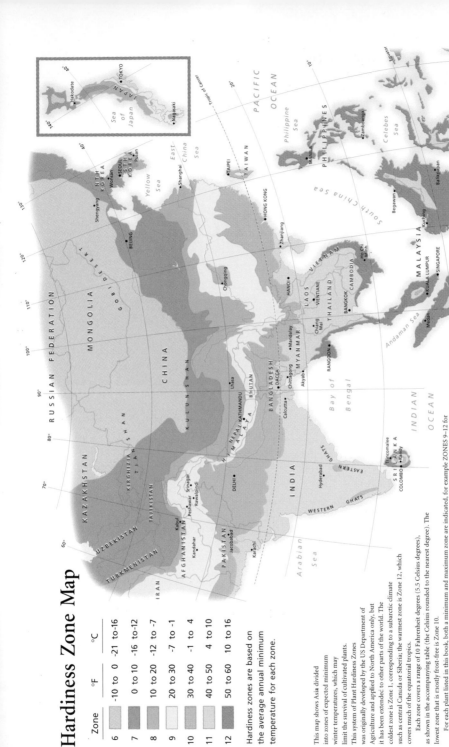

| Zone | °F | °C |
|------|-----|-----|
|  | -10 to 0 | -21 to -16 |
|  | 0 to 10 | -16 to -12 |
|  | 10 to 20 | -12 to -7 |
|  | 20 to 30 | -7 to -1 |
|  | 30 to 40 | -1 to 4 |
|  | 40 to 50 | 4 to 10 |
|  | 50 to 60 | 10 to 16 |

| 6 | 7 | 8 | 9 | 10 | 11 | 12 |

Hardiness zones are based on the average annual minimum temperature for each zone.

This map shows Asia divided into zones of expected minimum winter temperatures, which may limit the survival of cultivated plants. This system of Plant Hardiness Zones was originally developed by the US Department of Agriculture and applied to North America only, but it has been extended to other parts of the world. The coldest zone is Zone 1, corresponding to a subarctic climate such as central Canada or Siberia; the warmest zone is Zone 12, which covers much of the equatorial tropics.

Each zone covers a range of 10 Fahrenheit degrees (5.5 Celsius degrees), as shown in the accompanying table (the Celsius rounded to the nearest degree). The lowest zone that is mostly frost-free is Zone 10.

For each plant listed in this book, both a minimum and maximum zone are indicated, for example ZONES 9–12 for *Musa velutina*. This means that the plant will survive the average winter temperatures expected in at least the warmer parts of Zone 9, in which temperatures fall to 20°F (-7°C); but that it will also grow reasonably well in zones up to at least the cooler parts of Zone 12, where winter minimums are above 60°F (10°C). Of course, all the plants in this book are tropical plants and will not survive in cold climates unless they have the protection of a greenhouse.

These zones indicate only one part of a plant's climatic requirements. Other requirements are indicated in the text wherever possible.

What do we mean by 'tropical'? The tropics in the strict sense of the term are those parts of the world lying between the Tropic of Cancer and the Tropic of Capricorn; it is only here that the sun is ever directly overhead, so that a vertical pole casts no shadow. Because of their greater access to solar energy, the tropics are the hottest part of the world, and because the adjacent seas are warmer, they give off more moisture to the air and this is returned in the form of high rainfall in many parts of the tropics. However, this rainfall (and associated high humidity) can vary enormously, sometimes over quite short distances, and moreover is often strongly seasonal. Not all parts of the tropics are hot; the elevation of many land areas well above sea-level is accompanied by a rapid falling-off of both maximum and minimum temperatures—for example in Ecuador and Tanzania where there are snow-clad peaks virtually right on the equator.

Even the lowland tropics encompass very different garden environments. A week without rain in Singapore is rare, and for several months, it rains almost without stopping; high humidity is almost constant. In Bangkok, by contrast, the rainy season lasts for just six months and even then there are likely to be long dry spells; both the temperature and the humidity drop with noticeable effect during the so-called cool season. One visible result of such differences is that moisture-loving plants thrive in Singapore, growing with abandon almost everywhere, and at any time the island republic is far greener than the Thai capital. On the other hand, most flowering trees like the beautiful flamboyant *(Delonix regia)* and the

The placement of *Ixora chinensis, Bougainvillea, Typha* and *Coccoloba uvifera* around the pond give this garden a feeling of tranquility.

Indian laburnum, or golden shower (*Cassia fistula*), which need a prolonged dry season to bloom best, are in general far more spectacular in Bangkok than they are in Singapore.

Honolulu, far from Southeast Asia but also in the tropics, offers different conditions. Blessed with rich volcanic soil, constant warm temperatures, and quite varied topography, it supports a number of ornamentals that, so far at least, have frustrated the best efforts of eager Thai and Singaporean gardeners. But those plants are greatly outnumbered by many others that thrive in all three climates.

Whatever the problems of individual areas, and the adjustments that must be made because of them, there is no doubt that certain things are basic to nearly all tropical gardens. Or that with more than 200,000 different species native to the tropics and subtropics, a gardener in any warm-weather country has an extra-ordinarily rich and varied stock from which to draw in creating a memorable landscape.

## PLANT MATERIAL

The European fascination with tropical plants was a direct result of the epic voyages of early explorers. In search of India and the rare spices that commanded such high prices on Western markets, Christopher Columbus instead found the New World and, in it, such unknown wonders as *Ananas comosus*, the pineapple, and *Capsicum*, the chilli pepper. Neither, of course, was unknown to the natives of the places where they originated—the chilli pepper had been a part of the South and Central American diet for over 7,000 years—but they were new to Europe, and also to far more distant places like India and Southeast Asia, where they would appear in a remarkably short time.

Even before this, there had been a steady, if slower and less spectacular, movement of plants about the tropical world. Travelling in giant outrigger canoes, Polynesians had brought the green *Cordyline*, which they called the 'ti' plant, to Hawaii and made it an emblem of royalty. More systematic journeys by

Europeans were fascinated with tropical plants. The chilli pepper, *Capsicum annuum*, was one of the great wonders of the 'New World'.

The giant waterlily, *Victoria amazonica*, was a favorite in 19th century glasshouses.

Westerners accelerated this process, though they left few records of just when and how. We know that a brilliant Brazilian creeper was named after the eighteenth century French navigator Louis de Bougainville, but not how it spread so rapidly to every warm country in the world. Nor do we know what ship (probably Portuguese, possibly Spanish) carried the first branch of a frangipani *(Plumeria)* tree from its native central America to Asia, where it became a standard in both Buddhist and Hindu gardens. (We do know, however, that it was named after Charles Plumier (1646-1706), a French botanist.)

Once European countries acquired colonies in the tropics botanic gardens were established, originally for the purpose of experimenting with new economic crops. Pamplemousses, the first of such gardens, set up on the island of Mauritius in 1735, helped develop the sugar industry there, while Brazilian rubber *(Hevea brasiliensis)* famously transformed Malaya's economy after a handful of seedlings was successfully introduced to the Singapore Botanic Garden. But such establishments, which also included others in Java, India, Sri Lanka, and the West Indies, brought in new ornamental plants as well, often displaying them in imaginative ways far from their native habitats.

The perfection of glasshouses that could approximate tropical conditions in nineteenth century Great Britain, France, and other countries led to a passion for exotics. Serious botanists and collectors for commercial plant firms went out to bring back thousands of new specimens that were beautiful, rare, or, in some cases, like the evil-smelling *Amorphophallus*, simply odd. The Duke of Devonshire sent an agent to south India to acquire a seedling of *Amherstia nobilis*,

said to be the most beautiful of all flowering tropical trees, for which he built a special glasshouse at Chatsworth. From the wilds of South America came the giant waterlily, first christened *Victoria regia* but later renamed *V. amazonica;* it, too, was given a house of its own at Chatsworth and was first induced to bloom there.

For many of the most decorative plants, introduction into a glasshouse was the first step in a process that led on to intensive selection or hybridization and eventual acclaim as lovingly tended house plants. Those with unusual foliage—*Codiaeum,* for example, as well as *Caladium, Dracaena, Dieffenbachia,* and *Cordyline*—were particular favorites, but flowering shrubs and small trees—*Ixora, Hibiscus,* and *Plumeria*—also became popular. In due course these returned to the tropics in varieties often quite different from the original but just as welcome in a garden as in a drawing room.

Today, thanks to improved transportation and demand, tropical gardeners almost everywhere have an exceptionally wide choice of plant material, much of it introduced within relatively recent times. A garden in Bali, for instance, is likely to offer an international display—*Heliconia* from South America, red ginger *(Alpinia purpurata)* from Malaysia (but probably in the form of an Hawaiian hybrid), flamboyant *(Delonix)* from Madagascar, bottlebrush *(Callistemon)* from Australia, *Plumbago* from South Africa—all of them growing with the vigor of native plants.

## GARDEN DESIGN
Traditionally, most tropical gardens were very practical in content and almost non-existent in terms of design. Royal palaces, of course, were exceptions; as a rule, these did have usually rather formal

*Heliconia stricta* is a striking tropical plant and certainly adds vibrancy to the garden.

plantings aimed at creating a pleasurable atmosphere, with fragrant flowers and cooling water features. So, too, were some religious compounds like those of Buddhist temples, which incorporated plants with symbolic significance (the lotus, for instance, or the sacred bodhi tree, *Ficus religiosa*) and often attempted mini-forests that were conducive to meditation. Those of ordinary people, however, were on the whole devoted to specimens that served some useful function, culinary or medicinal, and little thought was given to the aesthetics of arrangement.

Though local touches may linger, like the Thai fondness for shrubs clipped into ornamental or grotesque shapes (a borrowing from the Chinese), it is clear that tropical-garden design as we know

it today is primarily the result of European colonization. It was then, mostly in the eighteenth and nineteenth centuries, that certain concepts were introduced, the effects of which can still be seen. These include the well-trimmed lawn—a feature previously unknown in the tropics or, for that matter, in India, China, or Japan—as well as the massed planting of specimens chosen for foliage or flowers or both. Many of the public areas of famous botanic gardens like those in Singapore and at Bogor in Indonesia seem to have been inspired by such great glasshouses as Kew's Palm House, which displayed their exotic specimens in combinations suggesting at once a 'tame jungle' and also a variation on an informal English country garden.

Early colonial gardens in the tropics were self-conscious efforts at creating familiar landscapes with unfamiliar material, sometimes extending to beds of unhappy temperate annuals to suggest the seasonal changes of back home. Nearly all contained lawns, herbaceous borders, clipped hedges, and the almost obligatory bed of mixed *Canna* in blazing colors. Few outside the often bold botanic garden experiments were very memorable, but they were sufficiently influential to erase any traditional styles, even in places like Thailand which never became a colony.

Over the years, however, these predictable arrangements have evolved into more imaginative landscapes, using tropical plants not merely as substitutes for those of colder places but rather for their own distinctive form and beauty. Though the underlying concept of a 'tame jungle' can still be found in many, the general effect is far more varied and individual.

Inevitably, the basic design depends on the size. This is true, of course, of gardens anywhere; but it acquires an added importance in the tropics, where growth is almost continuous and a seemingly modest shrub can triple in size over the course of a single rainy season. The days of huge compounds with half a dozen full-time gardeners—tropical gardens require an exceptional amount of pruning, weeding, mulching, and other work—are over in most places, and with them has gone the space to enjoy many of the larger flowering trees like angsana *(Pterocarpus)*, flamboyant *(Delonix)*, and rain tree *(Samanea)* that once spread their capacious branches over sweeping lawns. There are, however, other beautiful trees that can be equally rewarding in even a courtyard garden.

Before drawing up any plan, study the site carefully to answer certain questions. Are there neighboring buildings that need to be screened? How much sun does the garden receive (this will play an important role in plant selection)? Do you need or want an open area to set off plantings (the answer, except in very small gardens, is usually yes); and if so, should it be a lawn, a water feature, or perhaps merely an expanse of paving stones or pebbles? Do you want to have vines (some of the most effective tropicals fall into this category) and, if so, how do you want to display them—on a wall, a pergola, a trellis over a walkway? More than in most temperate places, tropical gardens are often extensions of the house, wrapping around verandas, patios, or living rooms and visible both night and day; decide what kind of effects—dense, sparse, dramatic, understated—you want to see from such vantage points and what plants might be used to achieve them.

It is always important to familiarize yourself as much as possible with the

*Canna* × *generalis* hybrids come in a glorious array of colors and are very robust.

plant material available. A book like the present one, giving the proper names and growing conditions, is essential. Others, showing planted gardens in various places, are helpful in determining how combinations are likely to look, especially when they reach mature size. (The annals of tropical gardening contain many a sad story of newcomers who thought *Ficus elastica*, or some other popular house plant, was a moderate-sized shrub, only to find it soon taking over both garden and house.)

Finally, visit as many local nurseries as you can and see the available stock. Thanks to their rapid growth, you will often find quite large specimens, including trees, that make it possible to install an almost 'instant' garden. Don't be afraid to experiment; one of the delights of tropical gardening is that anything can be taken out and replaced with something likely to grow just as fast and create a similar effect.

## PREPARING THE SITE

More often than not, you will have to do something about the soil in which your garden is to grow. Tropical plants need plenty of food and good drainage, and the lack of these is usually due to the medium provided. It may be heavy clay or porous sand; it may contain construction rubble or the invasive roots of a former or existing tree. Even in the best conditions, its nutrients may have been exhausted by overuse and heavy rains. Correction of such conditions is never easy and usually not cheap, but it is essential for healthy growth in the future and, if done properly, it will last for a long time.

Start by digging up and turning the existing soil, breaking up large lumps into smaller ones. The depths may vary depending on what is to be planted in different areas, but as a rule dig at least 6 in (15 cm) down for lawns and twice that for most beds.

Next, the turned soil should be improved by adding material that will

A good quality fertilizer is essential for tropical plants and should be applied both before planting and afterwards at regular intervals.

lighten it (in the case of clay) and enrich it. Sand from a riverbed (never from the seacoast) is good for lightening heavy soil, thus creating better drainage, though it usually contains little in the way of food. Old sawdust or grated coconut fiber (available in many tropical places) is also useful. Best of all is good topsoil if it can be obtained, or, if not, pre-mixed potting soil sold by the bag in most places. Whatever is used should be well mixed with the old soil in a ratio of about two parts of the new material to one part of the old.

At this point, some gardeners in heavy-clay areas recommend the addition of hydrated lime, which reduces acidity and helps break up the clay. This should not be dug in but sprinkled over and allowed to penetrate through rainfall or watering, at least a month before plants are installed.

The final step is adding fertilizers. These come in many forms, both organic and inorganic, and are vital for giving new plants the nutrients they need. It is also something that will have to be done at regular intervals in the future, particularly at the end and at the beginning of the rainy season; unlike those in temperate countries, tropical plants enjoy no winter rest period and so need frequent replenishment of their food supplies. Well-rotted poultry or cow manure is excellent, mixed at the rate of about 4 lbs (1.8 kg) to a square yard (0.8 square metre), and so is bone meal, which has a high phosphate content; if these are unavailable, use one of the several compound inorganic fertilizers available in pellet form, well watered into the soil.

Even a small tropical garden yields a steady supply of leaves, grass cuttings, and other soft material, and because of the warmth and moisture it is easy to start a compost heap. Find a place for this if at all possible (compact compost makers made of fiberglass can now be found in many places, taking up very little space), and once it starts acting— i.e. rotting—use the contents regularly to mulch various beds.

## PLANT SELECTION AND PLANTING

This is necessarily a very broad subject and depends on the size of the space, climate, location, and such personal matters as taste and whether you plan to work regularly in the garden or prefer something that requires minimum maintenance. A few general points would probably apply in any event, however. One of the most often overlooked is the importance of sunlight. Nearly all flowering shrubs and trees require a good deal of sun—at least half a day and preferably more—and so do lawns and most water plants; if you want reliable blooms, you have to allow for this, even if it means giving up that large handsome tree that seemed so appealing. On the other hand, a shady garden need not be relentlessly green; one of the glories of the tropics is the vast range of splendidly varied foliage plants, by means of which you can create a wide range of bold and subtle colors without a single prominent flower.

Another point, already mentioned, is the ultimate size of plants and their growing habits. A garden that looks well-established the day it is installed— quite easy to achieve in most places— isn't going to stay that way for very long. Trees are going to get taller and put out more horizontal branches, and specimens that multiply by spreading root tubers—for example, heliconias, gingers, and other members of that family are going to escape even a large bed unless kept carefully checked. Most

bamboos are going to spread rapidly, too, shrubs are going to increase in girth as well as height, vines are going to clamber into nearby trees—and all this is going to happen with what, to a temperate gardener, seems indecent speed. Allow for it in your plant selection, or be prepared for frequently changing effects.

### Trees and palms

Trees and palms are important not only for their intrinsic beauty but also for the scale they bring to a garden and the role they play in screening. Some of the large specimens that once graced spacious gardens of the past may not be feasible in more moderate sites, but there is no

The rich green of the leaves and the brilliant scarlet of the leaf bases make *Cyrtostachys renda* a very popular ornamental palm.

shortage of smaller ones to fulfil the same purpose.

Popular among medium-sized flowering trees are several species of *Cassia* (pink or yellow flowers), *Plumeria* (white, yellow, pink, or red), *Lagerstroemia* (pale to deep mauve or pink), *Tabebuia* (pink or yellow), *Saraca* (yellow-orange to scarlet), *Erythrina* (red-orange, red, apricot, or, in one species, white), *Bauhinia* (purple or white), *Cochlospermum* (yellow), *Jacaranda* (blue-mauve), and *Peltophorum* (yellow). All these are fairly fast growing and most require a pronounced dry season to bloom profusely; a few are deciduous, dropping their leaves usually just before flowering.

Both trees and palms can serve as useful screens along the perimeter of a garden. *Polyalthia longifolia*, for example, takes up relatively little room but grows to a height of 50 ft (15 m), with long, glossy-green leaves; a row planted close together will soon form a fairly solid wall to block an undesired view. Most of the taller, tufted palms, which grow in clumps, can be used for the same purpose — *Caryota mitis*, the fishtail palm, and *Ptychosperma macarthurii*, the Macarthur palm, are two of the most common.

Palms in general lend a truly tropical note to any garden, and certain specimens — *Bismarckia nobilis*, for example, with its huge, silvery, fan-shaped leaves; *Phoenix roebelenii*, the pygmy date palm, with feathery, fern-like fronds; and *Cyrtostachys renda*, with bright scarlet leaf sheaths — can be used as dramatic focal points.

The idea of being able to walk out and pick a ripe fruit from their own tree proves irresistible to many tropical gardeners, with the result that plantings often include a mango or two, an avocado, or a mangosteen. These are not always wholly satisfactory. Fruit trees often require special treatment, and the space they occupy, especially in a small garden, may not justify their seasonal bounty. The breadfruit *(Artocarpus altilis)* is a handsome specimen in its own right, providing excellent shade with its large, dark-green leaves, but it does require ample room to assume a good shape.

When planting a tree or palm, dig a large hole, about 3 ft (1 m) in diameter and depth, and fill it with good, rich soil to a height about 6 in (15 cm) above the desired level; water for at least a week to allow the soil to settle. Then plant the tree, making sure that the stem is not covered more than 2 in (5 cm) by soil. Taller trees should be firmly staked until their root systems are well established. Water regularly, and for the first year or so apply fertilizer every few months, each feeding being a little further away as the roots expand.

### Flowering shrubs and creepers
Given the right conditions — mainly sunlight and good drainage — there is almost no limit to the color combinations available to a tropical gardener through flowering shrubs and creepers. Those mentioned here are only some of the most widely used out of the thousands now under cultivation.

Few can beat the familiar *Hibiscus* for regular displays of blooms, especially on the two main species, *H. rosa-sinensis* and *H. schizopetalus*, and hybrids derived from them. Colors range from bright scarlet to mauve, and there are double as well as single varieties; *H. mutabilis*, on which the flowers change from pure white to dark pink during the course of a day, becomes a small tree given time and careful pruning. Other dependable bloomers are *Mussaenda* (red, pink, or white), *Barleria* (mauve and white),

No tropical garden is complete without a Hibiscus. *Hibiscus tiliaceus* flowers for most of the year.

*Pachystachys* (yellow), *Brunfelsia* (lavender blue when they open, white by the end of day), *Clerodendrum* (red on *C. paniculatum*, pale blue on *C. ugandense*), *Plumbago* (blue or white), *Ixora* (red, white, pink, yellow, and orange, in both large and dwarf forms), *Duranta* (mauve or white, with bright-orange berries), and the gardenia-like *Tabernaemontana* (pure white).

For fragrance, plant *Gardenia augusta* (which does not, however, like very hot climates), *Murraya paniculata* (popularly known as orange jessamine), *Cananga odorata* (actually a small tree, though there is a small variety), *Cestrum nocturnum* (a night-bloomer, as its name suggests, and very potently scented), or one of several varieties of *Jasminum*.

Undoubtedly the most famous of tropical creepers is *Bougainvillea*, the 'flowers' of which—actually bracts— bring vivid splashes of color to countless gardens. Over the years, cultivars have made it available in a rainbow spectrum, from magenta to snow white, sometimes two colors appearing on the same plant. Bougainvillea is commonly seen sprawling over walls or down from raised beds, but with frequent pruning it can be used for a hedge or as a standard.

Walls, trellises, or other supports can be transformed with such flowering creepers as *Solandra maxima*, the cup of gold; yellow *Allamanda*, which also comes in a shrub form; multi-colored *Ipomoea*, the morning glory; *Quisqualis indica*, the red, white, and pink Rangoon creeper; white or mauve *Thunbergia grandiflora*; or *Petrea volubilis*, with mauve-blue sprays that are the closest thing to a wisteria to be found in the tropics. Under the right conditions, two extraordinary jungle climbers worth trying are *Strongylodon macrobotrys*, with spectacular clusters of jade-green flowers, and *Mucuna bennettii*, the New Guinea creeper, on which similar blooms are bright red-orange. A creeping member of the *Ficus* genus, *F. pumila*, makes a solid, moss-like covering for walls in a sunny location.

### Foliage plants

Numerous tropical plants are grown primarily for their striking foliage, effective either in a mixed bed with flowering specimens or to create interesting color and texture on their own.

Some that can be used either in sun or partial shade include *Acalypha*, with leaves that range from green-and-white to brown with a pink edge; *Codiaeum*, also a popular house plant because of its seemingly endless variety of leaf colors and shapes; *Cordyline*, the Hawaiian 'ti' plant, of which numerous color variants have been raised; bromeliads, a large family that includes the pineapple and also some 50 other genera and 2,500 recognized species; *Philodendron bipinnatifidum*, a self-heading member of the family with huge, dramatic leaves; and *Dracaena*, which comes in many forms of which the familiar 'corn plant', seen in so many homes, is only one.

Foliage plants are particularly valuable in shady areas, where most flowering plants are not successful. Among the most often used for such purposes are *Dieffenbachia*, which has white, cream, or yellow markings on the leaves; *Aglaonema*, a low-growing specimen with patterned leaves that makes a good ground cover; *Maranta* and *Calathea*, two other low growers that look similar with their intricate markings; *Polyscias*, with leaves in a remarkable variety of shapes; *Asplenium*, popularly called the bird's nest fern; and *Schefflera*, which has over 700 species of assorted sizes and habits.

### Plants for tropical effect

There are a number of beautiful plants that are neither trees nor shrubs but that are essential in creating the sort of effects most people associate with a tropical garden. Orchids, for example, by far the largest family of flowering plants, are mostly native to warm, humid places and can provide wonderfully exotic splashes of color whether grown on trees or displayed in a special enclosure of their own. Bromeliads, too are a huge family of some 52 genera and more than 2,500 recognized species, and with their highly varied leaves and often spectacular flowers are effective in massed plantings (especially in small gardens) or as dramatic potted specimens on terraces. (In Hawaii, where they grow with notable vigor, there are gardens that consist almost entirely of various bromeliads and yet present a surprisingly wide range of textures and colors.)

Some of the most popular plants used to create a tropical mood are members of the large *Heliconia* genus, mostly native to South America but now found in gardens throughout the tropics. These range from low-growing to tall robust plants, some with erect displays of colored bracts, others with hanging flowers, still others grown principally for their decorative foliage. Given rich, moist but well-drained soil and adequate sunlight, heliconias always make a memorable display, though gardeners who favor a low-maintenance approach should remember that they tend to spread rampantly and can become invasive in small areas.

Close relatives to the heliconias are members of the Musaceae or banana family. A clump of real fruiting bananas outside a patio is a dramatic sight, but for smaller gardens some of the varieties grown for their flowers or leaves (*M. ornata*, for example) may be more suitable. Other popular exotics include *Alpinia*, grown either for its prominent flower bracts or for its striking variegated leaves; *Ravenala*, the traveller's palm, almost an emblem of the tropics and also useful for screening; the impressive torch ginger (*Etlingera elatior*), with flowers that rise straight from the ground; *Costus*, which grows in a spiral pattern with flowers at the tops of the stalks; *Strelitzia*, the famous bird of paradise; and various aroids, especially *Anthurium* and *Alocasia*.

## SEASIDE GARDENS

Planting a garden on a tropical seashore presents special problems. The soil is often little more than sand, water can be scarce (particularly on islands), and seasonal monsoon winds can be murderous on delicate ornamentals.

Proper conditioning of the growing areas is more important in such places than almost anywhere else. Plenty of humus and other organic material will make a dramatic difference; so will as much topsoil as you can afford to bring in from other places. In designing both house and garden, try to provide wind-screening for areas where you want arrangements that look attractive all year round; this can be done through planting, usually of native species able to withstand the sea winds (look around at wild areas to identify these) or architecturally with walls or other features.

In selecting plants, concentrate on drought-resistant species, a category that is far broader than many might suppose. The graceful coconut palm is an obvious choice, though it should be kept clear of buildings (or have ripening fruit regularly removed). Useful seaside trees that require little or no care include *Casuarina* species, *Hibiscus tiliaceus* (known as the sea hibiscus), *Coccoloba uvifera* (the sea grape), *Scaevola taccada* (both low tree and large shrub), *Terminalia catappa* (the sea almond), *Barringtonia asiatica* (excellent for screening), and several species of *Ficus. Plumeria, Cassia, Delonix, Lagerstroemia,* and *Erythrina* may need some protection from the wind, but bloom most spectacularly under such dry conditions.

Both *Bougainvillea* and *Allamanda* thrive by the sea, even in exposed situations, and so do species of *Crinum, Lantana, Adenium, Sansevieria, Catharanthus* (Madagascar periwinkle), most succulents like *Kalanchoe* and *Agave,* and several ground covers such as *Portulaca* and *Wedelia.*

## CONTAINER GARDENING

A considerable amount of tropical gardening is done in containers, not only small ones like pots on balconies and strategically placed around patios and terraces to show off prize specimens, but also large ones that are built-in features of many houses, hotels, and other structures.

The key to success with any container, as in the garden itself, is a good, nu-

The stately *Casuarina glauca* requires very little care and is ideal for a seaside garden.

tritious growing medium and adequate drainage. Pre-mixed potting soil is available in most places and saves a good deal of time and labor, though for really large containers it is probably still best to mix your own. This should consist of good earth (preferably baked to kill any weeds or pests it might contain), well-rotted manure or a good substitute, compost, and river sand, in a ratio of 2–1–1–1. At the bottom of the container there should be a layer of broken shards, gravel, or other material to prevent roots from clogging the drainage holes; the depth of this layer depends on the container size and may be 12 in (30 cm) or more in really large ones.

Most potted plants should be watered daily and regularly fed either with compost or inorganic fertilizers in pellet form; some, however, like *Bougainvillea* and other seaside plants—the best choices for high-rise balconies that receive wind and sun—need to dry out to bloom well. Water should never be allowed to stand in trays or saucers that may be placed under pots on terraces, which is not only bad for the plants but breeds mosquitoes as well.

## MAINTENANCE AND PROPAGATION

However careful the plant selection, there is really no such thing as a maintenance-free tropical garden. Continuous and often rapid growth means there is nearly always some chore to be done—weeding, pruning, raking up leaves, removing dead branches—and there are some otherwise desirable plants that require frequent attention. The stalks of heliconias and gingers, for instance, must be cut back to the ground after flowering, while some ground covers like *Wedelia* need regular trimming to keep them from becoming leggy.

Pruning is necessary to induce more flowering in many shrubs and creepers and also to maintain a desired shape. Invest in good equipment for this—

A layer of mulch conserves moisture, saves water and provides extra nutrition.

certainly strong hand shears, probably hedge shears, possibly a saw for larger tree branches—and keep them clean and sharp. In places where there is a pronounced division between wet and dry seasons, the best time for heavy pruning is when the rains stop, though in other areas it might go on more or less all the time when needed. Don't hesitate to prune drastically; most shrubs will quickly recover, flower more profusely, and have a better shape by this method than by the occasional removal of a few tall branches. Hedges, especially formal ones, should probably be shaped three or four times a year, informal ones at least twice.

Watering is important in prolonged dry periods, especially for more delicate plants, lawns, and ground covers. Ideally, this should be a good soaking rather than a light sprinkling, which mostly does little more than encourage surface root growth. A layer of mulch is a great help in conserving moisture and saving on water use.

Finally, there is the problem of pests, a whole multitude of them—mites, thrips, stem borers, leafminers, aphids, caterpillars, mealybugs, snails, and assorted fungi, to mention only some. Whether to spray or not to spray is a hotly debated topic among tropical gardeners, and the ultimate decision is up to the individual; with most, probably, it comes down to spraying only when absolutely necessary but admitting that occasionally it is necessary. It helps, though, to keep the garden as clean as possible, to inspect new plants carefully when buying them, and to hand-pick as many leaf eaters as possible; in a number of places, too, there are organizations that offer expert advice on pesticide-free gardening.

Propagation of tropical plants is by

one or another of a variety of methods.
Perhaps the easiest for shrubs is through
cuttings, either soft or hard wood, which
are then placed to root in a mixture of 3
parts river sand and 1 part compost; as
an alternative, some gardeners advocate
wrapping the base of the cuttings with
damp sphagnum moss and putting them
in sealed plastic bags until they root.
Dipping them into one of the now widely
available hormone rooting powders is
also beneficial.

Layering and marcotting are popular
methods with shrubs and trees that are
hard to root from cuttings. The first
involves simply pegging a low branch to
the ground and covering it with earth
until it roots. In marcotting (often used
to produce quite large plants of selected
fruit varieties) the outer bark of a
section of branch is removed with a
sharp knife and the area covered first
with moist soil, then with moss or
coconut fibre, finally with plastic, tied
tightly; the soil must be kept moist until
roots appear, after which the branch can
be removed below the marcot.

A number of plants, such as heliconias,
cannas, gingers, and some tufted palms,
are propagated by division of growing
shoots, or suckers, that emerge from the
underground roots. These should be
severed with a sharp tool and placed in
pots until they are of sufficient size to be
planted.

Seeds can be sown in pots or pans in
light soil—sterilized soil, compost, and
sand at a ratio of 1–1–2 is a good mixture
for all but very tiny seeds. It should be
kept in mind, though, that many seeds
quickly lose their viability in the tropics
and should be planted as quickly as
possible after collection; also that in the
case of some flowering trees seeds do not
always breed true as far as color is
concerned.

Layering is a popular method of propagation. Peg a low branch to the
ground and cover with soil until it roots.

## PLANT NAMES

The proper names of tropical plants, like
those of any other, consist of the genus
and the species, both in Latin, sometimes
followed by the name of a particular
cultivar, which may be in any language.
These names constitute a universal
language and are thus far more useful
than popular ones, which vary from
place to place and are usually more
colorful than accurate. It might be useful
to know, however, that many tropical
plant names have changed over the
years, some in quite recent times, so
older books on the subject may not agree
with newer ones. *Brugmansia*, for example,
used to be *Datura*, *Catharanthus rosea*
used to be *Vinca rosea*, and *Etlingera elatior*
(the torch ginger) has been, at one time
or another, *Nicolaia elatior*, *Phaeomeria
magnifica*, and *Phaeomeria speciosa*. In the
present book, these older names are
sometimes listed as synonyms under the
current ones.

CHAPTER 1

# Annuals & Perennials

## ACHASMA

This genus of gingers from tropical Southeast Asia is hardly known in cultivation but often catches the eye of travelers through rich lowland rainforests. It is one of several genera that characteristically have very tall leafy shoots springing at intervals from a thick, usually buried rhizome, and quite separate flowering stems, from the same rhizome but often far shorter or sometimes virtually sitting on the ground. They often have brilliantly colored flowers. Some botanists now regard *Achasma* as a synonym of *Etlingera*.

### Cultivation

They need very warm, humid and sheltered conditions beneath trees or in a courtyard, and a moist, humus-rich soil. Propagate by division of rhizomes.

### Achasma macrocheilos

syn. *Achasma megalocheilos*

### Yellow earth ginger

Native to Malaysia, this species has leafy stems up to 20 ft (6 m) tall, but the small head of several flowers sits just above the litter of the forest floor. The large 'lip' of each flower is strikingly bicolored in scarlet and yellow. ZONES 11–12.

*Achasma macrocheilos*

## AECHMEA

This genus consists of over 170 species from Central and South America. Most are epiphytes or rock-dwellers, conserving water in the vase-like structure formed by the rosette of stiff leaves, which may be barred, striped or otherwise patterned, and prickly margined in some such as *Aechmea agavifolia*. Flowers are small but often intensely colored, in dense spikes that vary greatly in size and structure but always with numerous overlapping bracts that usually contrast in color with the flowers—a typical example is *Aechmea* 'Mary Brett'. The berry-like fruits are often colorful as well.

### Cultivation

They grow happily outdoors, most preferring filtered sun. Despite being epiphytes, they will grow on the ground as long as soil is open and high in humus, and the bed is raised slightly. Propagate by division (separating 'pups' with a sharp knife), or from seed.

*Aechmea agavifolia*

Aechmea chantinii

Aechmea 'Mary Brett'

Aechmea chantinii 'Black'

Aechmea fasciata

### Aechmea chantinii

Known as the Queen of the Aechmeas, this species from northwestern South America has vivid red and yellow flowers rising above long, drooping, salmon orange bracts. The rosettes consist of olive green leaves often with silvery gray, dark green or almost black banding. The flowers are followed by blue or white berries. It has an upright, urn-like habit and reaches a height and spread of 12–24 in (30–60 cm). 'Black' is one of several cultivars. ZONES 11–12.

### Aechmea fasciata
#### Silver vase

Reminiscent of a formal flower arrangement, this Brazilian species has a 'vase' of silvery gray leaves irregularly barred green, from which emerges a short, broad cluster of mauve-blue flowers among crowded, spiky bracts of a most delicate clear pink. The rosettes, up to about 18 in (45 cm) high, do not clump up much. ZONES 10–12.

*Aechmea nidularioides*

*Aechmea pineliana*

### Aechmea nidularioides

This species has strap-like leaves about 24 in (60 cm) long; the flowering stalk terminates in a rosette of red bracts at the center of which sit yellow flowers in an eye-catching display. ZONES 10–12.

### Aechmea pineliana

Attractive grown in bright light or full sun where the foliage takes on a deep rose color, this south Brazilian species grows to a height and spread of 12–15 in (30–38 cm). It has a dense upright habit with stiff, pointed gray-green leaves edged with red spines. The yellow flowers form a short, cylindrical head and are borne above the scarlet stems and bracts. On maturity the flowers turn black. It is sun and cold tolerant and adapts well to outdoor conditions. ZONES 10–12.

### Aechmea 'Royal Wine'

This is a popular hybrid cultivar which has adapted well to indoor culture. It has strap-like, bright green leaves with red

Aechmea 'Royal Wine'

Aechmea 'Shining Light'

bases and a slightly branched, pendent inflorescence with dark blue petals. The fruit is orange. ZONES 11–12.

### Aechmea 'Shining Light'
This hybrid cultivar has a broad rosette of leaves that are glossy, pale green above and wine red on the undersides. It produces a large, about 24 in (60 cm) high, much-branched panicle, with bright red bracts and numerous small red flowers. ZONES 11–12.

## ALPINIA
### Ornamental ginger
Of Asian and Pacific origin, these plants are widely cultivated in tropical and subtropical gardens for their showy blooms, some as commercial cut flowers. They grow from fleshy rhizomes to form large clumps. The aboveground shoots are in fact pseudostems consisting of tightly furled leaf bases as in cannas and bananas. The large thin leaves form 2 rows. Although strictly speaking perennials, they do not die back and can be used in the garden like a shrub.

### Cultivation
Alpinias appreciate part-shade, a warm, moist atmosphere and rich soil. Propagate by division.

Alpinia galanga

### Alpinia galanga
#### Galangal, Thai ginger

Although most alpinias are grown for ornament and are not regarded as edible, this Southeast Asian species is the source of an important spice, a vital ingredient of Thai cooking in particular. It is the thick, white-fleshed rhizome that is used, either freshly grated, dried or powdered ('laos powder'), to add a subtle piquancy to dishes such as curries. The plant makes a clump of leafy stems 6 ft (1.8 m) high. The flowers, white with pink markings, are not very showy.
ZONES 11–12.

### Alpinia purpurata
#### Red ginger

From the Pacific Islands, this species produces showy spikes of small white flowers among vivid scarlet bracts throughout the year. The glossy leaves are narrow and lance-shaped. New plantlets sprout among the flower bracts and take root when the dying flower stems fall to the ground under the weight of the growing plantlets. The plants grow to 10 ft (3 m) tall.
ZONES 11–12.

### Alpinia zerumbet
syns *Alpinia nutans, A. speciosa*
#### Shell ginger

This evergreen, clump-forming perennial grows to around 10 ft (3 m) with a spread of 5–10 ft (1.5–3 m). It has long, densely massed stems with broad, green leaves. The drooping sprays of flowers, starting as waxy white or ivory buds, open one at a time to reveal yellow lips with pink- or red-marked throats. 'Variegata' has leaves irregularly striped yellow; it tends to be lower growing.
ZONES 10–12.

## AMORPHOPHALLUS

The inflorescence of these plants consists of a large encircling bract (spathe) from the center of which emerges a fleshy spike of tiny flowers, the male and female flowers arranged in separate zones. The spike is large and often knob-like, and is the source of the foul smell given off by many of the species when in flower. They are leafless in the tropical dry season,

Alpinia purpurata

Alpinia zerumbet

dying back to a large underground tuber. At the start of the wet season they send up their flowers, shortly followed by a single, deeply lobed leaf that may be quite large and long stalked.

### Cultivation

These plants prefer a sheltered, humid position and deep, fertile, humus-rich soil. Keep well watered in the growing season. After the foliage dies back, the tuber should be kept fairly dry. Propagation is mainly by transplanted tubers, which usually multiply by small offsets.

### Amorphophallus paeoniifolius
#### Elephant yam, telingo potato

This species has a solitary leaf up to 3 ft (1 m) long on a dark green, pale-spotted stalk. The purple and green, white-spotted spathe, up to 10 in (25 cm) across, has a protruding spadix with a very large, spongy, deep purple terminal knob. ZONES 11–12.

## ANTHURIUM
### Flamingo flower

This is a huge and diverse genus of evergreen, shrubby or climbing epiphytes in the arum family. Familiar as florists'

plants and cut flowers are 2 to 3 species with typically brilliant red flat spathes held above broad leathery leaves; selection and breeding has broadened the range of colors to include white, pink and orange. The actual flowers are the tiny bumps gathered around the central spadix.

### Cultivation

Anthuriums are easy to grow. Indoors, they need bright light, high humidity and constant warmth and moisture to flower. Plant outdoors in a humid position, in well-drained, peaty soil in full or part-shade out of the wind. Keep soil moist but not soggy. Propagate from rhizomes. Potted plants need dividing and repotting every few years.

### Anthurium andraeanum

Grown for its large, brilliantly colored spathe with raised veining, this species grows to about 24 in (60 cm) high, with large heart-shaped leaves. The plants only produce one or two flowers at a time but they bloom all year. The spathes, so glossy they appear varnished, are typically bright red, but other colors have been bred including pink, and green marbled with red. ZONES 11–12.

*Amorphophallus paeoniifolius*

*Anthurium andraeanum*

### Anthurium scherzerianum
### Flamingo flower

Growing to 24–30 in (60–75 cm), this species typically has red spathes, with curled spadices, but cultivars vary from white to pink to very dark red, sometimes with paler spots. The elongated, rather dull green leaves are very thick and leathery. ZONES 10–12.

## BAMBUSA
### Bamboo

This is a genus of around 120 species of clump-forming bamboos found in tropical and subtropical Asia. Many are very large, up to 80 ft (24 m) tall or even more, with strong, woody, hollow stems. The upper parts of the stems are often arching, and branch at the nodes into wiry branchlets with masses of grass-like leaves. The flowers are rather insignificant, often half-hidden among the foliage on slender, arching panicles which are usually produced rather intermittently.

### Cultivation

They thrive in tropical climates with humid conditions and deep, humus-rich soil. Plant young bambusas in part-shade. Propagate by division.

### Bambusa multiplex
syn. Bambusa glaucescens
### Hedge bamboo

A native of southern China, this variable species has gracefully arching stems usually 10–30 ft (3–9 m) tall and 1–2 in (25–50 mm) in diameter topped with plumes of narrow, 6 in (15 cm) long leaves with silvery undersides. It is mostly represented in gardens by yellow-leafed and variegated cultivars. 'Alphonse Karr' has yellow-striped stems, tinted pink when young. 'Riviereorum' is a relatively dwarf cultivar with 5–10 ft (1.5–3 m) stems. ZONES 9–12.

## BEGONIA
### Begonia

Many begonias are grown as indoor plants, prized either for their beautifully colored and textured foliage or showy flowers, sometimes both present in the one species or cultivar. Mostly evergreen, they have broad, usually asymmetrical leaves of rather brittle and waxy texture. Female flowers, as distinct from male flowers which are on the same plant, have broad, colored flanges on the ovaries which develop into winged fruits.

### Cultivation

As indoor plants they do well in standard potting mix with peat moss or leafmold added to increase acidity. Grow in bright to moderate light, with good

*Bambusa multiplex*

Begonia fuchsioides

Begonia × hiemalis

ventilation and high humidity. Pinch back young plants of the shrubby type to keep them compact and to encourage flowers. Propagate from stem or leaf cuttings (laying the cut leaf blades flat on damp sand and weighing them down with pebbles), or by division of rhizomes, or from seed. Watch for gray mold, powdery mildew and botrytis if conditions are too damp.

### Begonia 'Cleopatra'

A rhizomatous begonia, this is a popular, easy-to-grow plant with a dense mass of shortly creeping rhizomes that support crowded, sharply lobed, yellow-green and purplish brown leaves. It bears profuse, long-stalked sprays of pale pink flowers. It is a popular balcony plant, thriving in hot sun. ZONES 10–12.

### Begonia 'Erythrophylla'
syn. Begonia 'Feastii'
#### Beefsteak begonia

Grown chiefly for its attractive foliage, the large, leathery leaves are some 4 in (10 cm) wide, bright green above and deep red-brown underneath. The sprays of delicate pink flowers on 6 in (15 cm) stalks are a bonus. Apart from its popularity as an indoor plant, this easily grown cultivar makes an interesting garden plant for lightly shaded spots. ZONES 10–12.

Begonia 'Cleopatra'

### Begonia fuchsioides

This shrubby begonia has small, crowded, oval leaves, flushed pink on new growths. Small coral-red to pale pink flowers are borne in numerous short sprays over a long season. Suitable for outdoor use, it grows to 3 ft (1 m) tall with an erect, closely branched habit and gracefully drooping branchlets. It prefers good light. ZONES 10–12.

### Begonia × hiemalis
syn. Begonia × elatior

This name applies to a group of hybrid cultivars originating from crosses between Begonia socotrana and Tuber-hybrida Group begonias, resulting in a range of easily grown plants with single or double blooms in subtle colors from white through yellow and orange to red and pink. They have fibrous rather than

Begonia 'Pink Shasta'

tuberous root systems and tend to die after flowering, though some newer cultivars have overcome this drawback. ZONES 10–11.

### Begonia 'Pink Shasta'
One of the 'angel-wing' type of cane-stemmed begonias, 'Pink Shasta' grows to 3–4 ft (1–1.2 m) high with branching stems and leaves slightly silver spotted. It produces pendulous panicles of light salmon-pink flowers. It originated as a seedling of 'Shasta', which is derived from *Begonia coccinea*. ZONES 10–12.

## BILLBERGIA
### Vase plant
This genus of bromeliads consists of around 50 species of evergreen perennials from Central and South America. The majority of species are 'tank epiphytes', plants perched on trees with the bases of their broad, strap-like leaves tightly overlapping around a central hollow which fills with rainwater, providing a reservoir for the plant between rainfalls. The horny-textured leaves are often edged with small teeth and in many species have a coating of mealy, grayish white scales interrupted by greener bands. Showy, stalked flower clusters appear at any time of year from the centers of the leaf rosettes, with pink or red bracts often more conspicuous than the tubular flowers.

### Cultivation
Species of *Billbergia* are easy to grow and make ideal indoor plants, or they can be planted outdoors in sheltered, humid spots in the garden. A porous, fast-draining soil mix suits them, or they can be planted on a mound of stones. Some species soon form quite large clumps and can be propagated by division after flowering; the slower-growing ones are propagated by cutting off the basal 'pups', which are treated as cuttings. Scale insects and mealybugs can be a problem with these bromeliads, and brown leaves may be the result of too much sun.

### Billbergia nutans
### Queen's tears, friendship plant
This popular species from southern Brazil and Argentina can be grown outdoors in sheltered rockeries or tubs, even in full sun. Indoors it likes coarse potting mix and good light. Reaching a height of 24 in (60 cm) and spreading to make large dense clumps, its pale olive green leaves are grass-like, tapering into long thread-like recurving tips, and pendent clusters of flowers on long arching spikes. The curled-back petals are an unusual combination of pale green and navy blue, but it is the long pink bracts that really catch the eye. ZONES 10–12.

## BROMELIA
This genus gives its name to the large family Bromeliaceae (the bromeliads). The 50 or so species of *Bromelia* are scattered widely through South America and parts of Central America and the West Indies. They are mostly ground-dwelling perennials resembling pineapple plants, with strong, hooked

*Bromelia balansae*

*Billbergia nutans*

spines along the margins of their long, stiff leaves which generally turn a bronzy color in strong sun. The leaves form large rosettes, which in some species can multiply by sending out long rhizomes to make extensive clumps. A stout flower spike arises from the center of the rosette surrounded by leaf-like bracts that may be brilliantly colored; the flowers are tubular and densely packed and give way to large fleshy yellow fruits, which in some species are used medicinally.

### Cultivation

*Bromelia* species are mostly grown outdoors, thriving in full sun and well-drained soil. They are relatively free from diseases and pests. Propagate from offsets or seeds, keeping seedlings well ventilated to discourage damping off fungus.

### *Bromelia balansae*
### Heart of flame

This vigorous species reaches a height of 5 ft (1.5 m) and can spread extensively. Its flower spike is up to 3 ft (1 m) tall and is surrounded by glossy, brilliant scarlet, spiny-edged bracts, the longer, lower ones only colored at the base. The purple flowers are in a series of dense heads among shorter whitish bracts. The dull orange-yellow berries can form very large clusters, taking almost a year to

ripen. This plant has been used in South America as an impenetrable living fence. ZONES 10–12.

## CALADIUM

Now undergoing a slight revival in popularity, caladiums include some of the showiest but most tender tropical foliage plants, prized for the gorgeous colors and rich patterning of their large, thin leaves. Consisting of 7 species from tropical South America, the genus belongs to the arum family, resembling the taro genus (*Colocasia*) in growth habit with underground tubers and leaves of the 'elephant-ear' type. They are deciduous in the tropical dry season, the tubers going through a dormant stage. The flowering stems are typical of the arum type, not very showy, with a thin, greenish white spathe half-hidden under the leaves.

## Cultivation

They need bright light but not direct sun. Plant tubers in peat moss or sphagnum, transplanting when sprouted into a humus-rich soil.

*Caladium bicolor*

*Calathea burle-marxii*

### Caladium bicolor
syn. *Caladium* × *hortulanum*

**Angel wings, elephant's ears, fancy-leafed caladium**

Caladiums reached a height of popularity in the USA before World War II, when at least a thousand cultivars were listed. There has been debate as to whether the wild parents all belong to the South American *Caladium bicolor* in the broad sense, or whether they included several species (in which case many of the cultivars should correctly be treated as *C.* × *hortulanum*). Their leaves are typically arrowhead-shaped but some cultivars have narrower leaves, wedge-shaped at the base. Color varies from plain green with a red or pink center to intricate combinations of green, white, pink and red, usually with dark green veining. Plants reach 12–24 in (30–60 cm) high. In tropical climates they can remain in the ground year round, and may naturalize in damp areas. ZONES 10–12.

## CALATHEA

Consisting of 300 or so species of evergreen perennials of the arrowroot family, native to Central and South America and the West Indies, this genus is prized for its decorative foliage. At least one species is grown as a food crop, yielding small starchy tubers. The long-stalked, mostly upright leaves are usually large and often beautifully variegated in shades of green, white, pink, purple and maroon, and usually purplish on the undersides. The flowers are interesting but rarely showy, in short dense spikes with overlapping bracts that may be white or variously colored and often partly hidden beneath the foliage.

### Cultivation

In the wet tropics and subtropics calatheas make attractive foliage plants for outdoor landscaping in shaded areas beneath trees or in courtyards. Many will thrive in low light levels. Plant in humus-rich, moist but well-drained soil. Water freely in warmer weather and fertilize regularly. Propagate by division of rhizomes. The sheathing leaf bases often harbor mealybugs, and the foliage can be affected by aphids, spider mites and thrips.

### Calathea burle-marxii

Named in honor of the renowned Brazilian landscape designer, Roberto Burle Marx, whose gardens featured dramatic swathes of plants such as calatheas, this east Brazilian species grows rapidly up to 5 ft (1.5 m) high, with short bamboo-like stems growing erect from the rhizomes. The leaves may be over 24 in (60 cm) long and half as wide, bright green with a yellowish central stripe on the upper surface, duller gray-green beneath. The ¾ in (20 mm) long pale violet flowers emerge from waxy white bracts grouped in a large spike. ZONES 11–12.

### Calathea veitchiana

One of the taller growing calatheas, to 3 ft (1 m) or more in height, this species from Peru has leaves blotched light green along the center, the blotches bordered by scalloped bands of dull green; these in turn are bordered greenish yellow, while on the underside the dark green areas become purple. The small white flowers are borne in a club-shaped spike with green bracts. This species is named after a horticulturalist, James Veitch, whose famous English nursery continued throughout the nineteenth century. ZONES 11–12.

### Calathea zebrina
### Zebra plant

This vigorous species from Brazil is usually 24–36 in (60–90 cm) tall, and can develop into a broad clump of crowded stems, its habit reminiscent of a dwarf canna except that the large, velvety, deep green leaves are marked by parallel stripes or bars of pale chartreuse; the undersides are purplish red. The leaves can be trimmed away to reveal clusters of chocolate brown bracts which protect the flowers. ZONES 10–12.

*Calathea veitchiana*

*Calathea zebrina*

*Canna × generalis*

# CANNA

This genus of robust rhizomatous perennials consists of about 25 species, all native to tropical and South America. Slender flowering stems grow up through the centers of these false stems, emerging at the top with showy flowers of asymmetrical structure. Most of the wild species have rather narrow-petalled flowers in shades of yellow, red or purple. All garden cannas are hybrids. The colors range from the common reds, oranges and yellows through to apricots, creams and pinks. The leaves can be green, bronze or purple, or sometimes white or yellow striped. Plants range in height from 18 in (45 cm) to 8 ft (2.4 m).

### Cultivation

Cannas thrive outdoors. They are sun-loving plants and thrive in hot dry weather as long as water can be kept up to the roots, and they respond well to heavy feeding. Cut back to the ground after flowering has finished. Propagate by division.

### Canna × generalis

*Canna × generalis* is the name given to a large group of canna hybrids of unknown or complex parentage. Plants are extremely variable, ranging from dwarfs less than 3 ft (1 m) to large growers that reach 6 ft (1.8 m). Foliage is also variable and may be plain green, reddish, purple or variegated. Flowers come in all the warm shades, either in plain single colors such as the orange-red 'Brandywine', or spotted or streaked as in the yellow and red 'King Numbert'. 'Königin Charlotte' has dazzling red flowers. 'Lenape' is a dwarf hybrid cultivar with bright yellow flowers with a red throat and brownish red spots; it grows to a height of only 30 in (75 cm). 'Lucifer' is a most attractive hybrid cultivar with yellow-edged red petals and purple-toned leaves. It is one of the newer dwarf types, growing to 3 ft (1 m) high. ZONES 9–12.

### Canna indica
syn. *Canna edulis*
**Indian shot**

Despite the name, this species is native to northern South America although it is commonly naturalized in warm regions elsewhere. Growing to about 8 ft (2.4 m) tall, it has dark green leaves with purple tones and bears dark red to yellow flowers with very narrow petals, followed shortly by fleshy spined capsules containing black seeds—their hardness and smooth spherical shape allowed them to be substituted for shotgun pellets, hence the common name. Some strains, once distinguished as *Canna edulis*, have been cultivated for the edible starch in their rhizomes, known as 'Queensland arrowroot'. ZONES 9–12.

# CELOSIA
**Cockscomb, Chinese woolflower**

This genus of erect annuals, perennials and shrubs in the amaranthus family contains 50 or more species from warmer parts of Asia, Africa and the Americas, but only one *(Celosia argentea)* is widely cultivated as a bedding annual and for cut flowers. It has evolved in cultivation into several different forms, hardly recognizable as belonging to the one species. It has simple, soft, strongly veined leaves; the variation is almost wholly in the structure of the heads of the small flowers, which have undergone proliferation and deformation in the two major cultivated races.

*Canna indica*

## Cultivation

Species of *Celosia* are well adapted to hot climates, withstanding the fiercest heat. They require full sun, rich, well-drained soil and constant moisture. Propagate from seed.

### Celosia argentea

syns *Celosia cristata, C. pyramidalis*

Probably native to tropical Asia, this erect annual can reach 3 ft (1 m) or more in height. The leaves are mid-green; the silvery white flowers appear in dense, erect, pointed spikes with a silvery sheen. The species is best known in the guise of two strikingly different cultivar groups, which in turn are hardly recognizable as belonging to the species. These are the Plumosa Group, with erect, plume-like heads of tiny deformed flowers in a range of hot colors, and the Cristata Group (cockscombs), with bizarre wavy crests of fused flower stalks also in many colors. ZONES 10–12.

*Celosia argentea*

*Celosia spicata*

### Celosia spicata

Of uncertain origin, this annual species has appeared in recent years as a cut flower. Growing to 24 in (60 cm) or more, it has an erect, slender habit and much narrower leaves than *Celosia argentea*. The flowers are neatly crowded onto terminal spikes, opening progressively from the base with the buds purplish pink and the chaffy flowers ageing to pale silvery pink as the spikes elongate. The flowers last well when dried. ZONES 10–12.

### CHLOROPHYTUM

This is a large genus of lilies related to *Anthericum*, consisting of over 200 species scattered through parts of Africa, southern Asia, South America and Australia, though the vast majority are native to southern and tropical Africa. These are evergreen perennials with short rhizomes, the roots often swollen and fleshy. Grown for their foliage, the strap-shaped, sword-shaped or lance-shaped leaves vary in size, thickness and coloration, while the small starry white or greenish flowers are hardly showy. Only one species is widely cultivated; it is regarded as one of the hardiest of indoor plants.

#### Cultivation

They are not fussy about soil or growing medium as long as drainage is adequate and they thrive in light to medium shade. Water freely. Propagate from seed, by division, or by means of the plantlets that often form on flowering stems.

### Chlorophytum comosum
#### Spider plant, hen-and-chickens

Native to moist coastal regions of South Africa, this species is widely grown for its attractive grass-like foliage and is one of the most popular plants for hanging baskets. In mild climates it can make a ground cover in the shade of trees, growing to a height of 12 in (30 cm). Rosettes of narrow leaves up to 18 in (45 cm) long multiply to form dense, untidy clumps. The long, weak, branched flowering stems carry small star-shaped white flowers through much of the year, and small plantlets develop on the stems after flowering, enabling the plant's rapid spread. The wild, green-leafed form can be invasive but several forms with cream- or yellow-striped leaves are more popular as garden or indoor plants: 'Mandaianum' is a compact form, its narrower dark green leaves irregularly striped dull yellow-green; 'Picturatum' has leaves with a broad yellow central stripe; 'Vittatum' has leaves with a broad white central stripe, usually with finer stripes at the sides. ZONES 9–11.

Chlorophytum comosum

## CLIVIA
### Kaffir lily

This genus of southern African lilies consists of 4 species of evergreen perennials with thick, strap-like, deep green leaves springing from short rhizomes with thick roots. Flowers are borne in dense umbels terminating somewhat flattened stems and are funnel-shaped to trumpet-shaped, with 6 red to orange, sometimes green-tipped petals that are partially fused into a tube. They are sometimes followed by quite conspicuous, deep red, berry-like fruits.

### Cultivation

Plant in a shaded or part-shaded, position in friable, well-drained soil; they are surface-rooted and dislike soil disturbance. Propagate by division after flowering. Seed can also be used but plants can be slow to flower.

### Clivia caulescens

This is the rarest species in cultivation. The sheathing bases of the leaves form a basal 'neck' to each shoot, and the spreading, floppy leaves can sometimes reach as much as 6 ft (1.8 m) in length. Flowering stems are up to 18 in (45 cm) high, bearing an umbel of narrowly funnel-shaped, downward-curving flowers only 1½ in (38 mm) long, pale red with green tips and yellow protruding stamens. ZONES 10–11.

### Clivia miniata
### Bush lily, fire lily

This most commonly cultivated and showiest species is distributed widely in eastern South Africa. About 18 in (45 cm) in height, it has broad leaves, sometimes up to 3 in (8 cm) wide and bears clusters of broadly funnel-shaped flowers up to 3 in (8 cm) long, mostly orange to scarlet with a yellow throat. Many cultivars have been selected over

Clivia miniata

the years, including yellow and cream forms. There is a group of especially prized forms commonly called 'hybrids' with tulip-shaped, deep, rich scarlet blooms. ZONES 10–11.

## COLOCASIA

This genus of the arum family from tropical Asia consists of 6 species of evergreen tuberous perennials. The large leaves are arrowhead-shaped or heart-shaped, with prominent veins, supported on a tall stalk that joins the blade a little in from the edge. The flowering stems appear at any time of the year and are like small, pale yellow or cream calla lilies, with a delicate fragrance. At least

*Colocasia esculenta*

2 *Colocasia* species are grown for their edible tubers and others are occasionally grown as ornamentals.

### Cultivation

They like a sheltered but sunny position and fertile, humus-rich soil. Keep the soil around the base of the plant firm to support the slender stem. Water abundantly and harvest tubers 8 months after planting. Young shoots can be cooked and eaten like asparagus, while the starchy tubers can be boiled or roasted like potatoes. Propagate by division.

### *Colocasia esculenta*
syn. *Colocasia antiquorum*
**Taro, dasheen, eddoe, elephant's ear**
This evergreen species can stand 4–8 ft (1.2–2.4 m) tall, the long leaf-stalks supporting heart-shaped, mid- to dark green leaves which are up to 24 in (60 cm) long; the plants can spread by slender runners. *Colocasia esculenta* var. *antiquorum* (eddoe) has smaller but more numerous tubers. The attractive ornamental cultivar 'Fontanesii' has dark purple stalks and bronze-tinted leaves. There are innumerable edible cultivars of taro and one feature in which they vary is the presence and amount of irritant crystals in the tubers, which may need to be removed by repeated boiling. ZONES 10–12.

### *Colocasia gigantea*
This species from the Malaysian region has pale green leaves up to about 5 ft (1.8 m) long and 3 ft (1 m) wide, their undersides with a whitish bloom. The whole plant can stand about 8 ft (2.4 m) high with a short basal trunk at the apex of which are produced a continuous succession of narrow cream spathes. It grows in slightly boggy clearings in rain-forest and is easily cultivated. ZONES 10–12.

## COSTUS
### Spiral flag, spiral ginger
This genus of clump-forming evergreen perennials consists of some 150 species. They have ginger-like leaves arranged in an ascending spiral around the stem, and attractive terminal flowerheads with overlapping bracts, rather like a pine cone. The flowers which emerge between the bracts are orange, yellow, pink, red or white.

### Cultivation
Grow in humus-rich soil in a well-lit position, but not direct sunlight. Propagate by division or from seed. Plants grown indoors may be affected by red spider mite.

### *Costus speciosus*
### Crepe ginger, spiral ginger
This tall-growing species has short elliptic leaves running in a conspicuous spiral up the slender cane-like stems that are themselves gently twisted into a spiral, and up to 8 ft (2.4 m) tall. The large flowerheads consist of tightly overlapping green bracts tinged reddish, and white, sometimes pinkish flowers with yellow centers and petals like silky

crêpe, emerging one or two at a time over much of the year. ZONES 11–12.

## CRINUM

This genus of beautiful large bulbous plants, allied to *Amaryllis*, occurs wild in most warmer regions of the world. The lily-like flowers are borne in umbels at the apex of thick flowering stems and usually open progressively; usually white or pink, they have six broad petals, often upward-curving, and long stamen filaments. Globular, thin-skinned fruits contain large fleshy seeds that have no dormancy and will begin to germinate dry.

### Cultivation

Bulbs should be planted in rich, moist soil with the neck of the bulb above ground level. Some species do best in full sun, others appreciate a light shade. Propagation is best from seed as dividing the plants is difficult. The flowers usually take a few seasons to develop with either method. Most species are susceptible to caterpillars, slugs and snails.

### Crinum asiaticum
### Asiatic poison lily, poison bulb

This tropical Asian species likes damp soil, and can be placed at the margins of a pond. Its long-necked bulbs sit on the surface and produce evergreen, fleshy, very broad leaves making a clump up to about 4 ft (1.2 m) high. The stout flowering stem can carry up to 50 sweetly scented white flowers with very narrow petals, opening through much of the year. There is a rare form with pale pink flowers, another with soft golden yellow leaves, and one with its leaves boldly striped in green and cream. The poisonous bulbs were once used medicinally, as an emetic; they present little danger in the garden. ZONES 10–12.

Costus speciosus

Crinum asiaticum

### Crinum pedunculatum
### Beach lily, swamp crinum

This species is similar to *Crinum asiaticum* but is a more robust plant. It makes large clumps of evergreen foliage, the long basal necks hardly distended at the base into proper bulbs; the dull green leaves are very thick and leathery, up to 4 ft (1.2 m) long. It produces many stout flowering stems of up to 3 ft (1 m) high, each bearing a long succession of narrow-petalled white flowers with showy long stamens. The shiny greenish white fruit are up to 2 in (5 cm) wide. It thrives in almost any sunny situation, including exposed seashores and saline swamps. A mature clump can reach 6–8 ft (1.8–2.4 m) wide. ZONES 10–12.

## CROSSANDRA

This genus, of the acanthus family, has simple leaves arranged in opposite pairs and bear erect spikes of showy yellow to

*Crinum pedunculatum*

*Crossandra pungens*

red flowers, opening progressively from the base of the spike, each flower with the petals opened out flat, like a hand.

### Cultivation

Some species are popular as potted plants for indoors or a heated greenhouse. They need to be watered freely when in full growth. Shoots that have flowered should be cut back by about half. Propagation is from seed or cuttings.

### *Crossandra pungens*

This tropical African species has rather narrow dull green leaves with a pattern of paler veins. The flowers are borne in spikes with broad, spiny-edged bracts and are orange in color. ZONES 10–12.

## CTENANTHE

Around 15 species belong to this genus of tropical plants closely related to *Maranta* and *Calathea*. They are evergreen perennials or subshrubs with short rhizomes; the taller species produce forking, somewhat bamboo-like aerial stems with a single leaf at each node. The rather leathery, lance-shaped or almost oblong leaves are borne on slender stalks which broaden into sheathing bases. The flowers are borne in spikes with tightly overlapping bracts and are not showy.

### Cultivation

Several species are widely grown as indoor foliage plants, or outdoors in the shade of trees, requiring protection from drying winds. Indoors they require bright to moderate light but direct sunlight may cause the leaves to curl. They need ample water during the growing season and dislike low humidity. Propagation is usually from basal offshoots.

### *Ctenanthe oppenheimiana*

This widely grown species is normally about 18 in (45 cm) high but can grow taller under good conditions. Its 10–12 in (25–30 cm) long leaves are oblong and have a herringbone pattern of broad grayish bars on a dull green background, with dull red undersides. Most commonly grown is the cultivar 'Tricolor' with irregular blotches of creamy yellow on its leaves; the red undersides give it a reddish glow from above. ZONES 10–12.

## CYPERUS
### Umbrella sedge, papyrus

*Cyperus* is an enormous genus of over 600 species of sedges, including both annuals and evergreen perennials. They include some of the world's most troublesome weeds of crops and gardens, for example nutgrass, *Cyperus rotundus*. The broad clumps of thick, cylindrical or 3-angled, stems have grass-like leaves springing from the base and are topped by compact heads or large umbels of small chaff-like flower spikes.

### Cultivation

Most ornamental species do well at the water's edge or in boggy ground. Grow in rich compost and water well. Direct sunlight is tolerated. Repot when the plant fills the container. If the tips turn brown, the atmosphere may be too dry, while a lack of new stems may indicate too little light. Propagate from seed or by division.

### Cyperus papyrus
### Paper reed, papyrus

The papyrus of the ancient Egyptians is one of the stateliest of all water plants. It is extremely rampant, growing 5–8 ft (1.5–2.4 m) tall with an indefinite spread. Its long, sturdy, leafless stems carry great starbursts of fine branchlets that carry the tiny brown flowers. It will grow in very shallow water and prefers a sunny position. ZONES 10–12.

## DICHORISANDRA

This genus of about 25 species is related to the wandering Jew *(Tradescantia)*. The foliage may be glossy green or banded or striped with cream. The small cup-shaped flowers are purple or blue and are followed by fleshy orange fruits.

### Cultivation

They can be grown in well-drained, shady spots. They require adequate moisture at all times and high humidity. Propagate by division or from cuttings.

*Ctenanthe oppenheimiana*

*Cyperus papyrus*

Dichorisandra thyrsiflora

Dieffenbachia seguine 'Tropic Marianne'

### Dichorisandra thyrsiflora
#### Blue ginger, Brazilian ginger

The common name for this species arises from its ginger-like stems. The plant has glossy, dark green leaves 12 in (30 cm) long that are spirally arranged along the upright stems. It produces dense terminal clusters of deep purple-blue flowers, and grows to a height of 8 ft (2.4 m) and spread of 3 ft (1 m). ZONES 10–12.

## DIEFFENBACHIA
### Dumb cane

A genus of about 30 species, these evergreen, tufted perennials are often grown as houseplants. Their large oval leaves are often heavily marked with creamy white or yellow stripes or patches. Their sap makes the mouth and tongue swell, rendering speech impossible.

### Cultivation

Bright to moderate light suits them. Allow the surface soil to become dry in between thorough waterings as roots may rot if they are over-watered. Propagate from root cuttings or stem cuttings laid horizontally in compost.

### Dieffenbachia seguine
syns Dieffenbachia maculata, D. picta

This robust plant of up to 10 ft (1.3 m) high has large, paddle-shaped, deep green leaves marked sparsely with white spots and blotches along the lateral veins and insignificant, greenish white flowers. It flourishes in poor light. 'Amoena' has bold green leaves with creamy white bands and marbling between the veins; 'Rudolph Roehrs' grows to 3 ft (1 m) with chartreuse leaves with green midribs and green edges; 'Tropic Marianne' has yellowish green leaves, white midribs and green edges. ZONES 10–12.

## EICHHORNIA
### Water hyacinth

These aquatic perennials have rosettes of stalked, broadly oval or heart-shaped leaves and terminal spikes of showy, funnel-shaped flowers. They grow floating in water, with no need to anchor their roots; a raft of connected plants can rapidly cover a large area of water, choking rivers and blocking sunlight to other marine life. Never grow them in open watercourses.

### Cultivation
They thrive in warm, slowly moving water in full sun. Propagate by division.

### Eichhornia crassipes
This species spreads to 18 in (45 cm) or so. The pale violet flowers are marked with bright blue and gold, and occur in upright terminal spikes. The rounded, glossy green leaves are arranged in rosettes. Its cultivation is prohibited in most warmer countries. ZONES 9–12.

## EPISCIA
The 6 species of this genus are related to the African violet and make ideal plants for hanging baskets. Long runners bear tufts of ornamental leaves, which are hairy and produced in whorls or rosettes; they cascade down the sides of the pot or basket, and given the right conditions produce long-lasting, colorful flowers. The flowers, either solitary or in small racemes, have 5 lobes.

### Cultivation
Plant in African violet mix or porous, peaty, indoor plant mix in bright indirect light. Poor light may result in few flowers. They require constant warmth and humidity, so are well suited to a sunny bathroom or conservatory. Keep moist at all times, but take care not to over-water as it leads to rotting. Pinch back stems after flowering to encourage branching, and repot every year. Propagate by laying runners in compost, from cuttings or by division.

### Episcia dianthiflora
### Lace flower vine
This evergreen, low-creeping perennial has rooting stems that provide an easy means of propagation. Its small leaves, to 2 in (5 cm) long, are dark green often with red veins. Its pure white flowers

Eichhornia crassipes

Episcia dianthiflora

have purple spotting at the base and inside the spur. The edges of the petals are deeply and attractively fringed. ZONES 10–12.

## ETLINGERA
This genus of about 57 species has cane-like stems and linear or lance-shaped leaves. Small flowers surrounded by waxy, colorful bracts are borne in torch-like clusters at the tops of leafless stems arising from the rhizome.

## Cultivation

They need moist, humus-rich soil and a position in full sun or part-shade. Water well during growth and less when dormant. Indoors they require warmth, high humidity and plenty of water throughout the growth period. Propagate from seed or by division.

### *Etlingera elatior*

syns *Nicolaia elatior, Phaeomeria speciosa*

### Torch ginger

The oblong leaves to 3 ft (1 m) long are borne on 20 ft (6 m), bamboo-like leaf stalks. A cluster of small, white- to gold-rimmed, scarlet flowers appears, embedded in a waxy, pyramid-like cone of pink-edged, bright red bracts, sometimes opening to 10 in (25 cm) across. The inflorescence is borne on a 5 ft (1.5 m) leafless stem. ZONES 11–12.

## FITTONIA

### Nerve plant, painted net leaf

This genus consists of 2 species of evergreen, creeping perennials. They are grown mainly for their opposite, short-stemmed leaves, with their brightly colored veins, most often as conservatory and house plants. Occasionally white to reddish white, insignificant flowers are borne on short spikes. They make good ground covers or trailing plants.

### Cultivation

Grow in part-shade and provide a humus-rich, well-drained soil and plenty of water. Where temperatures drop below 50°F (15°C) grow indoors in a good potting mix and keep evenly moist. They make excellent hanging basket subjects. Cut back straggly stems. Propagate from cuttings or by layering stems.

### *Fittonia verschaffeltii*

This species reaches about 6 in (15 cm) high with an indefinite spread and has dark green oval leaves with conspicuous red veins. The insignificant flowers are irregular and best removed if they form. *Fittonia verschaffeltii* var. *argyroneura* (syn. *F. argyroneura*), the silver net leaf fig, has rooting stems and mid- to dark green leaves with conspicuous white veins. ZONES 11–12.

## GERBERA

This genus consists of around 40 perennial species. The showy flowerheads, in almost every color except blue and purple, are carried on bare stems 18 in (45 cm) long. They are ideal rockery

*Etlingera elatior*

*Fittonia verschaffeltii*

*Gerbera jamesonii*

*Gloriosa superba*

plants. Only one species, *Gerbera jamesonii*, is commonly cultivated, along with its numerous hybrids.

### Cultivation

They need full sun to part-shade in hot areas and fertile, composted, well-drained soil. Water well during the growing season. Gerberas make good greenhouse plants, where they require good light and regular feeding during the growing season. Propagate from seed, cuttings or by division.

### *Gerbera jamesonii*
### Barberton daisy, Transvaal daisy

Native to South Africa, this is one of the most decorative of all daisies and is an excellent cut flower. From a basal rosette of deeply lobed, lance-shaped leaves, white, pink, yellow, orange or red flowerheads, up to 3 in (8 cm) wide, are borne singly on long stems. Modern florists' gerberas derive from crosses between *Gerbera jamesonii* and the tropical African *G. viridifolia*. Some have flowerheads as much as 12 in (30 cm) across, in a wide range of colors, as well

as double, for example 'Brigadoon Red', and quilled forms. ZONES 8–11.

## *GLORIOSA*
### Glory lily, climbing lily

This genus contains one variable species of tuberous climbing lily. They climb over low shrubs and through long grass by means of the coiled, tendril-like tips of the leaves. They are widely grown for their decorative, brightly colored flowers which make long-lasting and most attractive cut flowers. The plants die back in the tropical dry season to dormant tubers.

### Cultivation

Glory lily is a tropical plant and will thrive outdoors. Plant the tubers in full sun and rich, well-drained soil, fertilizing as the stems begin to elongate. Protect from wind and provide support. Propagate from seed or dormant tubers.

### *Gloriosa superba*
### Tiger's claws

This tropical species can climb to a height of 6–8 ft (1.4–2.4 m) under

*Gloriosa superba* 'Rothschildiana'

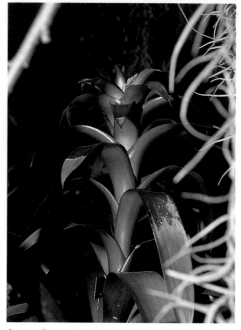

*Guzmania* 'Squarrosa'

suitable conditions. The brilliant red and gold flowers resemble tiger lilies in shape with reflexed, wavy edged petals and conspicuous stamens. 'Rothschildiana' has larger, pinkish red flowers with petals yellow-edged; 'Simplex' has similar but smaller flowers in deep orange and yellow. ZONES 10–12.

## GUZMANIA

The 120 species in this genus of evergreen, mostly epiphytic bromeliads have lance-shaped leaves that form funnel-shaped rosettes, and flowerheads of tubular white or yellow flowers usually surrounded by colorful bracts on yellow, orange or bright red stems. Guzmanias are mostly rainforest plants from the American tropics.

### Cultivation

They require a position in part-shade in a well-drained compost. Water moderately during the growing season, less at other times, but always keep the leaf vases filled with water. If potting, leave enough room for just one year's growth and then repot. They make good indoor or greenhouse plants where they need plenty of indirect light. Fertilize only when in full growth. Propagate from seed or offsets.

### Guzmania lingulata

This is the most commonly grown species. It has basal rosettes of strap-like, apple-green leaves and grows to 12–18 in (30–45 cm) tall. Striking colored bracts surround clusters of tubular, white to yellow flowers. *Guzmania lingulata* var. *minor* grows to 12 in (30 cm) high and across and has creamy yellow flowers and orange-red bracts; it is easily grown in a greenhouse. 'Indiana' has erect golden yellow bracts tipped with orange-red. ZONES 10–12.

### Guzmania 'Squarrosa'

This cultivar is a clump-forming epiphyte with rosettes of colorful bronzy leaves that grow up to 3 ft (1 m) in length. The center of the foliage flares a brilliant red for a short period during bloom time. The bright red inflorescence is borne on a short erect stem, and the flowers are white. ZONES 11–12.

Guzmania lingulata

Guzmania lingulata 'Indiana'

## HEDYCHIUM
### Ginger lily

Ginger lilies are associated with the tropics because of their lush foliage, glamorous flowers and heady scent. They are perennials that grow from rhizomes to form clumps up to 6 ft (1.8 m) high and 4 ft (1.2 m) wide, and for most of the year bear spikes or heads of fragrant flowers that last well and are good for cutting.

### Cultivation

They prefer humus-rich, moist but well-drained soil in a part-shaded position. Spent stems should be cut out each season to ensure vigorous growth—or blooms can be cut for indoors. Propagate from fresh seed or by division.

### Hedychium coronarium
### White ginger lily, garland flower

This species bears dense spikes of butterfly-like, satiny white flowers with pastel yellow blotches and a sweet scent. The leaves are lance-shaped with downy undersides. It has an upright habit and grows to about 5 ft (1.5 m) in height with a spread of up to 3 ft (1 m). ZONES 10–12.

### Hedychium gardnerianum
### Kahili ginger

This species from the Himalayas grows to 8 ft (2.4 m) tall with long, bright

Hedychium gardnerianum

green leaves clasping the tall stems. This is the most widely cultivated species; it prefers a warm climate although it will grow outside in temperate areas. It bears fragrant red and pale yellow flowers, held in dense spikes. *Hedychium gardnerianum* is considered a weed in some regions such as in the north of New Zealand. ZONES 9–11.

## HELIAMPHORA
### Sun pitchers

This genus contains 6 species of rhizomatous, carnivorous plants, allied to sarracenias, that are found on very wet mountains in Venezuela and Guyana. They have funnel-shaped, green to reddish leaves with, in most cases, a small overhanging cap. Each leaf has a nectar-secreting gland designed to attract small insects to their last meal. The flower stems may be up to 24 in (60 cm) tall, each with several delicate white flowers changing to pink with age.

### Cultivation

These plants grow naturally in wet, peaty soil and prefer warm, humid conditions, though preferably less than 86°F (30°C). They are best grown in a pot with a mixture of peat, sand and

*Heliamphora heterodoxa*

sphagnum moss placed in a saucer of water. Propagate by division of rhizomes or from seed.

### Heliamphora heterodoxa

This sun pitcher is from the swampy mountains of Venezuela and grows to about 15 in (38 cm) in height. It has funnels up to 2 in (5 cm) in diameter and white to pink flowers. There are a number of forms. ZONES 11–12.

### Heliamphora nutans

This is an intriguing sun pitcher with green, basal, pitcher-shaped leaves with red margins and a constriction in the middle. It grows 4–8 in (10–20 cm) high and has large, nodding white to pink flowers on 6–12 in (15–30 cm) stalks. ZONES 11–12.

## HELICONIA
### Lobster claw, false bird-of-paradise

From tropical America, Southeast Asia and some Pacific Islands, these beautiful, exotic plants have large leaves and spikes of colorful bracts enclosing relatively insignificant flowers. Planted *en masse*, heliconias create an eye-catching show of color all year round.

*Heliamphora nutans*

The bracts may be red, yellow or orange, or scarlet tipped with yellow and green, or lipstick red and luminous yellow. The leaves are spoon-shaped and grow to 6 ft (1.8 m) long. Heliconias make excellent cut flowers.

## Cultivation

Plant in humus-rich, well-drained soil in filtered sun. Water well during the growing season. To encourage new growth remove all dead leaves and flowers. Propagate by division of rootstock, ensuring there are two shoots on each division. Check for spider mites, snails and mealybugs.

### Heliconia bihai
**Firebird, macaw flower**
syns Heliconia humilis, H. jacquinii
The large, paddle-shaped, green leaves of this species surround a flower stem of pointed, scarlet bracts tipped with green and inconspicuous white flowers. This is the most familiar species and is popular for flower arrangements. ZONES 11–12.

### Heliconia caribaea
**Balisier, wild plantain**
As its specific name suggests, this plant is from the Caribbean Islands. It can

grow to 8 ft (2.4 m) with a spread of 6 ft (1.8 m) and has glossy dark green banana-like leaves. The inflorescence is 3–5 ft (1–1.5 m) long and has white, inconspicuous flowers within red or yellow spathes. ZONES 11–12.

### Heliconia collinsiana
**Collins' heliconia, hanging heliconia**
Growing to around 12 ft (3.5 m) tall, this heliconia grows into a dense clump

Heliconia collinsiana

Heliconia bihai

Heliconia caribaea

*Heliconia wagneriana*

*Heliconia rostrata*

of thin stems from which the pendulous flowers hang in long strings. Bracts are 8–10 in (20–25 cm) long, bright red and sheath the golden yellow true flowers. The whole plant is dusted with a staining, powdery bloom. ZONES 11–12.

### Heliconia psittacorum
#### Parrot flower
Ranging from eastern Brazil to the West Indies, this smaller *Heliconia* species is good for mass planting. It has long-stalked, lance-like, rich green leaves. Narrow, pinkish, orange or pale red bracts surround yellow or red flowers with green tips. It is usually 3–5 ft (1–1.5 m) tall. ZONES 11–12.

### Heliconia rostrata
#### Fishtail heliconia
Possibly the most striking of the heliconias, this species from Peru and Argentina has a large, pendulous cascade of alternating bracts of scarlet tipped with yellow and green. It grows 3–20 ft (1–6 m) in height. ZONES 11–12.

### Heliconia wagneriana
#### Rainbow heliconia, Easter heliconia
From steamy Central America, this magnificent heliconia with its cream, red and green bracts cannot fail to impress. It grows at least 12 ft (3.5 m) tall, but the flowering season is relatively short. ZONES 11–12.

## HYMENOCALLIS
syn. *Ismene*
#### Spider lily, filmy lily, sacred lily of the Incas
The unusual, beautiful white flowers of the spider lilies resemble daffodils except for the delicate, spider-like petals surrounding the inner corona. There are about 40 species of *Hymenocallis*. Some are evergreen and all are scented.

#### Cultivation
Most species can be grown as indoor pot plants. Bulbs should be planted about 6 in (15 cm) deep in well-drained soil. A part-shaded position is best. Water very well during growth and never allow to dry out completely. Offsets form quickly and should be divided.

*Hymenocallis caribaea*

*Impatiens*, New Guinea Hybrid, 'Concerto'

### Hymenocallis caribaea

This evergreen species from the West Indies has strap-like leaves to 24 in (60 cm) long. It bears large flowers, about 6 in (15 cm) across, with long, narrow petals that look like white spiders perched atop glossy green foliage. ZONES 10–12.

### IMPATIENS

This large genus of around 850 species of succulent-stemmed annuals, evergreen perennials and subshrubs is widely distributed, especially in the subtropics and tropics of Asia and Africa. They are useful for colorful bedding displays and for indoor and patio plants. The flowers come in an ever-increasing range of colors. Their botanical name, *Impatiens*, refers to the impatience with which they grow and multiply.

#### Cultivation

They will grow in sun or part-shade; many species do well under overhanging trees. They prefer a moist but freely drained soil, and need protection from

*Impatiens*, New Guinea Hybrid, 'Tango'

strong winds. Tip prune the fast-growing shoots to encourage shrubby growth and more abundant flowers. Propagate from seed or stem cuttings.

#### Impatiens, New Guinea Hybrids

Hybrids from a New Guinean species, members of this group of fast-growing perennials grow to a height and spread of 12–18 in (30–45 cm). The leaves are

*Impatiens pseudoviola*

*Impatiens pseudoviola* 'Woodcote'

oval, pointed and bronze green, or may be variegated with cream, white or yellow. The flat, spurred flowers are pink, orange, red or cerise, sometimes with white markings. Cultivars include 'Cheers', with its coral flowers and yellow leaves; 'Concerto', with crimson-centered deep pink flowers; 'Tango', with deep orange flowers and bronze leaves; and 'Red Magic', which has scarlet flowers and bronze-red leaves. They do well in brightly lit positions indoors or on enclosed verandahs or patios. ZONES 10–12.

### Impatiens pseudoviola
This semi-trailing East African species is a perennial. It produces white flowers suffused with rose pink, with violet-rose central stripes on the wing petals. 'Woodcote' is a shrubby, pale pink-lilac form. ZONES 10–12.

### Impatiens repens
#### Golden dragon
This evergreen, creeping perennial is native to Sri Lanka. It bears golden, hooded flowers with a large hairy spur; these stand out against the small, kidney-shaped leaves with red stems. *Impatiens repens* grows to a height of 2 in (5 cm). This species is especially suited to hanging baskets. ZONES 10–12.

### Impatiens zombensis
Another tropical African species, *Impatiens zombensis* comes from the highland region around Zomba in Malawi. It is a shrubby species that reaches about 3 ft (1 m) tall and bears purplish flowers with white-spotted throats. ZONES 10–12.

## LIRIOPE
This genus contains 5 species of clump-forming, rhizomatous, evergreen perennials native to Vietnam, China, Taiwan and Japan. Some cultivars are so dark in leaf they are practically black, a most unusual color for the designer to play with. They do not creep, and for ground cover have to be planted 6 in (15 cm) apart. *Liriope* flowers range from white through to pale purple.

### Cultivation
Grow in full sun or part-shade in well-drained soil. Cut back shabby leaves, just before the new ones appear. Propagate from seed or by division.

### Liriope muscari
syns *Liriope platyphylla, L. graminifolia*
This clumping, evergreen perennial is a useful casual ground cover or path edging. It has grass-like, shining, dark green leaves and bears erect spikes of rounded, bell-shaped, violet flowers.

*Impatiens repens*

It grows to 12–24 in (30–60 cm) high with a spread of 18 in (45 cm), with flower spikes held just above the foliage. 'Lilac Beauty' comes from China and Japan and is a larger example of the species; the leaves are 1 in (25 mm) wide and 12–18 in (30–45 cm) long with stiff lilac flowers rising above the foliage. 'Majestic' has large violet-blue flowers. 'Variegata' is the most common of the variegated forms—the leaf margins are lined with cream and it has lovely lilac flowers. ZONES 6–10.

*Impatiens zombensis*

*Liriope muscari* 'Variegata'

## MARANTA

This is a genus of 32 species of evergreen rhizomatous perennials from the tropical forests of Central and South America. Apart from the beautifully marked and textured leaves, they are known for their habit of 'going to sleep' at night. The leaves spread by day and stand erect at night. One species, *Maranta arundinacea,* is an important crop plant; it is better known to cooks as arrowroot.

*Maranta leuconeura 'Kerchoviana'*

*Musa velutina*

### Cultivation
They like humidity and bright light without direct sunlight. They make a good ground cover under large trees. Propagation is usually done by dividing established clumps or from basal cuttings struck on bottom heat.

### Maranta leuconeura
#### Prayer plant, Ten Commandments
This variable species contains most of the best foliage forms of this genus. It grows to 12 in (30 cm) in height and spread, and produces its inconspicuous white flowers with foliate spots in slender spikes. The dark green leaves are usually about 6 in (15 cm) long. They have silver to pink veins and the reverse side can be purple or gray-green. 'Kerchoviana', known as rabbit tracks, has oval, light green leaves with green to brown blotches on either side of the central vein; the insignificant white to mauve flowers appear intermittently. ZONES 11–12.

## MUSA
Many of the species belonging to this genus are fruit producers, and detailed information on the genus is given in the Fruit and Nut Trees chapter.

### Musa velutina
Banana flowers are admired more for their curiosity value than their beauty. This evergreen dwarf species grows no higher than 6 ft (1.8 m). It bears yellow flowers in summer which are highlighted by red bracts and small, velvety red bananas. The fruit unpeel themselves when ripe, hence one common name of self-peeling bananas. ZONES 9–12.

## NEOREGELIA
The members of this stemless bromeliad genus containing about 70 species vary greatly in size, texture and color. Native to South America, the genus was named after Edward von Regel, who was the Superintendent of the Imperial Botanic Gardens in St Petersburg, Russia. Many of the species turn a brilliant rose, violet or red color in the center of the rosette when flowering approaches. The flowers may be blue or white and the striking, spined foliage ranges from green to maroon, striped, spotted or marbled. The leaves form a wide funnel-shaped or tube-like rosette which ranges from 6 in (15 cm) to as much as 5 ft (1.5 m) across.

## Cultivation

Neoregelias prefer well-drained soil and dislike strong light, but they require some direct light to maintain their color. This genus thrives in a humid atmosphere and is best grown in pots or hanging baskets where it will enjoy good air circulation. Do not allow the center cup to dry out. Propagate from offsets.

### Neoregelia carolinae
#### Heart of flame, blushing bromeliad

This is the most widely cultivated species of the genus and forms a spreading rosette 15–24 in (38–60 cm) across, composed of light olive-green, strap-shaped, saw-toothed leaves. Immediately before flowering, which can be at any time of the year, the youngest inner leaves turn deep red. The cluster of inconspicuous, blue-purple flowers is surrounded by crimson-red bracts. 'Fendleri' has leaves neatly edged with bands of cream, although otherwise bright green. *Neoregelia carolinae* × *concentrica*, an unnamed cross between 2 of the most colorful species, displays the variegation found in some forms of *N. carolinae*, combined with the purple leaf tips of *N. concentrica*. 'Tricolor', seen more often than the species itself, has

cream-striped foliage; the inner leaves turn a rich crimson before producing purple flowers and the entire plant turns pink. 'Tricolor Perfecta' is similar. ZONES 10–12.

### Neoregelia chlorosticta
syn. *Neoregelia sarmentosa* var. *chlorosticta*

This species from Brazil is distinguished by its green-lilac-brown leaf blotching. The flowers are white, opening on short stalks 1 in (25 mm) long. ZONES 10–12.

### Neoregelia concentrica

This Brazilian species has a flat, outstretched funnel-shaped rosette

*Neoregelia concentrica* 'Aztec'

*Neoregelia carolinae* × *concentrica*

*Neoregelia chlorosticta*

*Nepenthes* × *coccinea*

*Nepenthes maxima*

30–36 in (75–90 cm) across. It has broad, leathery leaves with a center becoming deep purple as the flower buds form. The flowers are blue. 'Aztec' is possibly of hybrid origin, but shows a strong influence of this species; its leaves are heavily blotched with deep purple. ZONES 10–12.

## NEPENTHES
### Pitcher plant

These are perhaps the easiest of all the carnivorous plants to grow; they come from a genus of nearly 70 species, mainly from Indonesia and tropical Asia. They include some tall climbers, capable of ascending nearly 70 ft (21 m) into any handy tree, but their preference for swampy land means they often have to make do without support. Some species grow at lower altitudes, others in tropical highlands. They bear inconspicuous purple or brownish flowers in spikes among the upper leaves; the leaves often terminate in pendulous, colored 'pitchers' with lids strikingly tinted in shades of russet, green or even red and pink. Insects are attracted to them and drown in the liquid held in the pitcher before being absorbed into the plant as food.

### Cultivation

They require a very humid atmosphere, part-shade and moist, fertile soil. The species from tropical lowlands require higher temperatures (minimum temperature of 65°F/18°C) than those from the tropical highlands (minimum temperature of 50°F/10°C). Propagate from seed or from stem cuttings, although air layering may prove to be more successful.

### Nepenthes × coccinea

A garden crossing of 2 tall climbers, *Nepenthes* × *coccinea* produces pitchers measuring up to 6 in (15 cm) in length. These are yellow-green in color, mottled with purple-red streaks and blotches. ZONES 11–12.

### Nepenthes maxima

As its name implies, the pitchers on *Nepenthes maxima* are extremely large, often measuring up to 8 in (20 cm) in length. Because this species comes from the high-altitude regions of Indonesia and New Guinea, its temperature

Nymphaea gigantea

Nymphaea nouchali

requirements are lower than the lowland species. ZONES 11–12.

### Nepenthes rafflesiana

This is a tall, climbing species that can clamber up to 30 ft (9 m) by means of long tendrils, but it can withstand quite severe pruning in cultivation. The large leaves can camouflage the elegant green pitchers with their heavily spotted and ribbed mouths, often measuring up to 6 in (15 cm) in length. ZONES 11–12.

## NYMPHAEA
### Waterlily

This worldwide genus of 50 species of deciduous and evergreen perennial aquatic plants with fleshy roots is named after the Greek goddess Nymphe. They are grown for their rounded, floating leaves which are cleft at the base and for their attractive large flowers which come in shades of white and cream, brilliant yellows and oranges, pinks and deep reds, blues and purple. They may be night blooming, depending on species, and sometimes fragrant. The berry-like fruits mature underwater.

### Cultivation

Waterlilies grow in most climates and flower freely, both flowers and foliage floating on the water surface; remove faded foliage. They have large, scented flowers held above the water surface. All species need still water and annual fertilizing as they are gross feeders. Divide the tuber-like rhizomes and replant every 3 or 4 years. Check for insects, particularly aphids; goldfish kept in the pool will eat most pests. Propagate from seed or by separating plantlets.

### Nymphaea gigantea
### Australian waterlily

This tuberous-rooted plant from the tropical areas of Australia and New Guinea has large leaves, often up to 24 in (60 cm) in diameter. Day-blooming, 12 in (30 cm) flowers range from sky to deeper purple-blue. ZONES 10–12.

### Nymphaea nouchali
### Shapla

This tropical species has a wide distribution from southern Asia to northern Australia. Its flower is the national emblem of Bangladesh and it is used there and in India in perfumery and cosmetics. It is a rather small waterlily with floating leaves normally only 3–6 in (8–15 cm) across, and 3 in (8 cm) wide flowers held at or just above the water surface; they open during the day and have 10 or fewer pointed petals that may be blue, pink or white, with a distinct gap between the petals and the bunch of yellow stamens. ZONES 11–12.

*Nymphaea*, TDbH, 'Director Moore'

*Nymphaea*, TDbH, 'Bob Trickett'

*Nymphaea*, TDbH, 'Isabelle Pring'

*Nymphaea*, TDbH, 'Pink Platter'

*Nymphaea*, TDbH, 'Margaret Randig'

### *Nymphaea*, Tropical Day-blooming Hybrids

Tropical hybrids can bear day- or night-time flowers. 'Director Moore' has deep blue petals surrounding purple stamens and a yellow center. 'Margaret Randig' has mottled-purple foliage with fragrant large, open, sky-blue petals with yellow centers and blue-tipped stamens. Bright green leaves mottled with rich brown offset the open, soft pink daytime blooms of 'Pink Platter'; those of 'St Louis' are scented and pale yellow. 'St Louis Gold', has abundant daytime blooms of deep gold. 'Bob Trickett'

Nymphaea, TNbH, 'Emily Grant Hutchings'

Nymphaea, TDbH, 'St Louis'

Nymphaea, TNbH, 'H. T. Haarstick'

Nymphaea, TDbH, 'St Louis Gold'

and 'Isabelle Pring' are also wonderful varieties. ZONES 10–12.

### Nymphaea, Tropical Night-blooming Hybrids

Of the night-bloomers, 'H. T. Haarstick' and 'Wood's White Knight' are notable. Both have tall stems, the former carrying deep red flowers over deep coppery red leaves with very serrated edges, the latter bearing creamy white flowers over mid-green leaves, also with serrated margins. 'Emily Grant Hutchings' has enormous deep pink flowers; 'William B. Sure' has pale pink blooms. ZONES 10–12.

Nymphaea, TDbH, 'William B. Sure'

## *NYMPHOIDES*
### Fairy waterlily, water snowflake
Resembling miniature waterlilies, the
20 species of rhizomatous, aquatic
perennials in this genus are distributed
throughout the world. Their rootstocks
embed in the pond bottom while the
long-stalked, oval, round or kidney-
shaped, wavy-edged leaves float on the
surface. The foliage ranges in diameter
from 1–6 in (2.5–15 cm), and is usually
slightly glossy and olive green, and
occasionally purple mottled. The ½–1 in
(12–25 mm) diameter flowers, with
5 often fimbriated (fringed) petals, may
be white or yellow; they are held just
above the foliage.

### Cultivation
Plant in soil with a water depth of
4–18 in (10–45 cm) in full or half-day
sun. The runners can spread to 6 ft
(1.8 m), so allow room for development.
Propagate by dividing the rootstock.

### *Nymphoides indica*
### Water snowflake, false Indian waterlily
This hardy perennial has rounded
surface leaves 2–8 in (5–20 cm) across
with a heart-shaped base. The flowers

are white with a deep yellow center and
the petals have characteristic fringed
margins. ZONES 10–12.

## *OCIMUM*
### Basil
This genus of approximately 35 species
of annuals, perennials and shrubs is
widely cultivated for their highly
aromatic leaves, which are used for
medicinal purposes or to flavor salads,
soups, sauces, stews and curries. They
have mostly oval leaves in opposite pairs
and small tubular flowers borne in
whorls towards the ends of the stems.

### Cultivation
Grow in a protected, warm, sunny
position in a moist but well-drained
soil. Regularly pinch back plants to
encourage bushy growth and to prevent
them going to seed quickly. Propagate
from seed. Protect from chewing insects
and snails.

### *Ocimum basilicum*
### Basil, sweet basil
This species, with its cultivars, is the
most commonly grown and most widely
used basil. A favorite with cooks, it is

*Nymphoides indica*

*Ocimum basilicum*

one of the most widely used herbs in Mediterranean cooking. It is a tender annual plant growing to about 18 in (45 cm) with light green, oval leaves that have a delicious warm, spicy fragrance. Small white flowers are carried in whorls towards the ends of the stems. There are a number of varieties of basil including a compact small leaf type; a crinkled, lettuce leaf variety and the beautiful 'Dark Opal', which has rich purple stems and leaves. There are perennial varieties also, but their flavor is inferior. 'Minimum' is a dwarf form with tiny leaves, used in the Greek Orthodox Church for sprinkling holy water. ZONES 10–12.

## OPHIOPOGON
### Mondo grass, snakebeard, lilyturf

This genus contains 50 or so species. They are valued for their attractive, long-lived clumps of grass-like foliage springing from underground rhizomes. They are not grasses but lilies, allied to lily-of-the-valley *(Convallaria)*. The flowers are small and can be white or blue through to purple. The berry-like fruits each contain one seed. They are quite trouble-free plants that provide a

very attractive ground cover that effectively suppresses weeds.

### Cultivation

These plants will tolerate sun or part-shade in moist, well-drained soil. Propagate by division of clumps or from seed. To establish a quick ground cover, plant divisions at 8 in (20 cm) intervals.

### *Ophiopogon japonicus*
syn. *Liriope japonica*
### Mondo grass

This fine-leafed species has dark green recurving foliage that arises from deep rhizomes, spreading to form dense, soft mats up to about 8 in (20 cm) deep. Pale purple flowers are hidden among the leaves, followed by bright blue, pea-sized fruit. 'Kyoto Dwarf' is only 2–4 in (5–10 cm) high, with very short leaves. ZONES 8–11.

### *Ophiopogon planiscapus* 'Nigrescens'
syn. *Ophiopogon planiscapus* 'Ebony Night'
### Black mondo grass

This cultivar is grown particularly for its distinctive purple-black rather stiff leaves about ¼ in (6 mm) wide which form slow-growing, sparse clumps. Its

*Ophiopogon japonicus*

*Ophiopogon planiscapus* 'Nigrescens'

*Pachystachys lutea*

*Peperomia argyreia*

They are erect growers with large, bright green leaves and yellow floral bracts that almost hide the true flowers, which are small, white and tubular. The flowers themselves last only a few days, but the bracts remain quite colorful over several weeks.

### Cultivation

They like full sun and fertile, moist but well-drained soil. If used as indoor plants, they prefer warm, well-lit, humid conditions. Propagate from seed or cuttings.

### Pachystachys lutea

This small, shrubby plant forms a clump of upright stems with a 'candle' of bright golden yellow bracts at the tip of each stem. The creamy white flowers within do not reveal themselves until the bracts are fully developed. The leaves are a deep matt green, lance-shaped, up to 6 in (15 cm) long and have prominent veins. Widely grown as a house plant, it makes a cheerful display. ZONES 10–12.

## PEPEROMIA
### Radiator plant

This genus from tropical and subtropical regions worldwide contains 1,000 species of evergreen or succulent perennials. Ideal in terrariums or dish gardens, they have diverse and beautifully marked and shaped, fleshy, usually long-stalked leaves. Long-stemmed spikes of minute, greenish white to cream flowers are produced in late summer.

### Cultivation

Peperomias make good house plants. They like bright light (but not direct sun), especially near a window, with high humidity. Keep moist and be sure to water them from below as the leaves mark easily. Use a half-strength, soluble fertilizer once a month. Peperomias are

lilac flowers appear in clusters along the flowering stem. These are followed by black fruit. It reaches a height of 10 in (25 cm) and a spread of 12 in (30 cm). *Ophiopogon planiscapus* is native to Japan. ZONES 6–10.

## PACHYSTACHYS
### Golden candles

This genus of 12 species of evergreen perennials and small shrubs is native to tropical Central and South America, and the West Indies. In tropical and sub-tropical areas, they can reach 6 ft (1.8 m) in height and are grown for the splashes of bright yellow and red they add to gardens. Elsewhere they are popular as indoor or greenhouse plants.

easily propagated from leaf or stem cuttings and should be repotted annually. Watch for mealybugs, spider mites and white fly.

### Peperomia argyreia
#### Watermelon peperomia
Found from northern South America to Brazil, this is a compact, nearly stemless perennial with rosettes of glossy, rounded, 3–4 in (8–10 cm) long, gray-striped leaves on long red stems. The flower spikes are small, but extend beyond the foliage. ZONES 11–12.

### Peperomia caperata
#### Emerald ripple
This perennial species has oval, deeply corrugated and veined, heart-shaped, dark green leaves that are pale green underneath and about 1½ in (35 mm) across, carried on the pinkish stems. Tight clusters of white flower spikes appear irregularly. 'Silver Ripples' has silver-gray markings on the ridges of the corrugations. ZONES 11–12.

## PILEA
This genus of around 600 species of annuals and perennials is widely distributed in the tropics with the exception of Australia. They may be creeping or erect and are usually small, though the larger species can reach 6 ft (1.8 m) tall. The foliage is variable: many have simple lance-shaped leaves, others have heart-shaped peperomia-like foliage and a few have tiny, clustered, moss-like leaves. The flowers are tiny, cream to pink structures that are easily overlooked. They are sometimes followed by seed pods that forcibly eject their seed when ripe.

### Cultivation
Pileas are widely grown as house plants; the smaller species generally prefer warm, humid conditions and are ideal

Pilea involucrata

Peperomia caperata 'Silver Ripples'

candidates for terrariums. Outdoors, grow in moist, well-drained, humus-rich soil in part-shade. Propagate from seed or cuttings or by division.

### Pilea involucrata
#### Friendship plant
From Central and South America, this attractive trailing species which sometimes mounds to 12 in (30 cm) tall has hairy, toothed-edged, 2½ in (6 cm) long oval leaves. The foliage has a puckered surface and is usually reddish purple with bronze and silver markings. There are several interesting cultivated forms of *Pilea involucrata* with varying leaf colors, shapes and sizes. ZONES 10–12.

### Pilea nummulariifolia

Usually seen spilling from a hanging basket, this trailing perennial from tropical South America and the West Indies has 1 in (25 mm) long, rounded leaves with toothed edges. It produces small cream flowers in the leaf axils and at the stem tips. ZONES 10–12.

## PISTIA
### Water lettuce, shell flower

The sole species in this genus is an aquatic perennial widespread in the tropics and a noxious weed in some areas. The 6 in (15 cm) wide, floating rosettes of ribbed, wedge-shaped leaves resemble blue-green lettuce heads. The base of the leaves is spongy, which keeps them buoyant, and the fine roots emerging from the base of the rosette extract nutrients directly from the water. Although connected by stolons, the rosettes can survive independently. The arum-like inflorescence is enclosed in a leaf-like spathe that makes it inconspicuous.

Pilea nummulariifolia

Pistia stratiotes

### Cultivation

Water lettuce is easily grown in any pond or slow-moving water. It multiplies rapidly and can quickly clog streams. It is usually self-propagating.

### Pistia stratiotes

Forming large clumps of felted rosettes, this perennial is an aggressive colonizer that can easily smother a small pond. Although it does not oxygenate the water, fish will feed on its roots. It also helps to shade the surface and keep the water cool. ZONES 10–12.

## PORTULACA

There are about 100 species of semi-succulent annuals or perennials in this genus, indigenous to the warm, dry regions of the world. The fleshy leaves vary in color from white to green or red, but it is for their flowers that they are grown—cup-shaped, white, yellow, apricot, pink, purple or scarlet in color, and resembling roses in form.

### Cultivation

They are easily grown in all climates. Because they are plants of the deserts they need sun, well-drained soil and only occasional watering. Propagate from seed or cuttings. Check for aphids.

### Portulaca grandiflora
### Rose moss, sun plant

Native to South America and one of the few annual succulents, this low-growing plant reaches 8 in (20 cm) high and spreads to 6 in (15 cm). It has small, lance-shaped, fleshy, bright green leaves like beads on their reddish stems. Its large, open flowers, usually double, are 3 in (8 cm) wide and come in bright colors including yellow, pink, red or orange. The flowers close at night and on cloudy days. It is suitable as a ground cover or in a rockery or border. ZONES 10–11.

## SALVIA
### Sage

The largest genus of the mint family, *Salvia* consists of as many as 900 species of annuals, perennials and soft-wooded shrubs, distributed through most parts of the world except very cold regions and tropical rainforests. Their distinguishing feature is the tubular, 2-lipped flower with the lower lip flat but the upper lip helmet- or boat-shaped; the calyx is also 2-lipped and may be colored. The flowers come in a wide range of colors, including some of the brightest blues and scarlets of any plants, though yellows are very rare.

### Cultivation

Sages generally do best planted in full sun in well-drained, light-textured soil with adequate watering. Propagate from seed or cuttings. The foliage of many species is attacked by snails, slugs and caterpillars.

### Salvia tiliifolia

This slender perennial has very erect branching stems up to 3 ft (1 m) tall and rounded leaves that are 1–3 in (2.5–8 cm) long and are rather rough to the touch. The flowers may be white to blue to lilac and rather small, scarcely longer than the calyces. It comes from Mexico and tropical South America. ZONES 10–12.

## SCAEVOLA
### Fan flower

This genus from Australia and the Pacific region contains 96 species of mainly temperate origin, with a very few occurring in tropical and subtropical regions. They are mainly evergreen perennials, shrubs, subshrubs and small trees, with a number of ground-covering varieties that have proved to be adaptable to a wide range of garden conditions, including seaside gardens. Most have leaves that are fleshy, often hairy and occasionally succulent, borne on stout, sometimes brittle stems. Fan-shaped flowers, while generally fairly

*Portulaca grandiflora*

*Salvia tiliifolia*

Scaevola taccada

Solanum pyracanthum

from coastal or inland sandy areas of warm-temperate Western Australia. The leaves are thick and serrated, and the light blue to mauve flowers are in terminal heads. ZONES 10–11.

### Scaevola taccada
syn. *Scaevola sericea*
**Sea lettuce**
One of the few species occurring beyond Australia, this species grows on tropical beaches and atolls throughout the Pacific and Indian oceans. An attractive ever-green shrub, it grows to 5 ft (1.5 m) high and about as wide. The bright green leaves are 4 in (10 cm) long. The small white flowers, streaked with purple, are borne at the branch ends for most of the year. The fruit are small, succulent, purplish blue berries. ZONES 10–12.

## SOLANUM
Many species belonging to this genus are climbers, and detailed information is given in the Climbers and Creepers chapter. However, *Solanum pyracanthum* is treated here as a perennial.

### Solanum pyracanthum
This perennial from tropical Africa grows to 5 ft (1.5 m) tall. The lobed leaves are spiny along the central vein. The flowers are violet. ZONES 10–12.

## SOLENOSTEMON
**Coleus, flame nettle, painted nettle**
This genus comprises 60 species of low shrubby perennials, often hairy and with variegated leaves, from tropical Africa and Asia. The stems are 4-angled and the opposite leaves are often toothed. The flowers are small with an elongated lower lip.

### Cultivation
They like moisture and protection from hot sun. They prefer humus-rich, moist

small at ½–1 in (12–25 mm) across, are profuse and are held on the plant for long periods. The flower color ranges from white to blue, mauve and deep purple.

### Cultivation
Species of *Scaevola* tolerate a wide range of soils but prefer them light and well drained; they do best in sun or part-shade. Propagate from seed or cuttings.

### Scaevola crassifolia
**Thick-leafed fan flower**
This is a vigorous spreading loose plant 3 ft (1 m) high and slightly wider. It is

Solenostemon amboinicus

Solenostemon scutellarioides

but well-drained soil and need to be pinched back to promote bushiness. Propagate from seed or cuttings.

### Solenostemon amboinicus
syns *Coleus amboinicus, Plectranthus amboinicus*
#### Allspice, three-in-one spice
This short-lived creeping perennial has been cultivated for so long its true native area is now unknown. It has pairs of pale green, downy, rather fleshy leaves, almost circular but with scalloped edges; they are very aromatic with a pleasantly spicy smell and can be used as a flavoring herb in cooked dishes. The white flowers are rather insignificant and not always produced in cultivation. The plant is seldom more than 12 in (30 cm) high, with weak, fleshy stems that root as it spreads. ZONES 10–12.

### Solenostemon scutellarioides
syns *Coleus blumei* var. *verschaffeltii, C. scutellarioides*
Native to Southeast Asia, this fast-growing perennial has leaves that are a bright mixture of pink, green, red or yellow and are a pointed, oval shape with serrated edges. It grows 24 in (60 cm) high and 12 in (30 cm) wide. ZONES 10–12.

## SPATHIPHYLLUM
Most of the 36 species of this genus of evergreen, rhizomatous perennials come from tropical America, with some native to Malaysia. They are lush, with dark green, oval leaves that stand erect or arch slightly, and beautiful white, cream or green flowers resembling arum lilies that bloom reliably indoors. A NASA study of 'sick building syndrome' found spathiphyllums among the top 10 plants for their ability to 'clean' the air in air-conditioned offices.

### Cultivation
Grow in loose, fibrous, porous potting soil in filtered light away from the sun. Regularly sponge any dust from the leaves. Water regularly, keeping the soil moist but not soggy. Feed every 4 to 6 weeks with half-strength soluble

fertilizer. Propagate by division. They are generally pest free. Too much light may turn the foliage yellow.

### Spathiphyllum 'Mauna Loa'
#### Peace lily

The leathery, lance-shaped, glossy, mid-green leaves of this perennial reach lengths of 12 in (30 cm). Oval, white, papery spathes surrounding white

*Spathiphyllum wallisii*

*Spathiphyllum 'Mauna Loa'*

spadices are borne intermittently, turning green with age. It is the best known of a fairly large number of large-flowered cultivars; others are 'Clevelandii', which is shorter, and 'Aztec'. ZONES 11–12.

### Spathiphyllum 'Sensation'

This is the largest of the *Spathiphyllum* cultivars. It has dark green foliage with prominent ribbing and large, well-shaped white flowers, ageing to green. It is a very attractive plant even when not in bloom. ZONES 11–12.

### Spathiphyllum wallisii
#### White sails

This is a dwarf species with clusters of glossy green, lance-shaped leaves on reed-like stems growing to 12 in (30 cm). A white spathe encloses tiny, creamy white spadices of fragrant flowers tightly packed around an upright spike. The color changes to green with age. ZONES 11–12.

### STRELITZIA
#### Bird of paradise

The 5 species of clump-forming perennials that make up this genus have

*Spathiphyllum 'Sensation'*

*Strelitzia reginae*

exotic flowers which resemble the head of a bird. Each bloom consists of several spiky flowers arising from a boat-like bract. The leaves are large and dramatic. Strelitzias form large clumps of evergreen banana-like foliage. The fruits are capsules.

### Cultivation
They need full sun or part-shade and prefer well-drained soil enriched with organic matter and dryish conditions in cooler months. New plants can be produced by dividing a clump, but this is hard work as the clump and roots are very dense. They can also be propagated from seed or suckers.

*Strelitzia nicolai*

### Strelitzia nicolai
#### Wild banana, giant bird of paradise
The erect, woody, palm-like stems on this tree-sized species reach a height of 20 ft (6 m) and the clump spreads over 12 ft (3.5 m). It has large dull green leaves over 5 ft (1.5 m) long on long stalks. The flowers appear near the top of the plant from the leaf axils. These

striking flowers are greenish blue and white, and open a few at a time from a reddish brown bract. ZONES 10–12.

### Strelitzia reginae
#### Crane flower, bird of paradise
This shrub-sized species has blooms of bright orange and blue sitting in a pointed green bract edged with red. It grows to 6 ft (1.8 m) high and spreads over 3 ft (1 m), forming an erect clump of leaves and smooth flower stalks

*Strelitzia reginae 'Mandela's Gold'*

*Tacca integrifolia*

arising from underground stems. The leaves are grayish green and spoon-like. 'Mandela's Gold' has yellow-orange and purplish blue blooms. ZONES 10–12.

## TACCA

This genus of 10 species of rhizomatous perennials is widespread throughout tropical Southeast Asia and Africa. They have basal leaves close to the ground, from which rise a scape with greenish yellow flowers surrounded by bracts.

The strange, almost bizarre flowers have earned members of this genus names such as bat flowers, cats' whiskers and devil's tongue.

### Cultivation

They need a humid atmosphere, some shade and a peaty soil. Propagate by division of the rhizomes or from seed, if available.

### *Tacca integrifolia*
### Bat plant, bat flower

Found naturally in Southeast Asia and from eastern India to southern China, this upright species has lance-shaped leaves up to 24 in (60 cm) long. The flowers are carried in racemes of up to 30 blooms, purple-red to brown, and are backed by 4 green to purple-tinted bracts. Filaments up to 8 in (20 cm) long hang from the flowers. ZONES 10–12.

## TAPEINOCHILOS
### Indonesian ginger

Ranging in the wild from Southeast Asia to northern Australia, members of this genus are plants of the forest floor. There are some 15 tropical species in this genus and, like *Costus* and *Heliconia* species, they make their dramatic statement not so much from the insignificant flowers but from the brilliantly colored bracts that surround them. Unfortunately their splendor is often hidden beneath the handsome foliage. These evergreen perennials make excellent cut flowers, but their short stems and cultivation requirements have cost them popularity.

### Cultivation

These plants need heat and humidity to thrive. Plant in part-shade in humus-rich soil. Propagate from seed or bulbils, or by division.

### *Tapeinochilos ananassae*

syn. *Tapeinochilos queenslandiae*

As the botanical name suggests, this species resembles a hard, scarlet pineapple (*Ananas*), but without the deep green fronds at the top. The flower spike rises about 15 in (38 cm) directly from the ground and is overtopped by the considerably taller stems, which carry the foliage. The scarlet bracts almost hide the small, tubular, yellow flowers. This species is native to eastern Indonesia, New Guinea and north-eastern Australia. ZONES 11–12.

## TILLANDSIA
### Air plant

This genus contains more than 350 species of evergreen, mainly epiphytic plants, often rosette-forming and some with branching stems and spirally arranged leaves. They are found from southeastern USA to the southernmost tip of South America. These bromeliads are grown for foliage and their unusual flowers, which are usually carried on spikes, heads or panicles and range in color from white to purple and green to red. Plants vary from 2½ in (6 cm) to more than 12 ft (3.5 m) high. Foliage may be gray, green or red-brown and leaves are covered with silver scales. The fruits are small capsules.

### Cultivation

Generally, the stiff, silver-leafed varieties are grown in hardier conditions in full sun, while the softer, green-leafed varieties prefer part-shade. Plant in well-drained sphagnum moss or on slabs of bark or driftwood; equal parts of bark and coarse sand can be used. They are often placed high up in hanging baskets to catch the rising heat. Mist regularly and water moderately. Propagate from offsets or by division.

### *Tillandsia argentea*

This small bromeliad grows 4–6 in (10–15 cm) wide, with a bulbous base and heavily scaled, silver, thread-like leaves. The leaves are arranged spirally around the short stem so that they resemble an onion. The red to violet

*Tapeinochilos ananassae*

*Tillandsia argentea*

flowers, held almost perpendicularly, are offset by red stems and red and green bracts. The plant grows best when mounted on trees or driftwood in filtered sunlight. Ensure good air circulation and a moderately humid atmosphere. ZONES 10–12.

*Tillandsia lindenii*

*Tillandsia caulescens*

### Tillandsia caulescens

This species from Bolivia and Peru grows to 18 in (45 cm) high. It has compact, spiralled, gray-green foliage, red bracts and white to purple flowers; these are 1 in (25 mm) long with recurved tips to the petals. In its native habitat, it is epiphytic on trees or cliffs at high altitudes. It is an easy plant to grow. ZONES 10–12.

### Tillandsia flabellata

Native to the cloud forests of Mexico and Guatemala, this is a very decorative plant when in flower. The foliage is rosette-shaped and either red or green; the bracts are pointed and bright red. Its long, narrow flower spikes grow upright in a fan-like arrangement to a height of 15 in (38 cm). The flowers are blue with petals up to 2 in (5 cm) long, fused into a tube. It needs a moderately humid atmosphere. ZONES 10–12.

### Tillandsia lindenii

This species grows in a typical rosette. The arching leaves are thin, smooth, pointed, and marked with red-brown lines. A large flower spike of crimson or pink-tinted bracts overlaps dense

*Tillandsia flabellata*

Victoria amazonica × cruziana 'Longwood Hybrid'

clusters of pansy-shaped, deep blue or purple-blue flowers rising just above the leaves. ZONES 10–12.

## VICTORIA
### Giant lily, royal waterlily

This genus of just 2 species of rhizomatous, deep-water aquatic annuals or perennials comes from tropical South America. Their strong rhizomes support huge floating leaves and bear nocturnal, waterlily-like flowers. Joseph Paxton (1801–65), gardener to the Duke of Devonshire, was the first to make them flower in Britain, and based his design for the Crystal Palace on the structure of its leaves—so strong they could bear the weight of his 7-year-old daughter.

### Cultivation

These aquatic plants need at least 3 ft (1 m) of water in which to grow and a position in full sun. Plant them in containers of rich loamy soil with added organic matter. Propagate from seed.

### Victoria amazonica
syn. *Victoria regia*
### Amazon waterlily

This is the largest known waterlily, with leaves reaching to 6 ft (1.8 m) across. It grows quickly, achieving its huge size just 7 months after planting from seed. The flat, prickly leaves have upturned margins of 2–4 in (5–10 cm). Leaf size is determined by the depth of the water in which the plant is growing—the deeper the water, the bigger the leaves. The flowers, white outside and pink inside, have as many as 60 petals each; they are more than 12 in (30 cm) wide. Only one flower blooms at a time. 'Longwood Hybrid', a hybrid between *Victoria amazonica* and *V. cruziana*, has white flowers that age pink. ZONES 11–12.

*Vriesea splendens*

*Vriesea carinata*

## VRIESEA

This genus consists of around 250 species of epiphytes, among the most popular bromeliads and closely related to *Tillandsia*. The smooth-margined leaves are often coated in mealy scales and have colored cross-bandings. The spectacular flower spikes vary in shape, with petals free or fused into a tube. They can be red, orange or yellow. Different species flower at different times of the year. Many hybrid cultivars have been developed, for example 'Christine'.

### Cultivation

Plant in part-shade in well-drained orchid medium. Water moderately during growth periods, always ensuring the rosette centers are filled with water. Propagate from offsets or seed.

### Vriesea carinata
### Lobster claws

The striking flattened spike of crimson and gold bracts gives this Brazilian bromeliad its common name. It grows to 10 in (25 cm) and has soft, arching, light green leaves. An excellent pot plant, be aware that this species needs a big pot as it has a larger root system than most bromeliads. ZONES 11–12.

### Vriesea splendens
syns *Tillandsia splendens*, *Vriesea speciosa*
### Flaming sword

This very striking bromeliad earned its common name from its sword-shaped flower spike of bright red or orange. It has medium-sized, soft green leaves with purple-black bands and an 18 in (45 cm) high inflorescence. ZONES 11–12.

## WEDELIA

There are around 70 species of this genus of the daisy family distributed throughout the tropics and subtropics. They range from annuals or perennials through to small shrubs. The former often have prostrate stems which root at the nodes giving the plant a creeping form; some are scrambling climbers. The leaves are in opposite pairs with the uppermost sometimes alternate. The flowers are typical of the daisy family, with small bell-shaped bisexual flowers in the center and female ray flowers radiating out, both of which are yellow. They are either solitary or occur in small clusters on long stalks. They set single-seeded fruits.

### Cultivation
Wedelias prefer well-drained soil in either sun or shade. Propagate from seed or cuttings, or by division.

### Wedelia trilobata
#### Creeping daisy
This daisy is a trailing herb with many slender, flexible stems sometimes up to 6 ft (1.8 m) long rooting at the nodes. The leaves are elliptic to oblong, green, notched and a little fleshy. They can be up to 4 in (10 cm) long and slightly lobed. With its golden flowers, 1 in (25 mm) across, and sprawling habit, this species makes a popular ground cover or hanging basket plant. It also grows well under trees, provided the ground is dry. ZONES 10–12.

## WITTROCKIA
The 7 species in this genus of bromeliads are epiphytic, terrestrial or rock-dwelling plants that form stemless rosettes. Most species have colorful thinly textured linear leaves with a few marginal spines. Spikes of flowers nestled in the heart of the plant have colorful bracts and blue or white petals.

### Cultivation
They may be grown outdoors in an open, well-drained soil in filtered shade. When grown as pot plants use an open, porous bromeliad potting mix. Indoors they need warm humid conditions and

Wittrockia superba

bright, filtered light. Propagation is from seed or offsets.

### Wittrockia superba
syns Nidularium karatas, N. superbum, Canistrum cruentum
In its natural habitat this rosette-forming bromeliad, to 3 ft (1 m) high and across, grows on trees, on rocks or in leaf litter on the ground. The long stiff leaves are a glossy green with red tips and sharp terminal spines. The flowers, arranged in a cone-shaped spike, are nestled in the heart of the plant. These are blue and white and surrounded by red bracts. ZONES 11–12.

## WORSLEYA
#### Blue amaryllis, Empress of Brazil
This genus, closely allied to *Hippeastrum*, consists of only one species. The fat bulb has a long neck protruding above the ground, topped by a few strap-shaped leaves; a short-stemmed cluster of large trumpet-shaped flowers emerges from the leafless bulb.

### Cultivation
This bulb needs full sun and perfect drainage. Most gardeners grow it in tall pots, the favored potting mix being a

*Worseleya rayneri*

combination of granite chips with a little compost. Never allow the soil to dry out. Propagate from seed.

### Worsleya rayneri

syns *Hippeastrum procerum, Worsleya procera*
This quite striking species was discovered on a mountainside near Rio de Janeiro in 1860, but it was not until 1899 that it was introduced to gardens by the Englishman whose name it bears, Arthington Worsley (1861–1943); it remains an expensive rarity. In the wild *Worsleya rayneri* grows in crevices of granite cliffs, the long bulb necks lifting the flowers into the air and sunshine. The color of the 4 in (12 cm) wide trumpets varies, from almost white to deep lilac-blue, sometimes with spotted petals. ZONES 10–12.

## XANTHORRHOEA
### Grass tree
This is a small genus of evergreen plants with grass-like foliage, all indigenous to Australia; they are very slow growing but long lived. Mature plants are stemless or develop a thick, sometimes branching trunk topped by a dense crown of long, arching, rather rigid leaves. Young plants are stemless, and may take 20 years or more to form a trunk. Long, spear-like flower spikes are produced spasmodically, often in response to burning. The spikes, up to 5 ft (1.5 m) long, consist of many densely packed, small white flowers, held on woody stalks up to 6 ft (1.8 m) long. The fruits are leathery capsules, packed along the spikes and surrounded by the blackened floral bracts.

## Cultivation

Grass trees need an open, sunny spot and well-drained soil as they are susceptible to root rot. They can also be grown in containers. Propagate from seed.

### Xanthorrhoea preissii

From mild-climate areas of Western Australia, this species has an upright or slightly twisted trunk, often black and scorched, which can reach 20 ft (6 m) with maturity, with a crown of long, arching, grass-like leaves. The small, creamy yellow flowers are densely packed at the top of a long spike which stands high above the crown. Brownish capsular fruit follow. ZONES 10–11.

## ZINGIBER
### Ginger

This genus consists of about 100 species of evergreen perennials with thick, branching, aromatic rhizomes and leafy, reed-like stems. They bear flowers in axils of colorful, waxy bracts in short spikes or globular heads on stalks arising from the rhizomes. One species produces the culinary root and stem ginger.

### Cultivation

These plants need a hot position with high humidity and plentiful water. Give them plenty of space to spread. Propagate from rhizome divisions.

### Zingiber zerumbet
### Wild ginger

This clump-forming, upright species is native to India and Southeast Asia. It has narrow, 12 in (30 cm) long leaves. On separate, tall stems are overlapping green bracts ageing to red, surrounding white or gold flowers. The rhizomes are bitter to eat, but can be used in potpourri. ZONES 10–12.

Xanthorrhoea preissii

Zingiber zerumbet

CHAPTER 2

*Shrubs*

## ACACIA

Many of the species belonging to this genus are trees, and detailed information on the genus is given in the Trees chapter. However, *Acacia farnesiana* is treated here as a shrub.

### Acacia farnesiana
#### Mimosa bush, sweet wattle

This spreading, many-branched shrub growing to 15 ft (4.5 m) tall is believed to come from tropical America but has now spread to drier tropical regions of all continents. Bipinnate leaves up to 2 in (5 cm) long with tiny leaflets are carried on spiny branches. It has large golden, sweetly scented, globular flowerheads. It is widely grown in southern France for the perfume industry. It can be used as a hedge or screen plant. ZONES 11–12.

## ACALYPHA

This genus of evergreen shrubs and subshrubs consists of over 400 species from most warmer countries of the world, but only a handful are grown as ornamentals. Some of these are valued for the decorative, narrow spikes of crowded, feathery flowers on the female plants (males are on different plants),

while one species is grown only for its showy variegated foliage. The leaves are thin, usually with toothed margins.

### Cultivation

They need a sunny to semi-shaded position, well-drained, light soil with plenty of water and protection from wind. Prune lightly to shape, followed by additional feeding and watering. Propagate from cuttings. Keep a lookout for mealybug, red spider mite and white fly.

### Acalypha hispida
#### Chenille plant, red-hot cat-tail

Thought to be from Malaysia, this upright, soft-stemmed shrub is grown for its striking, tiny, bright red flowers that hang in pendulous, tassel-like spikes on the female plants. Leaves are large, oval and bright green to reddish bronze. It reaches a height and spread of 6 ft (1.8 m). Regular pruning will maintain a bushy shape. It does best in sheltered sites in full sun. ZONES 11–12.

### Acalypha wilkesiana
#### Fijian fire plant, copper leaf

Originating in Fiji and nearby islands, this shrub grows to a height and spread of 10 ft (3 m). With erect stems

*Acacia farnesiana*

*Acalypha hispida*

branching from the base, it is grown for its large, serrated, oval leaves which appear in a wide color range, some with contrasting margins. It has inconspicuous tassel-like catkins of reddish bronze flowers. It prefers a warm, sheltered position and the foliage colors are best in full sun. Cultivars include 'Macrophylla' with large leaves, each differently variegated with bronze, copper, red, cream and yellow blotches; 'Godseffiana' with narrow, drooping green leaves edged with cream; 'Macafeeana' with deep bronze leaves splashed with coppery red; and 'Marginata' with bronze-red leaves edged with cream or pale pink. ZONES 10–11.

## ADENIUM

The name of this small genus of succulent shrubs is taken from their Arabic name *aden*, and these plants may also have given their name to the port city of Aden on the Arabian Peninsula. Shrubs and occasionally small trees, they are deciduous in dry seasons, and some develop very fleshy, swollen trunks. They range widely through tropical and subtropical Africa, from South Africa's Cape Province to the Red Sea, as well as southern Arabia.

### Cultivation
Popular in tropical gardens, they prefer a position in full sun or part-shade and thrive best in climates with a well-marked dry season. Kept dwarfed and rootbound in a pot, they will often flower more profusely. As they are very prone to rotting, they require a gritty, well-drained soil. Propagate from seed or cuttings.

### Adenium obesum
syns *Adenium multiflorum*, *A. coetanum*
**Impala lily, desert rose**
In the wild this species can make a small tree of 12 ft (3.5 m) or more with

*Adenium obesum*

*Acalypha wilkesiana* 'Macafeeana'

*Acalypha wilkesiana* cultivar

swollen trunk and thick, crooked limbs, but in cultivation it seldom exceeds about 5 ft (1.5 m), with a sparse branching habit. Whorls of lance-shaped to oval, glossy leaves are grouped at the branch tips, but when in flower it is usually leafless. The very decorative, trumpet-shaped blooms are 1¹/₂–2 in (38–50 mm) long and vary considerably in coloring; most popular is a very pale pink or white with deep pinkish red margins. Cultivar names have been given to a number of the color forms, most of which appear to be derived from *Adenium obesum* subsp. *obesum*, which extends over the species' whole geographical range — some of the other subspecies are more succulent, and are sometimes grown by succulent collectors. ZONES 11–12.

## AGAPETES

syn. *Pentapterygium*

These evergreen shrubs from the moist forests of southern Asia, mostly in the higher mountains, have leathery leaves and tubular flowers of a rather waxy texture. Most of the species grow as epiphytes in the forks of large trees, or frequently on cliffs or boulders. In some species the stems arise from a rather curious woody tuber which gets quite large as it matures.

**Cultivation**

They adapt to growing in the ground, but demand a well-drained soil of open texture and need to be planted high, with the tuber or root bases exposed or covered only by coarse humus. They enjoy shelter and humidity, but adapt readily enough to garden conditions.

### Agapetes incurvata

syn. *Agapetes rugosa*

This species is native to the Himalayan slopes in Nepal and northern India. It is a shrub of about 3 ft (1 m) tall with long scrambling branches and strongly veined leaves 2–4 in (5–10 cm) long. From leaf axils near the branch tips it bears groups of pendent tubular flowers about ³/₄ in (18 mm) long, pale flesh pink with much darker transverse bars. 'Scarlet Elf' has flowers of a stronger red shade. ZONES 10–11.

## ALLAMANDA

Many of the species belonging to this genus are climbers, and detailed information on the genus is given in the Climbers & Creepers chapter.

*Agapetes incurvata 'Scarlet Elf'*

*Allamanda schottii*

*Aphelandra squarrosa*

*Aphelandra squarrosa* 'Dania'

However the species *Allamanda schottii* is treated here as a shrub.

### Allamanda schottii
syn. *Allamanda neriifolia*
#### Shrubby allamanda
The only true shrub in the genus, this upright evergreen grows to a height and spread of 6 ft (1.8 m) and has glossy green leaves. Its trumpet-shaped golden yellow flowers, occasionally streaked with orange, are sometimes followed by large, shiny seed pods. *Allamanda schottii* prefers a sheltered sunny position. Prune to control shape; it often benefits from the stems being tied to supports. ZONES 11–12.

## APHELANDRA

This is a genus of around 170 species of subshrubs and shrubs, all native to tropical America. They have large, deeply veined, pointed leaves, usually deep green, sometimes with contrastingly colored veins, always arranged in opposite pairs on the stems. Dense terminal flower spikes have large, often brightly colored bracts from which protrude tubular orange, red or yellow flowers with a broad, 3-lobed lower lip. A handful of species have long been cultivated as decorative indoor plants, valued for foliage and flowers.

### Cultivation
They can be planted outdoors in moist, humus-enriched, well-drained soil in part-shade; otherwise they require a position indoors in strong light, but not direct sun. Cut back stems after flowering. Propagate from seed or cuttings.

### Aphelandra squarrosa
#### Zebra plant
Widely grown as a house plant, this Brazilian species can grow to 6 ft (1.8 m) high under ideal conditions. It has green leaves up to 12 in (30 cm) long, white or cream veins and midribs. The flower spike is around 8 in (20 cm) long, bright yellow and often tinted red or maroon. There are a number of cultivars, varying in leaf size and pattern, and flower colors. 'Louisae' is the cultivar most commonly grown, with bright creamy white main veins and midribs. 'Dania' has yellow to orange-yellow flowers, which are rarely seen, and leaves with prominent white veins. ZONES 11–12.

*Barleria cristata*

*Bixa orellana*

## BARLERIA

This is a large genus of 250 or more species of evergreen shrubs and subshrubs from the tropics of Asia, the Americas and Africa. The plants have simple leaves arranged in opposite pairs on the stems. The flowers are generally tubular and 2-lipped, emerging from between overlapping bracts on short spikes on terminating branches or in the upper leaf axils. These are soft-stemmed, quick-growing plants, used in tropical and subtropical gardens for quick effect. They are also popular as bedding plants.

### Cultivation

Tip prune to encourage bushiness. The plants require full sun and fertile, moist but well-drained soil and look attractive when grouped together in a shrub border. They are very easily propagated from cuttings.

### *Barleria cristata*
### Philippine violet

Despite its common name, this well-known tropical shrub is not native to the Philippines but to eastern India and Burma. It grows to around 3 ft (1 m) high and wide and is densely branched from ground level. For much of the year it produces small clusters of 2-lipped flowers from among bristly edged bracts in the upper leaf axils. Flowers vary from violet-blue to mauve, pink or white. It prefers a sheltered, humid position in part-shade. ZONES 10–12.

## BIXA
### Annatto, lipstick tree

Only one species belongs to this tropical American genus. It is cultivated for its ornamental value in gardens and for the fat-soluble orange dye its abundant seeds yield. The dye (annatto) is used to color foodstuffs and fabrics. South American Indians used it as body paint. The plant is very distinctive, with its large heart-shaped, bronze-tinged leaves, erect clusters of small, pink, rose-like flowers and large almond-shaped fruit capsules covered in dense red bristles. However, it is illegal in some parts of the world.

### Cultivation

Easy to grow, it should be grown in a protected position, and may be trained into a small tree or kept as a bushy shrub. Propagation is most effective from cuttings, as seed-grown plants take longer to come into flower.

### Bixa orellana

This colorful tree can sometimes reach a height of 30 ft (9 m) but is more commonly seen as a spreading shrub of about 10 ft (3 m) or slightly less. The pink and white flowers overlap with the clusters of bristly red fruit that persist on the branches long after they have released their seeds. ZONES 10–12.

## BOUVARDIA

A genus of 30 or so species of soft-wooded evergreen shrubs and subshrubs from Mexico, Central America and far southern USA, they are popular with florists and are grown for their attractive, long-tubed, often fragrant flowers in a range of colors from white to red. The leaves are smallish, soft and smooth margined, arranged in opposite pairs on the stems or in whorls of 3 or more, while the flowers are held in loose to dense clusters at the end of the stems.

### Cultivation

These shrubs require a warm, sheltered position in part-shade, though in humid climates some can tolerate full sun. The soil needs to be fertile and well drained. Water well and feed regularly during the growing period. Cut back stems by half after flowering to maintain shape; plants can become straggly. Propagate from cuttings. They are susceptible to attack by sap-sucking insects such as white fly and mealybug.

### Bouvardia longiflora
syn. Bouvardia humboldtii
### Scented bouvardia

A favorite with florists, this tender, weak-stemmed evergreen shrub grows to a height and spread of 3 ft (1 m) or more. Very brittle, the plant is easily

*Bouvardia longiflora*

damaged by strong winds. The strongly perfumed, snow white flowers are up to 3 in (8 cm) long and 1 in (25 mm) wide. ZONES 10–11.

## BRUGMANSIA
syn. Datura
### Angel's trumpet

The large shrubs of this genus are grown for their very large, fragrant, pendent trumpet flowers. They are still often found under the name *Datura*, but the true daturas are short lived, herbaceous plants with smaller, more upright flowers and capsular fruits that are usually prickly (brugmansias have fleshy, un-armed fruit that may be very long and narrow). Brugmansias are evergreen or semi-evergreen and their leaves are large and soft, rather like tobacco leaves but smaller, and all parts of the plant are narcotic and poisonous.

### Cultivation

They prefer a warm to hot climate, a sunny sheltered site and a light, fertile, well-drained soil. Best grown as small trees, they can be shaped when young to obtain a single trunk or can be kept trimmed as dense, rounded shrubs. Water well during the growing season. Propagate from tip cuttings. Whitefly and spider mite can cause problems, as can snails.

*Brugmansia aurea*

*Brugmansia* × *candida*

### Brugmansia aurea

This species grows to about 20 ft (6 m) with large, soft, downy leaves, serrated at the margins when young but becoming smooth-edged as they mature. The cream to pale golden yellow trumpet flowers, 10 in (25 cm) long with very wide mouths, hang beneath the foliage and appear to glow in the evenings when lit softly by garden lights. ZONES 10–12.

### Brugmansia × candida
syn. *Datura candida*

This 10–15 ft (3–4.5 m) high shrub, of rather untidy habit, branches low from a short trunk and the long, oval, velvety leaves are confined to the branch tips. The pendulous white flowers, strongly scented at night, are up to 12 in (30 cm) long and have a widely flared mouth. Once the most commonly cultivated species, *Brugmansia* × *candida* is now believed to be a hybrid between *B. aurea* and *B. versicolor*. 'Plena' has an extra frill of petals inside the main trumpet and 'Grand Marnier' has flowers of soft apricot. ZONES 10–12.

### Brugmansia 'Charles Grimaldi'

Named after a Californian landscape designer, this 6 ft (1.8 m) tall hybrid cultivar ('Dr Seuss' × 'Frosty Pink') has very large, pendulous, fragrant, pale orange-yellow flowers. It has very large leaves and with age will form quite a thicket of stems. ZONES 10–12.

### Brugmansia 'Frosty Pink'

This hybrid has large, pale apricot-pink and white flowers and grows to around 6 ft (1.8 m) tall. It has large, pale green leaves and forms clumps of stems. 'Ecuador Pink' is very similar, but has pretty flowers of pastel pink. ZONES 10–12.

### Brugmansia suaveolens
syn. *Datura suaveolens*

This many-branched, spreading evergreen shrub or small tree, which reaches 15 ft (4.5 m), has downy, oval leaves up to 12 in (30 cm) long. The flowers are narrower than in *Brugmansia* × *candida*, and their tubes are heavily striped with green. They are profuse at various times

Brugmansia 'Charles Grimaldi'

Brugmansia 'Ecuador Pink'

Brugmansia suaveolens

Brugmansia 'Frosty Pink'

of the year. Widely grown in tropical gardens, they are sometimes seen pruned to round-headed shrubs. 'Plena' has semi-double blooms. ZONES 10–12.

## BRUNFELSIA

These evergreen shrubs or small trees from South and Central America bear delightfully fragrant flowers with a narrow tube flaring abruptly into 5 flat petals; these change color from their first day of opening through successive days, with flowers of different ages sprinkling the bush. Most species are slow growing and bushy, with simple, rather leathery leaves. The plants may all contain poisonous alkaloids, particularly in their berry-like fruits, which have been known to poison dogs.

### Cultivation

These shrubs like a site with full sun or with afternoon shade, and fertile, well-drained soil with adequate water during dry spells. They do well in pots. Prune after flowering to promote bushiness. Propagate from tip cuttings. Mealybug and white fly may present problems.

*Caesalpinia crista*

*Brunfelsia pauciflora*

### Brunfelsia pauciflora
syns *Brunfelsia calycina, B. eximia*
**Brazil raintree**
This small deciduous or semi-evergreen shrub is slower growing and less vigorous than *Brunfelsia australis*, with duller, dark green, leathery leaves, growing to about 5 ft (1.5 m) tall and wide but rather open branched. In bloom it is even more dramatic: large, abundant flowers open a rich purple and fade to mauve and white over successive days. 'Floribunda' has smaller leaves and extremely abundant pale purple flowers. ZONES 10–12.

## CAESALPINIA
Many of the species belonging to this genus are trees, and detailed information on the genus is given in the Trees chapter. However, the ones included here can be treated as shrubs.

### Caesalpinia crista
Widespread on the world's tropical coasts, this is a rampant, woody climber or scrambling shrub. Stems are somewhat thorny and the shiny, compound leaves, which can be up to 3 ft (1 m) long, are made up of up to 10 large leaflets, each 4 in (10 cm) long. The plant produces panicles of orange veined, yellow flowers at the tips of stems. These are both fragrant and showy. This species is best grown at or near the coast. ZONES 11–12.

### Caesalpinia pulcherrima
syn. *Poinciana pulcherrima*
**Peacock flower, Barbados pride, red bird of paradise**
Mostly seen as a shrub of about 8 ft (2.4 m), this tropical species can grow to 15–20 ft (4.5–6 m). Short lived and fast growing, it has an open, moderately spreading habit with coarse, prickly leaves and branches with a whitish waxy

bloom, which terminate in tall, upright sprays of vivid, usually scarlet and gold blossoms. There is also a yellow-flowered form and a darker red one. ZONES 11–12.

## CALLIANDRA
### Powderpuff tree

The great majority of the 200 or so species of this large genus of evergreen shrubs and small trees are native to the Americas, mainly in the tropical regions, but a few are native to India, Africa or Madagascar. A small number are cultivated as ornamentals, valued for their showy flowerheads with numerous long stamens. The flowers are like those of the related acacias and mimosas but generally on a larger scale, usually in spherical or hemispherical heads. The leaves are always bipinnate but vary greatly in both number and in the size of the leaflets; in most species the leaves 'sleep' at night or in dull, stormy weather, the leaflets folding together.

### Cultivation

Despite their often delicate appearance, many calliandras are tough, long-lived plants thriving in any well-drained, fertile soil in full sun. Water well in the growing season. Propagation is easiest from seed, but some produce few or no pods in cultivation and can be grown from cuttings.

### Calliandra californica
### Baja fairy duster

A native of Baja California (a state of northwestern Mexico), this is a shrub of about 4 ft (1.2 m) in height of rather upright habit and open branched, the branches with paired prickles at the leaf bases. The leaves are small, with narrow gray-green leaflets only ¼ in (6 mm) long. The flowerheads are small and deep red to purplish. ZONES 10–12.

### Calliandra emarginata

A low-growing shrub, or occasionally taller to 10 ft (3 m) or so, this species is distinctive in having leaves with only 4 to 8 rather large leaflets; these are smooth and glossy and up to 2½ in (6 cm) long. A native of Honduras,

*Caesalpinia pulcherrima*

*Calliandra emarginata*

*Calliandra californica*

*Calliandra haematocephala*

*Calliandra surinamensis*

Guatemala and southern Mexico, the plant is dotted with globular flowerheads through much of the year. The color varies from almost white to deep reddish pink; the bases of the flowers are usually paler. ZONES 10–12.

### *Calliandra haematocephala*
**Blood-red tassel-flower, pink or red powderpuff**
A native of tropical South America, this species produces large flower-heads around 3 in (8 cm) in diameter. The flowers appear almost year round. It makes a large, broadly spreading shrub to a height of 12 ft (3.5 m) and an even greater spread with age. The leaves consist of rather few oblong leaflets about 2 in (5 cm) long, pink-flushed when first unfolding. ZONES 10–12.

### *Calliandra surinamensis*
**Pink tassel-flower**
This tropical species comes from the Guianas region of northern South America. It is an elegant shrub of erect, open habit up to about 10 ft (3 m) tall with arching branches and ferny foliage. The flowerheads are distinctive, forming narrow inverted cones that are scattered along the uppersides of the branches, white at the base but tipped rose-pink.

They appear through much of the year and attract butterflies. ZONES 11–12.

## *CALLISTEMON*
### Bottlebrush
These evergreen Australian shrubs and small trees bear magnificent long-stamened, mostly red flowers in dense cylindrical spikes. The tips of the flower spikes continue to grow as leafy shoots, leaving long-lasting, woody seed cap-sules that eventually become half embedded in the thickening branch. Many species have a somewhat weeping habit and a few have striking papery bark, like that in the related genus *Melaleuca*. The flowers are nectar rich and attract birds, including small parrots (lorikeets) in their native regions.

### Cultivation
The shrubby callistemons make a fine addition to the shrub border, where they attract birds. They prefer full sun and moist soil; some, however, will tolerate poor drainage. A light pruning after flowering will prevent seed capsules forming and help promote bushiness and flowering. Prune to establish a single trunk on tree-like species. Propagate species from seed (preferably wild collected), cultivars and selected clones from tip cuttings.

*Callistemon formosus*

*Cerbera manghas*

### Callistemon formosus

Endemic to a small area of rocky forest country in southeast Queensland, this is a medium to tall shrub of up to 15 ft (4.5 m) in height. The new growths are red, maturing to stiff, flat, pointed, dull green leaves on pendulous branches. The small flower spikes are creamy yellow, rarely pinkish. ZONES 10–11.

### CERBERA

Belonging to the oleander family, this genus consists of perhaps 4 species of evergreen shrubs and small trees, native to tropical Asia and Australasia, Madagascar and the Seychelles. They have a milky sap and are poisonous in all parts; one species from Madagascar was notorious for its use there as an 'ordeal' poison, administered to criminal suspects to test their guilt or innocence. Linnaeus took the genus name from that of Cerberus, the 3-headed dog guarding the entrance to Hades. The plants have broad, smooth leaves arranged in opposite pairs, fragrant white flowers and large egg-shaped fruits.

#### Cultivation

They need good light and a moist, humid atmosphere to prosper. Plant in well-drained, humus-rich soil. Propagate from seed or cuttings.

### Cerbera manghas

syn. *Cerbera odollam*

Occurring over most of the range of the genus (except Madagascar), this species grows mainly at the edges of mangrove swamps. A shrub to 20 ft (6 m) in height it has narrow, leathery leaves and highly fragrant white flowers, with either a pink or yellow center, held in large bunches. The large, single-seeded, egg-shaped fruit are between 2–3 in (5–8 cm) long and ripen from green to red. ZONES 11–12.

### CLERODENDRUM

This genus of over 400 species ranges through the world's tropics and warmer climates. It contains trees, shrubs, climbers and herbaceous plants, both deciduous and evergreen, some with very showy flowers. The features that unite them are leaves in opposite pairs; tubular flowers, usually flared or bowl-shaped at the mouth and with 4 long stamens and a style protruding well beyond the tube; and fruit, a shiny berry sitting at the center of the calyx that usually becomes larger and thicker after flowering.

#### Cultivation

They appreciate a sunny position, though sheltered from strong wind and the hottest sun, and deep, moist, fertile soil. Propagate from cuttings, which strike readily; many species sucker from the roots and a large root cutting can produce much quicker results.

### Clerodendrum buchananii

This tropical species from Indonesia makes a tall, weak shrub of about 10 ft (3 m) with an open habit and large, heart-shaped leaves with downy undersides. The flowers appear through much of the year in terminal panicles, the stalks and flowers all scarlet. It is an unkempt shrub, fast growing but short lived. There may be confusion between this species and *Clerodendrum speciosissimum*. ZONES 11–12.

### Clerodendrum paniculatum
#### Pagoda flower

This fast-growing but short-lived species is popular in the wet tropics for its huge panicles of small salmon pink flowers that terminate the erect shoots, appearing through much of the year. Growing to 6–8 ft (1.8–2.4 m), it branches from the roots into coarse, vigorous shoots with very large, deeply veined, glossy deep green leaves on long stalks. ZONES 11–12.

### Clerodendrum splendens
#### Glory bower

From tropical West Africa, this evergreen, woody stemmed, twining plant grows to 10 ft (3 m) or more. It has rich green, oval or elliptic leaves and showy clusters of 1 in (25 mm) wide scarlet flowers. ZONES 10–12.

### Clerodendrum thomsoniae
#### Bleeding heart vine, bleeding glory bower

A climbing shrub from western tropical Africa, the popularity of this species derives from the clusters of deep crimson flowers emerging from pure white, bell-shaped calyces contrasted by large, oval, deep green leaves. The calyces persist in fruit, turning dull pinkish. Reaching 10 ft (3 m) in height, it requires high humidity. ZONES 10–12.

### Clerodendrum ugandense
#### Blue butterfly bush

This species from East Africa will take rather cooler conditions than most tropical clerodendrums. It is a rangy and open evergreen shrub to 10 ft (3 m) with a spread of 6 ft (1.8 m). Its slightly arching branches bear terminal sprays of butterfly-shaped flowers in two shades

*Clerodendrum paniculatum*

*Clerodendrum buchananii*

of clear blue. It can be pruned back continually to keep the long branches in check. ZONES 10–11.

### Clerodendrum zambeziacum

One of the lower-growing shrubby clerodendrums, this tropical African species puts up rather weak stems about 3–6 ft (1–1.8 m) tall from its spreading root system. The leaves are large, soft and heart-shaped. Throughout the year it produces a succession of pure white flowers with tubes about 4 in (10 cm) long and sometimes curled stamens. ZONES 10–12.

## CODIAEUM

This genus consists of about 15 species of evergreen shrubs and small trees native to southern Asia, the Malay region and Pacific Islands. One species, *Codiaeum variegatum*, has given rise to a large number of cultivars with highly colored and sometimes bizarrely shaped leaves. These are popular garden plants in tropical regions, the larger-growing cultivars making good hedging plants. The small yellow flowers and tiny seed pods are quite insignificant—the plants are grown strictly for their magnificent foliage.

Clerodendrum splendens

Clerodendrum ugandense

Clerodendrum thomsoniae

Clerodendrum zambeziacum

*Codiaeum variegatum 'Interruptum'*

*Codiaeum variegatum 'America'*

*Codiaeum variegatum 'Petra'*

## Cultivation

They prefer moist, humus-rich soil in sun or dappled shade. As indoor plants they are grown in a rich but freely draining potting mix, and watered and fed freely. Propagate from tip cuttings or by air-layering.

### *Codiaeum variegatum*
### Croton, garden croton

This shrub species occurs throughout the range of the genus, with plain green leaves in the wild. Cultivated forms, though, show enormous variation of leaf color and pattern with shades of green, red, yellow, orange and purple, sometimes on the one plant. Some cultivars can grow to 8 ft (2.4 m) or more tall, with leaves up to 12 in (30 cm) long; they must be propagated vegetatively, usually by cuttings, to maintain their foliage color. 'America' has green, red, orange and yellow leaves, the variegation following the veins and margins; 'Petra' is similar to 'America' but has more clearly defined margins; 'Imperiale' has yellow leaves with pink margins and green midribs; 'Interruptum' has yellow, recurved leaves with green margins and red midribs; 'Mrs Iceton' (syn. 'Appleleaf') has elliptic leaves, metallic purple at the edges, yellow to rose in the center. ZONES 11–12.

### *COFFEA*
### Coffee

This genus includes some 40 species of shrubs and small trees, native mainly to tropical Africa, with a few in Asia. Best known is *Coffea arabica*, the original source of coffee and still the most prized species. Most have tiered branches and deep green, smooth-edged leaves arranged in opposite pairs. Attractive white flowers are clustered in the leaf-axils, followed by small, fleshy, 2-seeded fruits that turn red as they ripen.

### Cultivation

The preferred growing environment is humus-rich soil with light shade and steady temperatures. Propagation is

*Coffea arabica*

*Cordyline fruticosa*

from seed or semi-ripe cuttings. They adapt well to being grown as house plants. Propagate from seed, which must be fresh but germinates very rapidly.

### Coffea arabica
### Arabian coffee

Originating in mountain rainforests of Ethiopia, this is the coffee of commerce and, while one or two are unlikely to supply your coffee needs, it is a very attractive evergreen shrub for gardens or for large containers. It can grow to around 15 ft (4.5 m) high. Small, fragrant white flowers are clustered along the branches behind the leaves and are followed by the dark red fruits; each contains 2 'beans' which when extracted, dried and roasted are our familiar coffee beans. ZONES 10–12.

## CORDYLINE
### Cabbage tree, ti

Centered in the southwest Pacific region (one species in tropical America), most species of this genus of 15 or so species of somewhat palm-like evergreen shrubs and small trees are tropical or subtropical. Cordylines resemble dracaenas in habit and foliage, but differ in the flowers which are small and starry, borne in large panicles, and in the red,

black or whitish fruits. A peculiarity is their underground rhizome that grows downward, sometimes emerging through the drainage apertures of a pot; its main function appears to be food storage.

### Cultivation

Cordylines do well in rich, well-drained soil. The narrower-leafed New Zealand species are the most sun hardy, and *Cordyline australis* tolerates salt spray near the ocean; the species with broader, thinner leaves prefer a sheltered position in part shade, though will tolerate full sun if humidity is high. Most can be kept in pots or tubs for many years as indoor or patio plants. They are easily propagated from seed or stem cuttings.

### Cordyline fruticosa
*syn. Cordyline terminalis*
### Ti ngahere

This well-known species probably originated somewhere in the vicinity of Papua New Guinea but was long ago spread through the Pacific by Melanesians and Polynesians, who valued its starchy rhizomes as food. It grows to at least 10 ft (3 m) high, forming quite a strong, branched trunk, but is more often seen as a 3–6 ft (1–1.8 m) shrub in gardens or as a house plant. The thin, lance-shaped leaves are up to 30 in

Cordyline stricta

Cuphea ignea

(75 cm) long and 6 in (15 cm) wide, clustered at the top of the stem. The 12 in (30 cm) panicles of small, scented, white to dull mauve flowers, may be followed by crowded red berries. The many colored and variegated foliage forms are favorite landscaping plants in the tropics; they vary also in leaf size and shape. 'Imperialis' has dark green leaves streaked pink and crimson. ZONES 10–12.

### Cordyline stricta
#### Slender palm lily
This shrub from subtropical eastern Australia makes a clump of weak cane-like stems to 6–8 ft (1.8–2.4 m) high with dark green, strap-like, floppy leaves no more than ¾ in (18 mm) wide. It reaches about the same height grown in a pot but makes a sparser plant. Long, drooping panicles of pale purplish flowers are followed by small black berries. It does best in moist, sheltered positions and is very shade tolerant. ZONES 10–12.

### CUPHEA
From Central and South America, this genus consists of over 250 species of annuals, evergreen perennials, subshrubs and shrubs. They are mostly rather low growing with weak stems and smallish, simple leaves. The flowers have a long tubular calyx and small circular red, pink, yellow or white petals, the latter sometimes hardly visible. They are fast growing and can be treated as annuals. The many species vary quite considerably in appearance, especially with regard to the flowers. They bloom almost throughout the year.

#### Cultivation
They prefer moist, well-drained soil in sun or very light shade. Propagation is usually from small tip cuttings, though they are also easily raised from seed, which often self-sows.

### Cuphea ignea
syn. Cuphea platycentra
#### Cigar flower, cigarette plant
This species from Mexico and the West Indies gets its common names from the flowers, which are small, orange and tubular. Each has a white tip with a touch of black, suggesting the ash at the tip of a cigar or cigarette. The leaves are small, elliptical and bright green. A bushy subshrub, it grows up to about 24 in (60 cm) high and benefits from occasional trimming to keep it compact. ZONES 10–12.

### DRACAENA
syn. Pleomele
This genus of some 40 species of ever-green trees and shrubs, many originating from equatorial Africa and Asia, is grown for foliage, often as indoor plants. Those species grown indoors are sometimes confused with species of Cordyline and are often termed 'false

*Dracaena marginata*

*Eranthemum pulchellum*

palms' because of their cane-like stems and crowns of sword-like leaves.

### Cultivation

Outdoors, dracaenas need full sun or part-shade and well-drained soil. Occasionally they can be cut back to almost soil level if desired. Propagate from seed or by air-layering or from stem cuttings. Watch out for mealybugs.

### Dracaena marginata

A slow-growing shrub from Madagascar, this species reaches 15–20 ft (4.5–6 m). Its narrow, sword-like leaves have red margins. The cultivar 'Tricolor' with a cream stripe and red edge is commonly grown as a house plant. This species tolerates some shade. ZONES 10–12.

## ERANTHEMUM

This genus of around 30 species of tropical Asian shrubs and subshrubs in the acanthus family are most often grown for their attractive pink or blue flowers or in some cases for their attractive decorative foliage. They have simple, smooth-edged leaves arranged in opposite pairs on the branches, and clustered flowers with tubular bases and 5 flat spreading petals. The fruits are small club-shaped capsules that split explosively into two halves.

### Cultivation

Eranthemums are easily grown in tropical and subtropical climates, preferring a sheltered, part-shaded position in good soil and plentiful watering during the growing season. If a more compact shape is desired they can be cut back fairly hard after flowering. Indoors, provide bright, indirect light and water freely. Propagate from cuttings.

### Eranthemum pulchellum

syn. *Eranthemum nervosum*
### Blue sage

This is a colorful evergreen shrub to 4 ft (1.2 m) from tropical India that has naturalized in many other countries. Its erect stems are well clothed with rich green leaves to 8 in (20 cm) long with conspicuous veins. The striking flowers are a violet blue and arranged in dense spikes. The individual blooms have a slender tube with widely flared lobes. ZONES 10–12.

## EUCALYPTUS

Many of the species belonging to this genus are trees, and detailed information on the genus is given in the Trees chapter. However, *Eucalyptus tetraptera* is treated here as a shrub.

### Eucalyptus tetraptera
#### Square-fruited mallee

In nature this species is a straggly, untidy shrub rarely more than 6 ft (1.8 m) tall, growing in poor sandy soil along the southern coast of Western Australia. Its large leaves are thick and leathery and

*Eucalyptus tetraptera*

*Euphorbia pulcherrima*

its big 4-winged flowers are bright red with pink stamens. Light pruning will moderate its straggly habit. ZONES 10–11.

### EUPHORBIA

Many of the species belonging to this genus are succulents, and detailed information on the genus is given in the Cacti & Succulents chapter. However, the euphorbias included here may be treated as shrubs.

### Euphorbia pulcherrima
#### Poinsettia, Mexican flame tree

Potted poinsettias are a familiar Christmas decoration all over the northern hemisphere, but this native of Mexico is a garden plant. It makes a rather open shrub up to 12 ft (3.5 m) tall, usually dropping its leaves as flowering commences. The broad bracts, which give each flower cluster the appearance of a single, huge flower, last many weeks. There are many named cultivars, which extend the color range from the original blood red to pink and cream. It thrives best in subtropical regions and likes fertile soil and sunshine. The leaves are large but not especially attractive. Cultivars of the normal tall-growing poinsettia include 'Henrietta Ecke' with additional smaller red bracts. Most cultivars now sold for indoor use are semi-dwarf: 'Annette Hegg' is red, while 'Rosea' (pink) and 'Lemon Drop' (pale yellow) are similar except for color. ZONES 10–12.

### Euphorbia viguieri

This spiny succulent from Madagascar grows to 5 ft (1.5 m) in height. Its stems are 6-angled and ridged and bear triangular leaf scars and rows of irregular spines along the ridges. The leaves, which are clustered towards the tips of the branches, are red in color with

*Gardenia augusta 'Magnifica'*

*Euphorbia viguieri*

green midribs. Its floral bracts are yellow-green. ZONES 10–12.

## GARDENIA

Evergreen shrubs or small trees with glossy deep green leaves and fragrant white or cream flowers, gardenias provide some of the most fragrant of all flowers and are popular in warm-climate gardens worldwide. The genus includes some 200-odd species, most of them from tropical Asia or southern Africa.

### Cultivation

They need well-drained, neutral to acid soil and prefer light shade. Generous water and a regular dressing of compost and fertilizer ensures good flowering and keeps foliage a deep glossy green. They are easily propagated from cuttings.

### Gardenia augusta
syns *Gardenia florida, G. grandiflora, G. jasminoides*
### Common gardenia, Cape jasmine
This is the best known species of the genus, an evergreen, glossy-leafed shrub from southern China, though long supposed native to the Cape of Good Hope, hence the name Cape jasmine. It is commonly seen in gardens and flower shops in one of its double-flowered cultivars, all with white, strongly perfumed

*Gardenia augusta*

flowers changing to pale yellow as they age. The best known is 'Florida', a 3 ft (1 m) tall shrub with flowers about 3 in (8 cm) wide; 'Magnifica' is larger in all its parts though less generous with its flowers; 'Radicans' is almost prostrate, with small flowers and leaves. The flowers appear over a long season. ZONES 10–11.

## GRAPTOPHYLLUM

Generally seen as house plants, this genus of evergreen shrubs in the acanthus family comprises 10 species from tropical Australia and the Pacific islands. They are admired chiefly for

Hakea nitida

Hamelia patens

their decorative foliage, which is often marked with various colors. It bears tubular, 2-lipped flowers.

### Cultivation

In tropical climates they do well as garden plants, liking dappled shade and fertile, well-drained soil. They respond well to gentle pruning to control their tendency to legginess. As house plants they need regular watering during the growing season. Propagate from cuttings at any time.

### *Graptophyllum pictum*
### Caricature plant

This species has an erect, open habit and reaches a height of 5 ft (1.5 m) with a spread of about 30 in (75 cm). Its leaf coloration varies but typically it has mid-green, oval leaves with creamy central blotches. The tubular purplish red flowers are borne on terminal spikes. 'Tricolor' has cream and green leaves,

heavily flushed pink especially when young; 'Purpureum Variegatum' is similar but replaces the pink with purple-red. ZONES 11–12.

### *HAKEA*

This genus consists of 130 species of evergreen shrubs and small trees from Australia. They are closely allied to the grevilleas and, like them, are well-regarded garden plants in their home country, though the most easily grown species are not necessarily the most spectacular. There is great variety in the foliage, from needle-like to broad, though the leaves are always stiff and leathery. The flowers are borne in small clusters, and the bracts are woody follicles, which are sometimes quite large.

### Cultivation

Fast growing but not always long lived, they like plenty of sunshine and well-drained soil and dislike phosphorus-rich fertilizers. Propagation is usually from seed; outstanding forms can be perpetuated from cuttings. Watch for root-rot in moist soil.

### *Hakea nitida*

One of the lesser known hakeas, *Hakea nitida* is indigenous to Western Australia.

The white flowers tend to hide among the dull green leaves, but the plant is of shapely, upright habit and makes a fine informal hedge about 8 ft (2.4 m) high. ZONES 10–11.

## HAMELIA
### Rat poison plant
This is a genus of about 40 evergreen shrubs and small trees from tropical America, of which only a few of the shrubby species are encountered in tropical and subtropical gardens. The attraction is the clusters of flowers, borne over a long season. The inelegant common name comes from the poisonous nature of the fruit.

### Cultivation
They prefer rich soil, light shade and plenty of moisture, and are propagated from cuttings.

### Hamelia patens
### Firebush, scarlet bush
This dense, soft-wooded shrub grows to about 10 ft (3 m). The leaves are pale green with downy undersides, and the bright scarlet tubular flowers are held in clusters towards the ends of the branches. The flowers are followed by yellow-green berries that ripen to purple-black. ZONES 10–11.

## HIBISCUS
While the genus name conjures up the innumerable cultivars of *Hibiscus rosa-sinensis*, the genus of around 220 species is quite diverse. The leaves are mostly toothed or lobed and the flowers, borne singly or in terminal spikes, are of characteristic shape with a funnel of 5 overlapping petals and a central column of fused stamens.

### Cultivation
Easy to grow, the shrubby species thrive in sun and slightly acid, well-drained soil. Water regularly and feed during the flowering period. Trim after flowering to maintain shape. Propagate from seed or cuttings or by division, depending on the species. Check for aphids, mealybugs and whitefly.

### Hibiscus calyphyllus
This spectacular tropical African species is a shrub of 3–6 ft (1–1.8 m) with 3–4 in (8–10 cm) blooms distinguished by a purple-brown eye contrasting with the bright yellow of the petals. ZONES 10–11.

*Hibiscus calyphyllus*

*Hibiscus cisplatinus*

Hibiscus insularis

Hibiscus rosa-sinensis

Hibiscus mutabilis

### Hibiscus cisplatinus
This is a shrub growing at least 10 ft
(3 m) tall with thorny branches and
curious, rectangular-petalled flowers.
These are large and pink with each petal
being longitudinally veined in a darker
pink. The leaves are dark green, up to
6 in (15 cm) long and somewhat variable
in shape. *Hibiscus cisplatinus* is native to
Argentina and Brazil. ZONES 10–11.

### Hibiscus insularis
#### Phillip Island hibiscus
Endemic to tiny Phillip Island, which
lies off Norfolk Island in the southwest
Pacific, this species is now close to
extinction in the wild. It is a spreading
shrub up to 12 ft (3.5 m) tall, branching

low into a tangle of very woody stems
supporting a twiggy canopy of fine
foliage. The leaves are coarsely toothed
and the 2 in (5 cm) diameter flowers
open lemon yellow with a maroon center
and age to dull pink. ZONES 10–11.

### Hibiscus mutabilis
#### Confederate rose, cotton rose
A multi-branched deciduous shrub with
a low-branching habit, the cotton rose
comes from China and grows to about
12 ft (3.5 m) tall and almost as wide.
The large flowers open white and age
from pale pink to deep pink; they are
held among the felty, multi-lobed leaves.
'Plenus', with its double flowers, is the
most commonly grown cultivar.
ZONES 8–10.

### Hibiscus rosa-sinensis
#### Chinese hibiscus, red hibiscus, shoeflower
The name shoeflower is Jamaican, from
the use of crushed flowers to polish
black shoes. It is a glossy leafed
evergreen shrub, sometimes as much as
15 ft (4.5 m) high and wide, with blood-
red flowers borne just about all year. It
is less often seen than its numerous
garden cultivars, some pure-bred and

*Hibiscus rosa-sinensis* 'Surfrider'

*Hibiscus rosa-sinensis* 'Covakanic'

*Hibiscus rosa-sinensis* Hawaiian Hybrid

others, like the enormous blooming Hawaiian hybrids, carrying the genes of other species. These plants grow 3–10 ft (1–3 m) high, and the flowers can be 5-petalled singles, semi-double or fully double, the colors ranging from white through pinks to red; the Hawaiian hybrids offer yellow, coral and orange, often with 2 or 3 shades in each flower. The flowers range upwards in size from about 5 in (12 cm). Each flower only lasts a day, but they appear in long succession. *Hibiscus rosa-sinensis* cultivars include 'Surfrider' with single flowers that are deep orange with a red center; 'Fiesta' with dark apricot flowers with

*Hibiscus schizopetalus*

*Hibiscus syriacus* 'Blue Bird'

red and white centers; 'Covakanic' with flowers in beautiful varying tones of orange and apricot; as well as 'Apple Blossom', 'Cooperi', 'Madonna' and 'Sabrina'. ZONES 10–12.

### Hibiscus schizopetalus

From tropical Africa, this evergreen shrub grows to 12 ft (3.5 m) with rounded, toothed, deep green leaves and long-stemmed, pendulous, scarlet flowers; their petals are recurved and much cut, and the staminal column hangs as though on a silken thread. Pruning is not necessary as its natural, somewhat slender, drooping habit is part of this plant's charm. This species is closely allied to *Hibiscus rosa-sinensis* and has interbred with it. ZONES 10–11.

### Hibiscus syriacus
#### Blue hibiscus, rose of Sharon

This upright, deciduous shrub (evergreen in warmer climates) from temperate Asia flowers freely in varying shades of white, pink, soft red, mauve and violet blue. The single, semi-double and double flowers are bell-shaped and are borne in the axils of the leaves. It has small, hairless leaves and grows to 12 ft (3.5 m) tall with a spread of 3–6 ft (1–1.8 m). Prune to shape in the first 2 years of growth, trimming lightly thereafter to maintain compact form. Popular cultivars include 'Ardens' with large, mauve flowers with crimson centers; 'Blue Bird' with single, violet blue flowers with red centers; 'Diana' with broad, pure white flowers; and 'Woodbridge' with 2-toned pink blooms at least 4 in (10 cm) across. ZONES 5–10.

### IXORA
#### Jungle flame

From tropical regions of Africa, Asia and islands of the Pacific, this is a large

*Ixora chinensis*

genus of about 400 species of evergreen shrubs and small trees, some with spectacular heads of scarlet, orange, yellow, pink or white flowers. They have glossy, deep green leaves. In Asia, the roots of ixoras are used to make a medicine said to alleviate stomach ailments and cure dysentery. These shrubs are used for massed bedding, hedges and screens, and can be grown in containers.

### Cultivation
In the tropics, they appreciate a part-shaded position. Humus-rich, moist but freely drained, friable soils and high humidity suit them best, and they need regular water. Light pruning after flowering will maintain shape; spent flowerheads should also be removed. Propagate from cuttings or from seed.

*Ixora chinensis* 'Prince of Orange'

### *Ixora chinensis*
This evergreen shrub grows to a height and spread of 4 ft (1.2 m), its densely packed, erect branches clothed with narrowly pointed, deep green leaves.

*Ixora coccinea*

*Ixora javanica*

The large terminal clusters of tubular flowers vary from bright orange-red, yellow and white to pink. 'Lutea' has yellow flowers; 'Prince of Orange' has larger orange-scarlet flowerheads that almost cover the bush. ZONES 10–12.

### Ixora coccinea
### Jungle geranium
From tropical Southeast Asia, this neat, rounded evergreen shrub reaches a height of 3 ft (1 m) with a spread of 5 ft (1.5 m). Small, scarlet, tubular flowers in dense, ball-like clusters among the 4 in (10 cm) long, dark green leaves may be followed by cherry-sized black fruit. ZONES 11–12.

### Ixora javanica
syn. *Ixora amoena*
### Red ixora, Javanese ixora
Native to Java and the Malay Peninsula, this evergreen shrub grows up to 15 ft (4.5 m) in the wild but rarely reaches more than 5 ft (1.5 m) in cultivation. Its heads of small, tubular flowers are usually red, although orange and pink forms are known. ZONES 11–12.

## JATROPHA

This genus of evergreen and deciduous shrubs, small trees and herbs originates in warm-temperate and tropical regions of Asia and the Americas. The plants have a distinctive milky sap and are grown primarily for the unusual, large, deeply divided leaves which can have 5 lobes. The flowers may be yellow, purple or scarlet, and male and female flowers are generally borne on separate plants. Due to their strong sculptural form, some *Jatropha* species are often cultivated as part of a collection of succulents—although they are not related.

Jatropha multifida

### Cultivation

They do best in full sun, but will tolerate light shade, and need fertile, humus-rich, well-drained soil. Propagation is from seed or cuttings.

### Jatropha multifida
#### Coral plant, Guatemala rhubarb

This shrub from Central America grows to 6 ft (1.8 m) tall. Its large leaves, up to 12 in (30 cm) wide, are deeply incised, with as many as 12 narrow lobes. Clusters of red flowers are borne on long, thin stalks high above the foliage. It likes a sheltered position; it tends to shed leaves as a response to either dryness or cold. All parts of the plant are highly poisonous. ZONES 10–12.

## JUSTICIA

syns *Adhatoda, Beloperone, Drejerella, Jacobinia, Libonia*

This genus of about 420 species of shrubs and evergreen perennials is found in subtropical and tropical areas of the world, especially the Americas. They are widely grown in gardens in most warm areas. The leaves are simple and in opposite pairs, and the tubular flowers, in shades of cream, yellow, pink, orange or red, are mostly held in upright terminal spikes or clusters.

Justicia carnea

### Cultivation

They prefer well-drained soils in full sun or bright filtered light. They require shelter from the wind as many species have somewhat brittle stems. Plants can be kept neat and bushy by pinching out the growing tips. They are easily propagated from cuttings of non-flowering shoots.

### Justicia carnea
syns *Jacobinia carnea, J. pohliana*
#### Brazilian plume

This handsome, evergreen shrub bears dense, erect spikes of white, pink or

*Justicia spicigera*

*Lantana camara*

rose-purple flowers. It grows to a height of 5 ft (1.5 m) with a spread of 30 in (75 cm), and has pointed, veined, deep green leaves. Potted specimens need to be watered freely in full growth, less so at other times. Prune back hard to encourage branching. Caterpillars and snails can be a problem. ZONES 10–12.

### *Justicia spicigera*
syn. *Justicia ghiesbreghtiana*
#### Mohintli
Found from Mexico to Central America, *Justicia spicigera* is an erect, bushy shrub growing to 6 ft (1.8 m) tall. The mid-green leaves are oval and deeply veined. Loose, few-flowered terminal clusters of orange to red tubular flowers, about 1½ in (35 mm) long, are produced in succession. ZONES 10–12.

## LANTANA
This genus of the verbena family consists of around 150 species of evergreen shrubs and cany stemmed perennials, native to warmer parts of the Americas except for a few in southern Africa. Several species are notorious weeds of tropical and subtropical regions, most notably *Lantana camara*. The plants have rough, slightly prickly stems with oval leaves in opposite pairs, their surfaces

harsh and closely veined. Very small, trumpet-shaped flowers in compact button-like heads open progressively from the center of each head, their color changing in the older flowers towards the perimeter. Tiny fruits like blackberry drupelets may follow. In warm-climate gardens they are grown as outdoor shrubs or ground covers.

### Cultivation
These plants prefer fertile, well-drained soil and full sun. Plants in containers should be top-dressed annually and watered well when in full growth, less at other times. Tip prune young growth to promote a bushy habit and propagate from cuttings or from seed. The plants are generally little affected by pests, but check regularly for white fly and spider mite.

### *Lantana camara*
#### Common lantana, shrub verbena
This plant is reviled in warmer, wetter parts of the world for its rampant invasion of forests and pastures and poisoning of cattle, but valued as an ornamental es-pecially in cooler or drier regions. Much of this split personality is accounted for by its great variability. At least 25 weedy strains have been identified in Australia, only a few of which were introduced as

*Lantana montevidensis*

*Malpighia coccigera*

ornamentals; many of the ornamental cultivars show no signs of becoming weedy. The weedy forms produce long scrambling canes and can mound up to 20 ft (6 m) even without trees to climb over, but garden forms are mostly rounded or spreading shrubs 2–6 ft (0.6–1.8 m) high. The tiny flowers typically open cream, yellow or yellow-red and age to pink, red, orange or white, the heads appearing in a long succession. There are many cultivars ranging in color from the golden orange and red of 'Radiation' and the yellow of 'Drap d'Or' to the white blooms of 'Snowflake'. 'Chelsea Gem' is one of the oldest, an excellent compact shrub with profuse orange and red flowerheads—it makes an attractive standard. ZONES 9–12.

### Lantana montevidensis
syn. *Lantana sellowiana*
### Trailing lantana
The slender, weak stems of this trailing species mound up into a dense mass making it a wonderful plant for a ground cover or low hedge. It grows 18–36 in (45–90 cm) tall and 6 ft (1.8 m) wide or often more, with small, neat, closely veined dark green leaves. Throughout the year it bears bright mauve-pink flowerheads, each with a yellow eye.

A white-flowered cultivar has recently appeared and can make an attractive combination planted with the pink. ZONES 9–11.

## MALPIGHIA
Several of the 45 species of this genus of hot-climate evergreen trees and shrubs are grown for their delicate flowers and attractive foliage. Originating in the West Indies and Central and South America, they have distinctive flowers— pink, rose or red, with 5 slender-stalked petals—which are followed by edible berries in shades of orange, red or purple. The leaves are leathery and are usually toothed.

### Cultivation
These plants need regular feeding and watering, and do best in an open, sunny position in well-drained, moderately rich, moist soil. If desired, prune to maintain a dense habit. Propagate from seed or cuttings.

### Malpighia coccigera
### Barbados holly, Singapore holly
This beautiful little shrub from the West Indies grows slowly to a height and spread of 30 in (75 cm). It has small, shiny, holly-like leaves and neat, pale pink flowers with fringed petals and

golden stamens appear crowded along the branches. These are followed by the red berries. It makes an excellent miniature clipped hedge. ZONES 10–12.

## MEGASKEPASMA
### Brazilian red cloak, megas
Originally from Venezuela, the single species in this genus is a hot-climate, spreading shrub grown for its display of red flowers. It can reach 10 ft (3 m) in height and has simple, entire leaves.

### Cultivation
Plant this shrub in sun or part-shade and light, moist, well-drained soil rich in organic matter. It benefits from regular watering and fertilizing. Protect from snails. Propagate from seed or cuttings.

### Megaskepasma erythrochlamys
The mid-green, oval leaves of this evergreen shrub are up to 12 in (30 cm) long, with prominent veining. It forms spreading clumps, and the erect stems bear spikes of deep red flowers; these are up to 12 in (30 cm) long and are held above the foliage. ZONES 10–12.

*Megaskepasma erythrochlamys*

## MURRAYA
Allied to *Citrus*, this small genus of evergreen trees and shrubs comes from India and Southeast Asia. They have aromatic foliage and attractive creamy white flowers, which resemble those of their relative the orange and are often strongly scented. The fruits are small, oval berries. They were named after John Andrew Murray, a pupil of Linnaeus.

### Cultivation
Species of *Murraya* flourish in full sun or part-shade and humus-rich, moist but well-drained soil. Early pruning ensures a shrub thickly branched from the ground up; clipping after the late flowering season will keep their shape. Propagate from seed or cuttings.

### Murraya koenigii
### Curry leaf tree, karapincha
The leaves of this species are used in curries and other spicy dishes. From the Indian subcontinent, this aromatic shrub grows to about 10 ft (3 m). Loose sprays of small, fragrant, creamy white flowers

*Murraya koenigii*

stand out against the fresh green foliage and are followed by small black fruit. ZONES 10–12.

### Murraya paniculata
syn. *Murraya exotica*
#### Orange jessamine, mock orange
Widely distributed in tropical Asia, this compact, rounded bush up to 10 ft (3 m) tall is densely covered with shiny, dark green leaflets. The small, creamy white, perfumed flowers are held in dense clusters at the branch tips. It flowers repeatedly. Red berries may appear after each flowering. ZONES 10–12.

## MUSSAENDA
This is a genus of about 100 species of evergreen shrubs, subshrubs and climbers from tropical Africa, Asia and the Pacific Islands, widely cultivated throughout the tropics and subtropics for their year-long display. Their chief feature is not so much the petals of the small red or yellow flowers but the way a single sepal is greatly enlarged into a kind of bract, which can be white, red or pink. The shrubs themselves are attractive, with bright green leaves, but tend to become straggly and need regular trimming to keep them compact and 3–5 ft (1–1.5 m) tall.

### Cultivation
They prefer a sunny or part-shaded position and fertile, well-drained soil. Propagate from seed or cuttings. Spider mite and white fly may be troublesome.

### Mussaenda 'Aurorae'
syn. *Mussaenda phillippica* 'Aurorae'
This is a shrubby hybrid with evergreen rounded leaves to 6 in (15 cm) long. The small trumpet-shaped flowers are bright golden yellow surrounded by large white bracts to 3 in (8 cm) long. These flower clusters can be seen all year round in warm climates. ZONES 11–12.

### Mussaenda erythrophylla
#### Ashanti blood, red flag bush
Occurring naturally in tropical west and central Africa, this twining woody shrub usually climbs to 6 ft (1.8 m) on slender strong stems. It bears large, rounded,

Murraya paniculata

Mussaenda erythrophylla

bright green leaves covered with silky hairs and clustered creamy yellow flowers with a red-felted middle accompanied by blood red bracts up to 3 in (8 cm) long. ZONES 11–12.

### Mussaenda philippica
#### Lady flowers

The name is a botanical convenience, applied to a group of presumed hybrids. These have much tighter flower clusters than usual, so the 'bracts' resemble large, many-petalled flowers and are usually pink. Most are named after prominent ladies, hence the common name. Cultivars include the bright pink 'Dona Imelda'; 'Dona Luz', which is pink with red edges; and the pale pink and crimson 'Queen Sirikit'. They may have been derived from *Mussaenda erythrophylla* and *M. frondosa*. ZONES 11–12.

### NERIUM
#### Rose laurel, oleander

This small genus consists of one or two species of evergreen shrubs native to northern Africa and southwestern Asia. They bear brightly colored, funnel-shaped flowers with 5 broad petals;

*Nerium oleander 'Album'*

these are followed by bean-like seed pods containing plumed seeds. The leaves are narrow, leathery and lance-shaped. *Nerium oleander* and its cultivars are those plants most commonly seen in gardens. All neriums are very poisonous; all parts of the plant are so very bitter that even goats will not eat them.

#### Cultivation

Plant these shrubs in full sun and in well-drained soil. If they become over-grown and leggy, they can be re-juvenated by severe pruning. They can be grown in containers. Propagate from seed or cuttings.

### Nerium oleander

Depending on the cultivar selected, these plants can grow from 6–12 ft (1.8–3.5 m) tall. As the species is often used for hedging, it is wise to keep the varying growth habits of the cultivars in mind if a uniform appearance is wanted. The blooms can be single or double, and some cultivars have variegated foliage. Some popular cultivars include: 'Album', with single, white flowers and a cream center; 'Little Red', with single red flowers; 'Luteum Plenum', with creamy yellow double flowers; 'Mrs Fred Roeding', with salmon-pink double blooms and a relatively small growth habit; 'Petite Pink', with single pale pink flowers and growing only 3–6 ft (1–1.8 m) tall; 'Punctatum', a vigorous plant with single, pale pink blooms; 'Splendens Variegatum', with pink double flowers and variegated gold-green foliage borne at the expense of the profuse flowering habit of its parent 'Splendens'; 'Algiers', with its flowers of the darkest red; and 'Madonna Grandiflora', which has white double flowers. 'Casablanca' (syn. 'Monica') has single, very pale pink, almost white flowers. ZONES 9–11.

## OCHNA

The 90 or so species of this genus of evergreen and deciduous trees and shrubs occur wild in tropical and subtropical regions of Africa and Asia. The leaves are mostly finely toothed and may be shed briefly, the new growth flush being translucent bronze. Flowers are mostly yellow, like small hypericums but in tight clusters. Fruits consist of an enlarged red calyx and receptacle with several green to black drupelets, each containing one seed.

### Cultivation

Grow in full sun in any fertile, moist but well-drained soil. Prune regularly. Propagate from seed or cuttings.

Mussaenda philippica

### Ochna serrulata
#### Carnival bush, Mickey Mouse plant

A native of southern Africa, this shrub can grow up to 8 ft (2.4 m) with a rather open habit and has narrow, glossy mid-green leaves. The flowers are butter yellow and are followed by red and black fruit; these are eaten by birds which distribute the seed widely causing the plant to become a pest in warm climates. ZONES 9–11.

## PENTAS

This genus of around 40 species of biennials, perennials and subshrubs is found in tropical parts of Arabia and Africa. They have bright green, lance-shaped, 3–8 in (8–20 cm) long leaves, sometimes coated with a fine down or tiny hairs. The small, starry, long-tubed flowers are massed in flat-topped heads and appear throughout the warmer months. They are usually bright pink, but also occur in red and purple shades, as well as white.

### Cultivation

Pentas are easily grown as house plants; the new dwarf strains can be treated as

Ochna serrulata

Pentas lanceolata

### Pentas lanceolata
syn. *Pentas carnea*
**Egyptian star, star cluster**
This erect, straggling shrub grows to a
height of 2–3 ft (0.6–1 m) with a slightly
wider spread. It is grown for its clusters
of tubular, red, pink, lilac or white
flowers, set among bright green, hairy
leaves. ZONES 10–12.

## PHILODENDRON
Many of the species belonging to this
genus are climbers, and detailed
information on the genus is given in the
Climbers & Creepers chapter. However,
*Philodendron bipinnatifidum* is treated here
as a shrub.

### Philodendron bipinnatifidum
syn. *Philodendron selloum*
**Tree philodendron**
This upright, robust species from Brazil
grows to 10 ft (3 m) tall. It is noted for
its shiny, oval, deep green leaves, 15–24 in
(38–60 cm) long and many-lobed; in
some hybrids, the leaves can be up to
3 times as large. The flowers are white
or greenish. This species is variable in
leaf outline; the common form with
irregular lobing is sometimes known
under the synonym. Other cultivars and
hybrids include some of the most spectacular of all foliage plants. ZONES 10–12.

## PLUMBAGO
**Leadwort**
This genus of 10 to 15 species of
annuals, perennials, evergreen shrubs
and scrambling climbers and semi-
climbers is found in warm-temperate to
tropical regions. The blue, white or red
flowers have 5 petals narrowing to a
long slender tube and are massed on
short stems near the tips of the arching
branches. The leaves are arranged
alternately.

Philodendron bipinnatifidum

bedding or pot annuals. Plant in moist,
well-drained soil in full sun or part-
shade and pinch back regularly to
maintain a compact habit and to encourage bloom. Deadhead as required
and trim lightly. Water well when in full
growth. Propagate from seed or from
softwood cuttings. Watch for aphids and
red spider mites.

## Cultivation

Plumbagos require well-drained soil, perhaps enriched with a little organic matter. Established plants are tolerant of dry conditions, but soil should be kept moist for a good flowering display. Prune to tidy their vigorous stems and remove old wood to encourage new growth and the next crop of flowers. Propagate from tip or semi-hardwood cuttings.

### *Plumbago indica*
syn. *Plumbago rosea*
#### Scarlet leadwort
This species from India is a first-rate pot plant for a lightly shaded spot. Its flowers are a beautiful deep glowing pink. ZONES 10–12.

## *RHODODENDRON*

syn. *Azalea*

The rhododendrons are a spectacular genus of around 800 evergreen semi-deciduous and deciduous shrubs and trees. They are woody stemmed plants grown mainly for their massed display of flowers, which vary greatly in size from tiny thimbles to 8 in (20 cm) trumpets. As far as gardeners are concerned there are 3 main categories of rhododendrons,

namely: azaleas (deciduous and evergreen); tropical or Vireya rhododendrons; and the temperate climate plants we might call 'true' rhododendrons, which includes the small alpine or arctic rhododendrons.

## Cultivation

A compact root ball and no tap roots make rhododendrons ideal for container cultivation and easy to transplant. They need loose, open, well-aerated, acidic soil with plenty of humus to retain moisture. They thrive with regular mulching. In wet areas or gardens with alkaline soil it is best to plant in raised beds filled with specially blended compost. Vireya rhododendrons are superb plants for tropical or subtropical gardens. Rhododendrons are propagated from seed or cuttings or by layering.

### *Rhododendron aurigeranum*
Native to New Guinea and found in forest clearings, rocky areas or grassy slopes at moderate altitudes, this Vireya rhododendron grows to 8 ft (2.4 m) tall with orange to orange-yellow funnel-shaped flowers. It is popular with hybridizers of modern Vireya cultivars. ZONES 10–12.

*Rhododendron aurigeranum*

*Plumbago indica*

*Rhododendron brookeanum*

*Rhododendron jasminiflorum*

### Rhododendron brookeanum

Native to Malaysia and Indonesia, this Vireya may be epiphytic or terrestrial. At low altitudes it is found as an epiphyte on mangroves and other trees, and terrestrially on sandstone rocks at up to 4,660 ft (1,400 m). It reaches 6–15 ft (1.8–4.5 m) tall with fragrant funnel-shaped flowers that are orange, orange-pink or red, with white to golden yellow centers. 'Titan' has flowers fading to light pink. ZONES 10–12.

### Rhododendron jasminiflorum

Native to the Malay Peninsula, this Vireya species can grow to 8 ft (2.4 m) tall. It has 2½ in (6 cm) long, bright green leaves in whorls of 3 to 5. Throughout the year it

*Rhododendron javanicum*

produces 5- to 8-flowered trusses of 1½–2 in (3.5–5 cm) long, scented, tubular white flowers. ZONES 10–12.

### Rhododendron javanicum

This 6–12 ft (1.8–3.5 m) tall epiphytic or terrestrial Vireya native to Malaysia and Indonesia has oval leaves up to 8 in (20 cm) long. The often fragrant, large-lobed, funnel-shaped flowers in loose trusses are 1½ in (35 mm) long and wide and are orange to orange-pink or red with cream or yellow centers. ZONES 10–12.

### Rhododendron laetum

From New Guinea, this Vireya is 5 ft (1.5 m) tall with 3 in (8 cm) long elliptical leaves. Its flowers are wide

*Rhododendron laetum*

*Rhododendron zoelleri*

open, funnel-shaped and 2½ in (6 cm) long, usually deep yellow, sometimes suffused pink, orange or red and occasionally scented. ZONES 10–12.

### Rhododendron zoelleri
Usually seen as a 4–6 ft (1.2–1.8 m) tall shrub, this Vireya from Indonesia, New Guinea and the Moluccas can reach 20 ft (6 m) tall. Its trumpet-shaped flowers are particularly bright shades of yellow and orange with orange-red lobes. It is popular with hybridizers for its vivid color. ZONES 10–12.

## RUSSELIA
Consisting of around 50 species of evergreen and deciduous subshrubs and shrubs, this genus ranges from Mexico and Cuba to Colombia. The handsome plants produce showy, narrow, tubular flowers, which come in red, pink or white. The scale-like leaves appear on pendent stems.

### Cultivation
They prefer full sun and humus-rich, light, well-drained soil. Propagate from cuttings or by dividing rooted layers.

### Russelia equisetiformis
syn. *Russelia juncea*
### Coral plant, coral fountain
This erect, slender subshrub with wiry, near-leafless green stems is from Mexico. It is grown for the clusters of red flowers it bears all year, set among tiny, green leaves. Fast growing, it is well suited to spilling over a wall, or as a seaside specimen. It grows to a height and spread of just under 3 ft (1 m). ZONES 9–12.

## SANCHEZIA
Native to Central and South America, *Sanchezia* is a genus of some 20 species of

*Sanchezia speciosa*

*Russelia equisetiformis*

large, bushy perennials, shrubs and scrambling climbers. They bear eye-catching spikes of tubular, showy, yellow, orange, red or purple flowers, each with 5 lobes and often colored bracts, and have opposite pairs of simple leaves.

### Cultivation
Plant in full sun in fertile, well-drained soil. Tip prune young plants to encourage a branching habit. Propagate from cuttings. Watch for attack by scale insects.

### *Sanchezia speciosa*
syn. *Sanchezia nobilis*
This species has multicolored flowers with yellow petals, bright red bracts and purple stems. An erect, evergreen shrub, it has glossy leaves with white or yellow veins. ZONES 10–12.

### *SCHEFFLERA*
Many of the species belonging to this genus are trees, and detailed information on the genus is given in the Trees chapter. However, *Schefflera arboricola* is treated here as a shrub.

## Schefflera arboricola
### Hawaiian elf schefflera

Endemic to Taiwan, this smaller version of *Schefflera actinophylla* makes a shrub 6–15 ft (1.8–4.5 m) tall with a similar spread. It produces many branches near the ground and can be pruned to a rounded shape, making it a popular pot plant for indoors and out. The leaves consist of 5 to 10 leaflets radiating from the leaf stalk; each is shiny green and up to 6 in (15 cm) long. Greenish yellow flowers in sprays appear near the branch tips, followed by orange fruit that ripen to purple. 'Renate' has variegated leaves, as does 'Samoa Snow'. ZONES 10–12.

## SOLANUM

Many of the species belonging to this genus are climbers, and detailed

*Schefflera arboricola 'Samoa Snow'*

*Schefflera arboricola*

information is given in the Climbers & Creepers chapter. However, *Solanum mauritianum* is treated here as a shrub.

### Solanum mauritianum
This shrub originates in Argentina. It grows up to 15 ft (4.5 m) and has gray-green hairy branches and oval leaves up to 12 in (30 cm) long that are softly hairy. The flowers are blue, and the fruit are hairy yellow balls to ½ in (12 mm) long in clusters. ZONES 10–12.

## TABERNAEMONTANA
Widespread throughout tropical and subtropical regions, this genus consists of around 100 species of evergreen shrubs and small trees. Some resemble gardenias in both leaf and flower but differ in having milky sap. The leaves are deep green and roughly oval; the funnel-shaped flowers are usually white. They are often used as informal hedging.

### Cultivation
They grow best in humus-rich, moist, well-drained soil, in a sheltered position in sun or dappled shade. Water well all year round. Propagate the species from seed and the cultivars from cuttings.

### Tabernaemontana divaricata
syns *Ervatamia divaricata, E. coronaria*
**Crepe jasmine, crepe gardenia**
Occurring naturally from northern India to China's Yunnan province and northern Thailand, this twiggy, heavily foliaged shrub grows to about 6 ft (1.8 m) high. It has leathery leaves up to 4 in (10 cm) long. White tubular flowers in terminal clusters open throughout the year; their

*Solanum mauritianum*

scent is strongest in the evening. 'Flore Pleno' is a double-flowered cultivar and is much more widely grown than the species. These beautiful shrubs are excellent container plants and can be lightly trimmed to shape. ZONES 11–12.

## TECOMA

syn. Stenolobium

This genus of mainly evergreen shrubs and small trees consists of around 12 species native to Central and South America, and closely related to *Tecomaria* and *Tabebuia* — in fact a recent botanical revision includes the African tecomarias in an expanded *Tecoma*. They bear clusters of showy yellow to orange, tubular to trumpet-shaped flowers. Their leaves can be simple or compound with an odd number of leaflets. The fruits are smooth, bean-like capsules.

### Cultivation

*Tecoma* species thrive in full sun with shelter from strong winds, and need adequate soil moisture. Propagate from seed or cuttings. Look out for spider mite.

### Tecoma stans

syns Bignonia stans, Stenolobium stans

**Yellow bells, yellow trumpet flower, yellow elder**

This evergreen shrub or small tree reaches a height of 15–20 ft (4.5–6 m),
but can be pruned heavily after flowering to keep it compact. The leaves are composed of 5 or 7 leaflets, each 2½–3 in (6–8 cm) long with deeply serrated edges. This species features bright yellow, trumpet-shaped flowers, 2 in (5 cm) long, arranged in sprays at the branch tips. It has a long flowering season. The fruit is a capsule about 8 in (20 cm) long, ripening to chocolate brown. ZONES 10–12.

## TECOMARIA

A single, variable species of semi-climbing evergreen shrub constitutes this genus, native to southern and eastern Africa. Some botanists now merge it with the American *Tecoma*. It has showy trumpet-shaped flowers in shades of yellow, orange or scarlet, which appear in clusters at the ends of shoots. The pinnate leaves are arranged opposite each other or in whorls of 3, and have an odd number of leaflets. The fruits are oblong, narrow capsules.

### Cultivation

These plants grow best in full sun in a position where they are protected from wind; they should be provided with some form of support. Thin out crowded stems as necessary. The soil should be well-drained with added organic matter.

Tecoma stans

Tecomaria capensis

They need to be watered regularly. Propagate from seed or cuttings.

### Tecomaria capensis
### Cape honeysuckle
syn. *Tecoma capensis*

The Cape honeysuckle is a scrambling shrub able to climb to a height of 15–25 ft (4.5–8 m). The branches are slender and sprawling, forming roots where they touch the ground. The glossy green leaves are 6 in (15 cm) long, divided into 5 to 9 rounded to oval leaflets with serrated edges. Orange-red to scarlet, curved flowers, each 2 in (5 cm) long are borne in short spikes. 'Aurea' has yellow flowers. ZONES 10 12.

## THUNBERGIA

Many of the species belonging to this genus are climbers, and detailed information on the genus is given in the Climbers & Creepers chapter. However, the ones included here can be treated as shrubs.

### Thunbergia natalensis

This very attractive species from South Africa is not a climber but a soft-wooded shrub that reaches 3 ft (1 m) in height. It bears soft blue flowers. Subtropical and warm-temperate climates suit it best. ZONES 10–11.

### Thunbergia togoensis

This semi-climbing African shrub produces hairy buds. They open into dark blue flowers with yellow centers. ZONES 10–12.

## TIBOUCHINA

### Lasiandra, glory bush

There are more than 300 species in this genus of evergreen perennials, shrubs, small trees and scrambling climbers from South America. The flowers are large and vivid, commonly purple, pink or white, with 5 satiny petals. They are borne either singly or in clusters at the shoot tips, and sometimes the whole plant is smothered with blooms over several months. The flower buds are rounded and fat, while the leaves are simple and hairy, deeply marked with 3 to 7 veins. New growth is often a contrasting reddish bronze, and stems are square; the fruits are capsules.

### Cultivation

They prefer full sun and do best in light soil with added organic matter and a

*Thunbergia togoensis*

*Thunbergia natalensis*

*Tibouchina heteromalla*

*Tibouchina clavata*

### Tibouchina clavata
This rather straggling species, native to Brazil, grows to 8 ft (2.4 m) tall. It bears attractive lilac or white flowers. The blooms are not very large, but are gathered in elegant open clusters. ZONES 10–12.

### Tibouchina heteromalla
This evergreen spreading shrub grows to a height of 3 ft (1 m) with a spread of 4 ft (1.2 m). The erect stems rise directly from the base; the 4–6 in (10–15 cm) long leaves are velvety and whitish green on the underside. Five-petalled, violet-petalled flowers are produced in terminal panicles which may be up to 8 in (20 cm) long and 2–3 in (5–8 cm) in diameter. ZONES 10–12.

### Tibouchina lepidota
Native to Ecuador and Colombia, this leafy shrub usually has a short trunk to 12 ft (3.5 m) high. However, it can become tree-like, growing to 40 ft

slightly acidic to neutral pH. Keep plants moist during the growing season. Prune after flowering. They have brittle stems and need shelter from wind. Propagate from cuttings.

Tibouchina lepidota

Wigandia caracasana

(12 m) tall with a neat round canopy. The leaves are dark green and shiny, oblong to lance-shaped, with 5 main veins and 2 outer minor ones; they are paler and hairy underneath. Its violet to purple flowers are borne in clusters; the flower buds are enclosed by pink silky bracts and the stems have reddish hairs. 'Alstonville' has particularly vibrant flowers. ZONES 10–12.

## WIGANDIA

These 5 species of striking, evergreen shrubs from Central and South America have huge, oval to heart-shaped, scalloped, deep green leaves with white, often stinging hairs beneath. The leaves are 18 in (45 cm) long and the bushes grow to 10 ft (3 m) or more tall, although they can be pruned. Violet-blue flowers appear in large terminal panicles of one-sided spikes. *Wigandia caracasana* from Venezuela is probably the best known of the 5 species.

### Cultivation

Plant in moist but well-drained soil in full light. They can be grown in pots and need abundant water during the growth period, moderate amounts at other times. Propagate from seed or cuttings. Sometimes white fly can be a problem.

### *Wigandia caracasana*
syn. *Wigandia urens var. caracasana*

Native to Mexico and South America, *Wigandia caracasana* is a variable species of erect evergreen shrub that grows to 10 ft (3 m) or even more. It has leaves which are very large, up to 18 in (45 cm) long, oval and wavy edged and deep green above with a hairy white underside. The hairs can be sticky and sometimes mixed with longer stinging hairs. The flowers are violet to purple, in large terminal clusters. This species is often grown for its 'jungle effect' on a garden. It can grow in full light in a protected situation. ZONES 10–12.

CHAPTER 3

*Trees*

## ACACIA
### Wattle

This large genus contains over 1,200 species of trees and shrubs, some deciduous but mostly evergreen. Over 700 are indigenous to Australia. They are also common in tropical and subtropical Africa. Acacias have either bipinnate leaves or their leaves are replaced by flattened leaf stalks, known as phyllodes, which perform the function of photosynthesis. The tiny flowers, deep golden yellow to cream or white, and crowded into globular heads or cylindrical spikes, are often fragrant and produce abundant, bee-attracting pollen. Fruit are either round or flattened pods.

### Cultivation

The hard-coated seeds remain viable for up to 30 years. They should be treated by heating and soaking for germination. Some need fire to germinate. In cultivation many species are fast-growing but short-lived (10 to 15 years). They do best in full sun and well-drained soil. Some will take part-shade.

### Acacia auriculiformis
### Ear pod wattle

Native to far northern Australia and New Guinea, this tree grows to 30 ft

*Acacia auriculiformis*

(9 m) or more and has a broadly spreading crown. Its sickle-shaped phyllodes are 4–6 in (10–15 cm) long. Rods of dull golden flowers, 3 in (8 cm) long, are followed by twisted woody pods. It prefers an open sunny position. Exceptionally fast-growing (though short-lived), it can drop most of its leaves in the dry season; fallen leaves and pods may thickly cover paths and lawns. ZONES 10–12.

### Acacia mangium

From the tropical rainforests of far north Queensland, Australia, this acacia is a fine ornamental tree, notable for the size of its large, conspicuously veined phyllodes, up to 12 in (30 cm) long and 4 in (10 cm) wide. Planted in a sunny position, it makes a medium-sized tree with a straight trunk and dense pyramidal crown. Closer planting produces a tall, straight tree, reaching 80–100 ft (25–30 m). The cream flowers are not very showy. The pods are long and tangled together. ZONES 11–12.

## AMHERSTIA
### Pride of Burma

The one species in this genus, considered among the most beautiful of all flowering trees, was named in honor of Lady Sarah Amherst, an early nineteenth-century botanist and collector whose husband became Viceroy of India. In its native Burma handfuls of *Amherstia* flowers are offered at Buddhist shrines.

### Cultivation

A tropical tree, it is not common due to difficulties in propagation. Seed is almost impossible to obtain and cuttings are very difficult to strike, so layering of branches using pots raised on stands is usually the only way. *Amherstia* likes a very sheltered position, even part-shaded by larger trees.

### Amherstia nobilis

This spreading tree grows to 40 ft (13 m), with large bipinnate leaves up to 3 ft (1 m) long. Briefly deciduous in the dry season, the drooping leaflets have whitish undersides; new leaves are coppery pink. In the wet tropics, through much of the year, it bears sprays of orchid-like flowers 4 in (10 cm) across with spreading crimson petals, the upper ones gold-tipped. ZONE 12.

## BARRINGTONIA

This is a large genus of evergreen or dry-season deciduous trees with species scattered throughout the tropics, from Africa to northern Australia and the Pacific Islands. Their branches have a distinctive habit of repeatedly forking in a candelabra-like fashion, terminating in rosettes of paddle-shaped leaves. The striking flowers appear on usually pendulous spikes from the branch tips, with short petals and numerous long stamens. In many countries barringtonias are used as fish poisons: the bark, leaves or fruits are pounded or grated and then thrown in the water to stupefy the fish.

### Cultivation

They do best on sites with permanent subsoil moisture. Propagate from the large seeds which may take several months to germinate.

### Barringtonia asiatica
syn. Barringtonia speciosa
**Fish-killer tree**

Large brown seeds that are egg-shaped in outline but square in cross-section and with sharp angles are washed up on beaches all around the Pacific and Indian oceans. They are the fruit of this evergreen tree, which grows in coastal areas of tropical Asia, the Malay Archipelago and northern Australia. The buoyant seeds enable its dispersal across short ocean gaps. It normally grows to a height of about 20 ft (6 m) with multiple trunks and a vase-shaped crown. The leaves are dark green and glossy and the large flowers, appearing at the end of the dry season, are red and white. ZONE 12.

## BAUHINIA

This is a variable genus of legumes, consisting of some 250 species of

Barringtonia asiatica

Amherstia nobilis

Bauhinia × blakeana

Bauhinia monandra

evergreen and dry-season-deciduous trees, shrubs and climbers, occurring in most tropical and subtropical regions of the world. Some botanists take a narrower view of the genus, splitting off about two-thirds of the species into other genera. All have characteristic 2-lobed leaves, but they are grown for their beautiful perfumed flowers whose likeness to orchids or butterflies has given rise to the common names of several species. The flattened brown seed pods that follow often persist on the branches for months.

### Cultivation

Bauhinias like full sun and light, fertile, well-drained soil. Pruning is not usually necessary, but vigorous growth may be thinned out after flowering. Propagate from seed.

### Bauhinia × blakeana
### Hong Kong orchid tree

*Bauhinia × blakeana* is a presumed hybrid between *B. variegata* and the rather similar *B. purpurea*. It was first found in China in 1908, and was later adopted as Hong Kong's floral emblem. It resembles the more widely grown *B. variegata* but makes a taller, more densely foliaged and evergreen tree, with broader leaves. The slightly fragrant

flowers, up to 6 in (15 cm) across on a healthy specimen, are a purplish red except for darker streaks on the inner petals, and are borne in shorter sprays than on *B. variegata*. It sets few seed pods. ZONES 10–12.

### Bauhinia monandra

A rank-growing tropical species from the West Indies and northern South America, this species makes a multi-stemmed small tree to 20 ft (6 m) high. It has spreading branches and coarse foliage, with large pale green leaves. At the end of the dry season and well into the wet it produces a succession of flowers at the branch ends, with the large petals opening cream but ageing to flesh pink with a dramatic red splash on the upper petals. They are unusual in having only a single stamen. ZONES 11–12.

### BRACHYCHITON

This genus is made up of around 30 species of warm-climate, evergreen or dry-season deciduous trees and shrubs, all Australian except one or two found in New Guinea. Some brachychitons have spectacular flowers, which are bell-shaped. The leaves are diverse in shape but are commonly lobed, though lobing tends to disappear on adult trees. The

Brachychiton discolor

Caesalpinia ferrea

fruits consist of 5 stalked, boat-shaped carpels, rather woody when mature and splitting to release nut-like seeds that are edible but are surrounded by irritant hairs.

### Cultivation

Noted for their drought-resistant qualities, brachychitons require light, well-drained soil, preferably acidic. They prefer a sheltered position with protection from salty winds. Propagate from fresh seed or by grafting for selected clones.

### Brachychiton discolor
### Lacebark kurrajong

A massive tree, to 80 ft (24 m) or more in its native rainforest, the lacebark kurrajong is smaller when seen in parks and gardens, though retaining its distinctive form. Its thick trunk has greenish bark and supports a dense canopy of large, maple-like leaves, dark green above and silvery beneath. It bears clusters of deep pink, velvety, bell-shaped flowers. ZONES 10–12.

## CAESALPINIA

*Caesalpinia* is a diverse genus of legumes found in the warmer regions of the world and includes 70 or so species of trees, shrubs and scrambling climbers, the latter often very thorny. Most are evergreen, but some lose leaves in the tropical dry season. Some shrub species from the Americas have been distinguished in the past as the genus *Poinciana* (not to be confused with the 'poinciana' tree, now *Delonix*). The leaves of all caesalpinias are bipinnate, some very large with numerous leaflets; the flowers are in spikes from the upper leaf axils and may be quite showy, mostly in shades of red, yellow or cream, with separate petals and often conspicuous stamens. The seeds are in typical leguminous pods.

### Cultivation

Most species appreciate a sheltered sunny spot and deep, sandy soil. Propagation is from seed, which may need abrading and hot-water soaking to aid germination.

### Caesalpinia ferrea
### Leopard tree, Brazilian ironwood

A long-lived tree of up to 40 ft (12 m) high, native to eastern Brazil, this species is grown for its elegantly sinuous limbs, their smooth cream bark dappled with gray-green. The umbrella-shaped crown consists of ferny, un-armed, deep green leaves; it bears short, erect spikes of yellow flowers. Fast growing, the leopard tree is often untidily branched when young and should be trained to a single trunk at the base. ZONES 10–12.

## CANANGA

This genus consists of 2 fast-growing evergreen tree species from tropical Southeast Asia, the Pacific Islands and the north of Australia. They are prized for their 6-petalled, wonderfully fragrant flowers borne in pendent clusters. A perfumery oil is distilled from the flowers.

### Cultivation

Like their relatives the custard apple and soursop, they are easily cultivated in a sheltered, shaded position in tropical and warmer subtropical areas. They prefer a moist, humus-rich soil. Propagation is from seed or cuttings.

### Cananga odorata
### Ylang ylang

This handsome tropical tree reaching 80 ft (24 m) in the wild has pendulous, rather brittle branches and large, glossy green leaves. The flowers, with their long, twisted, drooping, greenish yellow petals and extraordinarily heavy perfume,

*Cananga odorata*

appear in thick clusters at the leaf axils, and are followed by small greenish fruit. The ylang ylang (its Malay name) is widely cultivated in Hawaii for the perfume industry. ZONES 11–12.

## CASSIA

This genus, as now understood, consists of over 100 species of shrubs and trees from tropical and subtropical regions around the world. (Previously, *Cassia* was interpreted in a much broader sense, including a very large number of shrubs, small trees and herbaceous plants now separated as the genus *Senna*.) Some are evergreen, some deciduous. Most have ferny, pinnate leaves and clusters of simple, bright golden yellow flowers with prominent stamens, often borne for a long period; these are followed by bean-like seed pods which are often very large.

### Cultivation

Cassias grow under a wide range of conditions, but most prefer well-drained soil and a sunny position. Propagation is from pre-soaked seed or cuttings.

### Cassia fistula
### Indian laburnum, golden shower tree, pudding pipe tree, monkey-pod tree

Native to tropical Asia, this widely cultivated species is a deciduous to semi-evergreen tree that can grow to around 60 ft (18 m) high though often only half that height or less in cultivation. It has pinnate leaves made up of 3 to 8 pairs of large leaflets. It produces large, drooping clusters of fragrant, bright yellow flowers. ZONES 10–12.

### Cassia javanica
### Apple blossom tree

This deciduous tree is native to Southeast Asia, where it may reach a height of 80 ft (24 m). Cultivated specimens are usually

Cassia fistula

Cassia javanica

Casuarina equisetifolia

half that height, with a broad, flat-topped crown. *Cassia javanica* has long, pinnate leaves made up of very long, narrow leaflets covered in fine down when young. The showy flowers are carried in large clusters and range from pale pink to red. ZONES 11–12.

## CASUARINA
### She-oak, Australian pine
This genus consists of 6 species of wide distribution in Australia, and about as many again in islands to the north. Many other species previously placed here are now classified under *Allocasuarina* or *Gymnostoma*. Despite bearing only inconspicuous (male and female) flowers, casuarinas are graceful trees, fast growing, tolerant of strong winds and adaptable, often to very dry conditions. Casuarina wood makes excellent firewood. They are grown as shade or amenity trees and are valued by some farmers for the shelter they provide for stock, while others maintain that they poison the ground.

### Cultivation
Plant in full sun in fertile, moist, well-drained soil. Water well during the growing period. Propagate from seed or cuttings. Pruning is rarely necessary.

### Casuarina equisetifolia
#### Beach she-oak, horsetail tree

This tree of around 40–60 ft (12–18 m) tall, depending on soil and exposure, has a short trunk and long, weeping, silvery gray branchlets. It grows naturally on beaches and exposed coastal headlands, being very resistant to salt-laden winds and tolerant of poor, sandy soil. Reputedly one of the best fuelwood trees in the world, beach she-oak is also used for boatbuilding, house construction and furniture-making. It has the widest natural distribution of any casuarina, occurring on tropical seashores around most parts of the Pacific and Indian oceans. ZONES 10–12.

## CECROPIA
#### Cecropia

These fast-growing trees with large, umbrella-like leaves are a striking feature of the Amazonian rainforest. They are soft wooded, with large, open crowns that often project above the surrounding trees. The thick branches are often hollow, containing a series of chambers that are inhabited by fierce ants which attack intruders on the tree, including both humans and leafcutter ants that

*Cecropia palmata*

feed on the foliage. Some Amazonian Indians made trumpet-like instruments from the hollow stems. The genus is widespread in tropical America, including some species of smaller size and less striking form.

#### Cultivation

These trees are easily enough cultivated in sheltered, sunny positions and deep, moist soil, but the rampant saplings are weak and easily damaged. Propagation is from seed.

### Cecropia palmata
#### Snakewood tree

This species from the West Indies and northeastern South America is particularly fast growing; the snakewood tree makes a tall, lanky tree of up to 50 ft (15 m) with few branches. The stems have a waxy blue coating and the leaves are about 24 in (60 cm) across, deeply segmented into 8 to 10 oblong lobes with rounded tips. The whole leaf is colored greenish white on the underside. ZONES 11–12.

## CLUSIA

This is a very large genus of tropical American evergreen trees and shrubs. The leaves of *Clusia* species may be quite large and are generally smooth and fleshy or leathery. The flowers, borne singly or in short sprays at the branch tips, are often large and showy, with male flowers more conspicuous than female ones though both appear on the same tree. They are cup or bowl shaped, often with 6 or more overlapping petals, and a dense, doughnut-shaped ring of stamens in the center; in females this is replaced by a broad, domed ovary with shiny stigmas fused to its surface.

#### Cultivation

Some species are vigorous trees tolerant of exposed coastal conditions, and these adapt well to street or park planting in tropical cities. All species prefer rich, moist but well-drained soil in a sheltered position. Propagation is from cuttings under heat, or by air-layering.

### Clusia rosea
#### Copey, balsam apple
syn. *Clusia major*

From the Caribbean region, this is one of the most widely planted species. It makes a tree of about 30 ft (9 m) tall with a broadly spreading crown of irregular shape and rather dense foliage, often forked into several trunks from ground level and sending down aerial roots, like some figs. The thick, olive-green leaves are paddle-shaped with broad, rounded tips. Pale pinkish flowers 2–3 in (5–8 cm) in diameter dot the crown. ZONES 11–12.

## COCCOLOBA
About 150 species of mainly evergreen shrubs, trees and vines make up this tropical American genus. They have leathery leaves of variable shape and produce spikes or panicles of very small separate male and female flowers. The flowers are succeeded by segmented purple fruit, edible in some species and of economic importance locally.

#### Cultivation
These tropical plants do best in moist, well-drained soil in full sun. Some are highly adapted to seashore conditions. Propagate from seed or cuttings.

### Coccoloba uvifera
#### Sea grape, Jamaican kino
From seashores of tropical America as far north as southern Florida, this striking small tree can grow to 30 ft (9 m) high, usually with a single trunk and broad crown. The glossy leaves are almost circular, about 8 in (20 cm) long, with prominent white or pinkish veins; new leaves are an attractive translucent bronze. It produces erect 8–12 in (20–30 cm) spikes of small white flowers, followed by green-spotted, edible purple fruit. It grows in the forefront of beach and dune shrubs. ZONES 11–12.

## COCHLOSPERMUM
The 30-odd species of this genus of shrubs and small trees are scattered

*Clusia rosea*

*Coccoloba uvifera*

throughout the tropics, growing mainly in regions of strongly seasonal rainfall, and are mostly deciduous in the dry season. The leaves are lobed, rather like grape or maple leaves, and beautiful large cream to golden yellow flowers are borne in clusters terminating the branches. The large seed pods are globular to sausage-shaped and split open in a most unusual pattern to reveal masses of seeds embedded in a kapok-like down. The roots of *Cochlospermum* are swollen and fleshy and are sometimes used as a food source, and other parts of the plants yield fibers and medicinal gums.

### Cultivation

Although not difficult to cultivate under tropical conditions, these are shrubs of very open, ungainly habit, but respond to cutting back with denser growth. They need full sun and moderately fertile, well-drained soil. Propagate from seed or root-tuber cuttings.

### Cochlospermum fraseri
### Yellow kapok

This, one of 3 species indigenous to far northern Australia, makes a crooked small tree up to 30 ft (9 m) high. The leaves

are slightly hairy, up to 6 in (15 cm) wide, with 3 to 7 shallow lobes. The flowers are bright golden yellow, up to 3 in (8 cm) across, borne on leafless branches late in the dry season. If kept watered in a garden the leaves may persist and be present with the flowers. ZONES 11–12.

## CORDIA

This genus is made up of around 300 species of evergreen and deciduous shrubs and trees from most tropical and subtropical regions of the world. Some are used as timber trees, others are hollowed out for canoes, and the leaves of a few species are used to make dyes. Most have large, smooth, oval leaves and small to moderately large, trumpet-shaped flowers that stand out against the dark foliage. The fruit is typical of the genus.

### Cultivation

These plants require steady, warm temperatures and moist, well-drained soil. They are propagated from seed or semi-ripe cuttings.

### Cordia sebestena
### Geiger tree, scarlet cordia

This small evergreen tree is native to the West Indies, Florida and Venezuela and

*Cordia sebestena*

*Cochlospermum fraseri*

is widely cultivated for ornament in the tropics. It grows to around 25 ft (8 m) high and has 8 in (20 cm) long, oval leaves. It produces tight clusters of bright orange-red flowers through much of the year, followed by 1 in (25 mm) oval, white, edible fruit. ZONES 10–12.

### Cordia wallichii

A native of tropical Asia, this small spreading tree grows 12–20 ft (3.5–6 m) high. The leaves are broad and dark green. Flowers, borne in dense panicles in the upper leaf axils, measure rather less than 1 in (2.5 cm) across. It makes a bushy shrub that could be used as a screen or shelter plant in subtropical to tropical gardens. ZONES 10–12.

## COUROUPITA

Three species of trees from northern South America make up this genus. They have large, elliptical leaves, usually clustered at the branch tips. The flowers are large and complex in structure, usually 6-petalled, and sometimes smell like garlic. They are followed by spectacular large, spherical fruit.

### Cultivation

They prefer to grow in deep, moist, humus-rich soil in full sun but in a sheltered position. Propagation is normally from seed.

### Couroupita guianensis
### Cannonball tree

This species is an upright, evergreen tree capable of growing to 100 ft (30 m) high, though 30–40 ft (9–12 m) is a more usual size. Pendulous flowering branches emerge directly from the trunk, right

*Couroupita guianensis*

*Cordia wallichii*

*Couroupita guianensis*

*Crateva religiosa*

down to the ground, and all year produce 3 in (8 cm) diameter, brilliant red and orange fragrant flowers with hundreds of stamens arranged in 2 groups, one in the flower's center and the other on a lower petal. Showy as the flowers are, the fruit are the main feature—they are brown spheres up to 10 in (25 cm) across filled with a smelly, soft red pulp, and one tree may bear hundreds of them. They look like small cannonballs and burst explosively on falling from the tree. ZONES 11–12.

## CRATEVA

Six or more species of evergreen shrubs and small trees make up this genus, widely distributed through the tropics. They are closely related to the herbaceous genus *Cleome*, as is obvious from the flower structure. The flowers have large, stalked petals and very long, protruding stamens. Leaves are usually compound with leaflets radiating from a common stalk, also like *Cleome*. The foliage of some species can cause a form of contact dermatitis in humans.

### Cultivation

These plants need warm, even temperatures year round and prefer rich, moist,

well-drained soil with plenty of water in hot weather. Propagate from seed or cuttings.

### *Crateva religiosa*
### Spider tree, temple plant

Native to Southeast Asia, the Pacific region and northern Australia, this ornamental small tree grows to 20 ft (6 m) or more high. It has smooth gray bark with white spots and distinctive pale green young branches. Its handsome leaves are composed of 3 oval leaflets up to 6 in (15 cm) long. It bears large flowers with creamy white petals ageing to dull orange-yellow and long, dark red to violet stamen filaments. The flowers are followed by smooth green berries. ZONES 11–12.

## DELONIX

Ten species make up this genus of tropical deciduous, semi-evergreen or evergreen trees from Africa, Madagascar, Arabia and India. The 5-petalled flowers appear in terminal racemes, and the elegant leaves are bipinnate and fern-like. The fruits, typical of the legume group, are large, flattened, woody, bean-like pods. They do well as shade trees.

### Cultivation

Plant in full sun in fertile, moist but well-drained soil and provide shelter from strong winds. Prune only when young to establish a single trunk. The vigorous roots can damage paths and foundations. Seedlings vary considerably in flower shape, color and size, and may take 10 or more years to flower. Propagate from seed or cuttings.

### *Delonix regia*
### Poinciana, royal poinciana, flamboyant tree, fleur-de-paradis, Gul Mohr, flame of the forest

This native of Madagascar grows only about 40 ft (12 m) tall, but its canopy may be wider than its height. The long, feathery leaves have lighter green undersides. It bears clusters of brilliant red or orange flowers, with one white petal marked with yellow and red, followed by dark brown pods up to 12 in (30 cm) long. ZONES 11–12.

## DILLENIA

A genus of some 60 species of evergreen trees and shrubs, mostly from tropical Asia, Africa, Madagascar and Australia. The large leathery leaves have prominent veins, and the showy yellow or white, 5-petalled flowers are produced singly or in loose panicles. They are followed by fleshy fruits enclosed by enlarged, fleshy sepals. They make good shade trees and are grown for their handsome foliage, showy flowers and decorative fruits. The fruits are used in tropical countries for curries, jellies and preserves.

*Delonix regia*

### Cultivation

They are moderately fast growing, transplanting easily when young. They need sun, fertile, humus-rich, moist but well-drained acidic to neutral soil, ample water and some shelter when young. Propagate from seed.

### Dillenia indica
### Elephant apple

This spectacular tree found in India and Southeast Asia grows to 50 ft (15 m) tall, with a broad canopy of large, dark green leaves up to 30 in (75 cm) long, with prominent parallel veins. The 6 in (15 cm) wide creamy yellow flowers are fragrant. The developing fruit resemble green apples. Mature fruit, measuring up to 6 in (15 cm) across, are edible, and so are the mature fruit bracts. ZONE 12.

## DRACAENA

Many of the species belonging to this genus are shrubs, and detailed infor-

*Dillenia indica*

mation on the genus is given in the Shrubs chapter. However, *Dracaena draco* is treated here as a tree.

### Dracaena draco
#### Dragon's-blood tree, dragon tree

This slow-growing tree from the Canary Islands is long lived. It may reach 30 ft (9 m) high with a trunk to 3 ft (1 m) in diameter and a crown of rosettes of stiff, lance-shaped, blue-green leaves to 24 in (60 cm) long and nearly 2 in (5 cm) wide. It bears insignificant flowers followed by orange berries. ZONES 10–11.

## DURANTA

This is a genus of about 30 species of evergreen trees and shrubs from the

*Dracaena draco*

*Duranta erecta*

American tropics and subtropics, although only one of its many species is commonly grown. The more vigorous growths have spines; the whorled or opposite leaves are smallish, often toothed; and the 5-petalled flowers, narrowing to a short tube, appear in delicate sprays from the upper leaf axils. The firm, fleshy, orange berries are allegedly poisonous.

#### Cultivation

*Duranta* species are vigorous. Grow in a fertile, well-drained soil in full sun. They can be trained to become small trees or kept cut back as shrubs; they make useful hedges. Propagate from seed or cuttings. They may be bothered by whiteflies.

### Duranta erecta
#### Golden dewdrop, sky flower
syns *Duranta plumieri, D. repens*

This species, with dense, slightly pendulous branches, can reach to 15–25 ft (4.5–8 m) if trained to a single-trunked tree. The flowers are a pale mauve-blue with darker streaks on the two lower petals and a cream 'eye'. The fruits, ½ in (12 mm) long, overlap with the flowers. The cultivar 'Variegata' has cream-edged leaves with purple tinges. The white-flowered 'Alba' has almost entire leaves. ZONES 10–12.

## ERYTHRINA
#### Coral tree

The 108 species of deciduous and semi-evergreen trees and shrubs in this genus occur wild in tropical and subtropical regions around the world, though with most species in the Americas and Africa. Belonging to the bean tribe of the legumes, they are grown as ornamentals for their vividly hued flowers. Their trunks and branches are protected by short, sharp prickles; many species have weak branches that tend to fall in storms. The

*Erythrina crista-galli*

leaves are compound with 3 broad, often diamond-shaped leaflets. Bean-like flowers in scarlet, crimson or orange are borne in racemes towards the ends of the branches at varying times of the year, followed by narrow seed pods that dry and brown as they ripen.

### Cultivation
They all enjoy full sun and well-drained soil. Spider mites may be a problem. Propagation is from seed or cuttings.

### *Erythrina crista-galli*
#### Common coral tree, cock's comb
This species is the best known coral tree. It grows into a gnarled, wide-crowned tree 15–30 ft (4.5–9 m) tall and bears scarlet or coral-red flowers. ZONES 8–11.

### *Erythrina fusca*
Found in many tropical areas, this deciduous tree grows to 80 ft (24 m) tall

*Erythrina fusca*

with a crooked trunk. Its pinnate leaves are 8 in (20 cm) long. The flowers are rich scarlet with creamy green wings and keel. They are followed by slim pods which are up to 12 in (30 cm) long. ZONES 10–12.

Erythrina haerdii

Erythrina variegata

### Erythrina haerdii

This small, deciduous tree from eastern Africa grows to 15 ft (4.5 m) or more tall with a wide, dense canopy of glossy green leaves. The large, spiky clusters of elongated pea-flowers, borne on bare branches, are brilliant crimson and produce a nectar that is especially irresistible to birds. They are followed by bumpy seed pods. ZONES 10–12.

### Erythrina livingstoniana

A spreading 80 ft (24 m) tree from Mozambique, Malawi and Zimbabwe, this species has 8 in (20 cm) long leaves made up of large oval leaflets. The bright scarlet flowers, borne in arching racemes, are followed by 15 in (38 cm) seed pods. ZONES 10–12.

### Erythrina variegata

This strongly branched, deciduous tree occurs naturally from eastern Africa and the Indian Ocean islands eastwards to Polynesia, reaching heights of up to 80 ft (24 m). The leaves are about 8 in (20 cm) long with large oval to rhomboidal leaflets. Although its floral racemes are only 8 in (20 cm) long, they are densely packed with bright scarlet to orange (rarely white) flowers, followed by 15 in (38 cm) pods. 'Parcellii' has leaves strongly variegated with yellow. ZONES 11–12.

## EUCALYPTUS
### Eucalypt, gum tree

Native mainly to Australia, the eucalypts are possibly the world's most widely planted trees, especially in drier sub-tropical and tropical regions. The leaves contain aromatic oil in small translucent cavities, eucalyptus oil being an important product of certain species. The nectar-rich flowers are abundant, mostly white, but yellow, pink or red in a minority of species, with the massed stamens the most conspicuous part. The fruits are woody capsules, mostly quite small. The bark of many eucalypts is smooth and shed annually, and the new and old bark can make a colorful contrast while this is happening.

### Cultivation

With rare exceptions eucalypts are grown from seed, which germinates freely. They should be planted out into the ground when no more than 18 in (45 cm) high, ensuring that roots have not coiled in the container at any stage. They seldom survive transplanting, and are not long-lived as container plants. They prefer full sun at all stages of growth.

### Eucalyptus grandis
### Flooded gum

One of the noblest of the large eucalypts, flooded gum comes from high-rainfall regions of the Australian east coast and can achieve a height of 200 ft (60 m) and a trunk up to 10 ft (3 m) in diameter in suitably deep, rich, moist soil. The base of its shaft-like trunk is blackish and rough, with smooth, whitish or blue-gray bark above. The thin leaves are dark green and shiny on top, paler beneath. It bears clusters of white blossoms. ZONES 10–11.

### Eucalyptus papuana
### Ghost gum

syn. *Corymbia aparrerinja*

Found near watercourses over much of northern inland Australia and around Port Moresby in Papua New Guinea, the ghost gum is a broad-crowned, single-trunked tree to 50 ft (15 m) high with an open, domed canopy of light green, lanceolate leaves. Its common name comes from the white, smooth, chalky bark. It bears small clusters of white flowers, followed by urn-shaped fruit. Liking a well-drained soil, it is tolerant of quite dry conditions. ZONES 10–12.

## FAGRAEA

This genus contains about 35 species of evergreen trees and shrubs, the latter generally epiphytic. Species are found naturally throughout the Pacific region, East and Southeast Asia. The opposite leaves are large and leathery and the

Eucalyptus papuana

Eucalyptus grandis

terminal clusters of tubular, fragrant flowers are followed by fleshy, multi-seeded, often brightly colored, berry-like fruits. While *Fagraea* species are relatively uncommon in cultivation, they make fine ornamentals and shade trees; they are also suitable to control soil erosion.

### Cultivation
They prefer a shady, somewhat protected situation and freely draining, sandy soil. Propagate from seed or cuttings.

### Fagraea fragrans
From India and Southeast Asia, this tree grows to 70 ft (21 m) tall and has a wide-spreading crown of leathery, elliptic leaves to 6 in (15 cm) long. It bears clusters of fragrant long-tubed flowers that open white and fade to cream. ZONES 11–12.

*Fagraea fragrans*

## FICUS
### Fig
This large, varied genus consists of about 800 species of evergreen and deciduous trees, shrubs and climbers from tropical and subtropical areas throughout the world. It includes the common fig, *Ficus carica*, which bears edible fruit, but most species are grown for their ornamental foliage and for shade. The tiny flowers are completely enclosed in the developing fruits which are borne in the leaf axils and are produced all year. Ripe fruits are eaten by bats and birds and the seeds of many species are often dropped into the branches of other trees where they germinate, sending down roots to the ground. These eventually form secondary trunks that kill the host tree.

### Cultivation
Some grow to great heights in gardens and most have vigorous, invasive root systems. Many make excellent pot and house plants when young. Figs prefer full sun to part-shade and humus-rich, moist but well-drained. Water potted specimens sparingly. Propagate from seed or cuttings, or by aerial layering.

*Ficus aspera 'Parcellii'*

### Ficus aspera 'Parcellii'
#### Mosaic fig

The wild form of this species comes from islands of the southwest Pacific. This small tree has large, roughly oval, dark green leaves mottled with white and with rather hairy undersides. Reaching 10 ft (3 m) in height, it is sometimes grown as a house plant. This cultivar has pronounced foliage markings and pink to purple instead of orange-red fruit. ZONES 11–12.

### Ficus aurea
#### Golden fig, strangler fig

This tree from the West Indies and Florida reaches 60 ft (18 m) high, sometimes originating as a strangler. It has thick elliptic leaves to 4 in (10 cm) long and it bears tiny yellow figs. ZONES 11–12.

### Ficus benghalensis
#### Banyan, Indian banyan

From southern Asia, the banyan is out-standing for its aerial roots, which descend from the branches to the ground and eventually form secondary trunks. An old tree, though reaching only about 70 ft (21 m) in height, can spread widely enough to shelter an entire village. The

banyan has pale gray bark, large glossy mid-green leaves, bronze when young, and round red figs borne in pairs. ZONES 11–12.

### Ficus benjamina
#### Weeping fig, weeping Chinese banyan

A tropical Asian evergreen tree, the weeping fig can reach 50 ft (15 m) in

*Ficus aurea*

*Ficus benghalensis*

*Ficus benjamina 'Exotica'*

Ficus cordata subsp. salicifolia

Ficus dammaropsis

height and a much greater spread, sometimes supported by aerial roots. It has shiny, pointed, oval leaves, insignificant fruit and an invasive root system. This species and its cultivars are used extensively as potted house plants. 'Exotica' has twisted leaf tips; 'Variegata' has rich green leaves splashed with white. ZONES 10–12.

### Ficus cordata subsp. salicifolia
**Willow-leafed fig**
This small tree has leathery oval leaves to 6 in (15 cm) in length with a rounded or heart-shaped base. The small fruit are shining red with white specks when ripe and are borne singly or in pairs in the leaf axils. They are an important food source for birds, monkeys and baboons in tropical Africa. ZONES 10–12.

### Ficus dammaropsis
**Dinnerplate fig**
From the mountains of New Guinea, this small tree grows to 30 ft (9 m). Unlike many *Ficus* species it is single-trunked, forming neither buttresses nor aerial roots. The large rough leaves, up to 24 in (60 cm) long, with deeply corrugated surface, are deep green above and paler beneath, sometimes with red veins. The large figs ripen to a deep purple and are clothed in overlapping scales. ZONES 10–12.

### Ficus elastica
**India rubber tree, rubber plant**
From tropical Asia, this tree can reach 100 ft (30 m) tall and forms massive aerial roots and high buttresses with age. *Ficus elastica* has an aggressive root system and a site must be chosen with care. Outside the tropics it is usually seen as a potted plant. Its rosy new leaves make an attractive contrast to the deep green mature leaves. Cultivars include 'Decora' with bronze new leaves, and 'Doescheri' with variegated gray-green and creamy white leaves with light pink midribs. ZONES 10–12.

### Ficus lyrata
**Banjo fig, fiddleleaf fig**
syn. *Ficus pandurata*
This spreading, evergreen tree from tropical Africa can reach a height of 100 ft (30 m). It features broad, violin-shaped leaves: they are bright glossy green, heavily veined, and up to 15 in (38 cm) long. Figs are long and green. *Ficus lyrata* is often seen as a house plant. ZONES 10–12.

### Ficus macrophylla
**Moreton Bay fig, Australian banyan**
This large, spreading evergreen tree occurs in coastal rainforests of eastern

Ficus elastica 'Decora'

Ficus lyrata

Ficus macrophylla

Ficus opposita

Australia. It grows to about 130 ft (39 m) tall with a spread nearly as great and a buttressed trunk. It bears large, leathery, dark green leaves with rust-toned undersides, and abundant figs that turn reddish brown when ripe. ZONES 10–12.

### Ficus opposita
### Sandpaper fig

Widely found in tropical northern Australia, this small tree to 30 ft (9 m) has mid-green leaves. Their raspy surfaces were used by Aborigines for smoothing wooden implements. The small, edible fruit are pear-shaped. This tree may become completely deciduous during the dry season. ZONES 11–12.

### Ficus religiosa
**Bo tree, peepul, sacred fig**

Indigenous to India and Southeast Asia, this species resembles the banyan

*Ficus virens*

although not as tall. It has an open crown and poplar-like leaves with long thread-like tips and bears small purple figs. It is believed that Buddha was meditating beneath a bo tree when he received enlightenment. Many trees have been propagated from the tree at Anaradhapura, Sri Lanka, recorded as having been planted in 288 BC. ZONES 11–12.

### Ficus virens
**Gray fig, Java willow, spotted fig, strangler vine**

Ranging from India to the Solomon Islands and northern Australia, this briefly deciduous strangler often starts life as an epiphyte. Cultivated plants, however, are usually more conventional single-trunked trees growing to about 50 ft (15 m) tall with a broad crown and heavy limbs. It has pointed-tipped, poplar-like leaves up to 6 in (15 cm) long and produces pairs of small, red-spotted white figs at the branch tips. ZONES 10–12.

### GARCINIA

This is a genus of some 200 species of slow-growing evergreen trees or shrubs mostly from tropical Asia with a few from Africa. They are grown for their thick foliage and edible fruits. The mangosteen, *Garcinia mangostana*, is considered by many to be one of the world's most delicious fruits. Some are cultivated for the yellow latex in their

*Ficus religiosa*

stems, which has been used in dyeing and is said to have medicinal properties.

### Cultivation
Plant in part-shade in moist, well-drained soil and water regularly. Male and female flowers are on separate trees, but male trees are rare and most fruits are formed without fertilization. They thus contain no seeds. Propagation from cuttings or by layering is difficult and the trees bear fruit only in equatorial climates, so they are rarely seen away from their origins.

### Garcinia xanthochymus
### Gamboge
A straight-trunked tree from northern India and the western Himalayas, this species reaches 40 ft (12 m) with a dense, rounded, low canopy. The glossy green, narrow leaves are up to 18 in (45 cm) long. It bears small white flowers and dark yellow fruit, the sap of which yields the yellow pigment gamboge, now

superseded by the more durable chrome and cadmium yellows. ZONES 11–12.

## HEVEA
Nine species make up this tropical American genus, which includes the rubber tree, *Hevea brasiliensis*, the major source of natural rubber. All species, as with others of the euphorbia family, have a milky sap. The flowers are small, fragrant and pale yellow, and the leaves are compound with 3 large leaflets.

### Cultivation
Tropical heat and humidity are essential to the commercial cultivation of these trees. They need moist, free-draining soil and part-shade. Propagate from seed, which must be very fresh.

### Hevea brasiliensis
### Para rubber tree
This tree, native to the Amazon and Orinoco rivers in South America, reaches 120 ft (36 m) but elsewhere it

*Garcinia xanthochymus*

*Hevea brasiliensis*

*Hibiscus tiliaceus*

seldom exceeds 60 ft (18 m). The thick, leathery leaves are divided into 3 leaflets and the greenish white perfumed flowers appear before or with the new growth, which is a distinctive bronze-purple. It is rarely grown other than in commercial plantations or in botanical gardens. ZONES 11–12.

## HIBISCUS
Many of the species belonging to this genus are shrubs, and detailed information on the genus is given in the Shrubs chapter. However, *Hibiscus tiliaceus* is treated here as a tree.

### Hibiscus tiliaceus
#### Cottonwood tree, mangrove hibiscus, sea hibiscus
This evergreen tree from tropical seashores of the Indian and Pacific Oceans grows to a height and spread of about 30 ft (9 m). It has large, heart-shaped, soft mid-green leaves with whitish undersides and bears scattered clear yellow flowers with large crimson centers turning orange as they fade. There are cultivars with purple and variegated leaves. It flowers for most of the year. ZONES 10–11.

## JACARANDA
This genus consists of about 50 species of medium to large deciduous and evergreen trees from Brazil and other parts of tropical and subtropical South America. All species have fern-like, bipinnate leaves and bell-shaped flowers which may be white, purple or mauve-blue. The best known species, the mauve-blue *Jacaranda mimosifolia*, is one of the most widely planted and admired of all warm-climate flowering trees. It yields a richly figured timber, although as the tree is so valued as an ornamental it is rarely cut; the timber, Brazil rose-wood, is usually that of *J. filicifolia*, a larger but less decorative species with white flowers.

### Cultivation
They grow in fertile, well-drained soil and full sun. Potted specimens should be watered freely when in full growth, less so at other times. Propagate from seed or from cuttings.

### Jacaranda mimosifolia
#### Jacaranda
syns *Jacaranda acutifolia, J. ovalifolia*
From the high plains of Brazil, Paraguay and Argentina, this fast-growing, deciduous tree can reach 50 ft (15 m) in height with a spread of up to 40 ft (12 m), and has a broad, rounded crown. The vivid green, fern-like foliage is bipinnate, with 12 or more leaflets. Depending on climate, the leaves may be shed before the flowers—mauve-blue to lilac terminal clusters of trumpet-shaped blossoms—appear; flat, leathery seed pods follow. Pruning is not desirable; if branches are removed, they are replaced by vertical shoots which spoil the shape of the tree. The trees are shallow rooted, which can pose problems for underplanting. ZONES 9–11.

## KIGELIA
This African genus consists of a single species of tropical and subtropical trees,

extending into northern South Africa.
The pinnate leaves are made up of oval
leaflets and the large, bell-shaped flowers
are borne in long pendent racemes and
are mostly orange or red. They are
adapted for pollination by bats. The
large, woody, sausage-shaped fruit have
a smooth skin enclosing a woody, fibrous
pulp which contains many large seeds.

### Cultivation
They require full sun, well-drained soil
and plenty of water, and do best in areas
of high humidity. Propagate from seed or
cuttings.

### Kigelia africana
#### Sausage tree
syn. *Kigelia pinnata*

This evergreen tree grows to about 40 ft
(12 m) and has a wide crown of spreading branches. The leaves are about 12 in
(30 cm) long. The flowers, borne in panicles up to 6 ft (1.8 m) long, open at night
and are crinkled and rich dark red inside,
but duller outside. They have an un-
pleasant smell which attracts the bats
that pollinate them. The light brown
fruit, up to 18 in (45 cm) long and
weighing up to 8 lb (4 kg), are not
edible. It grows vigorously in fertile,
well-drained soil with adequate water.
ZONES 10–12.

## LAGERSTROEMIA
### Crape (or crepe) myrtle
From southern and eastern Asia and
ranging as far as northern Australia, this
is a genus of around 50 species of
evergreen and deciduous small to large
trees, a few grown in warm and hot
climates for their showy flowers. Their
most distinctive feature is the crinkly
margin and slender basal stalk of each of
the 5 petals that make up a flower; the
flowers in turn are massed into large,
dense panicles at the branch tips. The

*Jacaranda mimosifolia*

*Kigelia africana*

'crape' (alternatively crepe) in the name
arose from the flowers' texture being
reminiscent of the once popular fabric
crape, while 'myrtle' alludes to their
being close relatives to the large myrtle
family. They make fine garden plants
and are easily grown. Some species have
attractive smooth bark, colored green,
brown or reddish.

### Cultivation
They thrive in full sun in well-drained,
humus-rich soil. Shelter from strong
winds, which destroy the delicate

Lagerstroemia speciosa

flowers. Propagate from cuttings or from seed. Watch for powdery mildew.

### Lagerstroemia speciosa
#### Queen's flower, queen crape myrtle
syn. *Lagerstroemia flos-reginae*
This deciduous species from the humid jungles of India, Sri Lanka and Burma can reach a height of 80 ft (24 m) in the wild, with a single trunk and a spreading broad head. It has long, leathery leaves that turn copper red before dropping. It bears showy panicles of large, rose-pink to lilac and lavender-purple flowers. The bark is shed in irregular patches, giving the smooth gray trunk a yellowish, mottled appearance. ZONES 11–12.

### MELIA
#### Bead tree, Chinaberry, Persian lilac, rosary tree, white cedar
This genus of only one very variable species of deciduous tree ranges across Asia from Iraq to Japan and south to Australia. *Melia azedarach* has many common names; 2 of them, bead tree and rosary tree, arise from the way the seeds

have a hole through the middle, convenient for bead-making. The trees were formerly grown in southern Italy for making rosaries. *Melia* is Greek for 'ash' *(Fraxinus)*, although the only connection is that the pinnate or doubly pinnate leaves are vaguely similar.

#### Cultivation
It grows in warm climates and readily tolerates dry conditions and poor soil. It is a favorite street tree in arid climates. Propagate from seed.

### Melia azedarach
syn. *Melia azedarach var. australasica*
This is a fast-growing, spreading tree which grows to 30 ft (9 m) tall. The young leaves appear with large sprays of small, delicately scented lilac flowers; these are followed by bunches of pale orange or cream berries, each containing a single woody seed, which persist after the leaves fall. They are poisonous to humans but much eaten by birds. 'Umbraculiformis' has a curious yet attractive habit, like a blown-out umbrella. ZONES 8–12.

### MICHELIA
Closely related to the magnolias, the 45 or so species of *Michelia* are found in tropical and subtropical Asia, with a few species in the cooler foothills of the Himalayas. They range from shrubs to substantial trees, mainly evergreen, and many bear intensely fragrant flowers. Some species are widely cultivated in India for their fragrant oil, which is extracted from the blooms for use in perfume and cosmetics.

#### Cultivation
They like a position in full sun or part-shade in humus-rich, well-drained, neutral to acid soil; they resent being trans-planted. Propagate from seed or cuttings.

*Melia azedarach*

*Michelia champaca*

### Michelia champaca
#### Champak, champaca
From the lower Himalayas, this upright,
conical tree reaches 100 ft (30 m) in its
native habitat, but cultivated trees
usually reach only a third of this height.
Its long, slender, mid-green leaves droop
from the somewhat horizontal branches.
Cup-shaped creamy orange petals on a
bed of recurved sepals are borne upright
on the branch tips. The flowers are
particularly fragrant. ZONES 10–11.

### PANDANUS
#### Screw pine
This large genus from East Africa,
Malaysia, Australia and the Pacific
contains about 600 species, a few of
which make decorative trees for seaside
gardens and swampy areas. Palm-like
evergreens, some grow 50 ft (15 m) or
more tall. They may appear shorter, as
they often lean at an angle. The sword-
shaped, spiny-edged green leaves, are
long and narrow and arranged spirally at
the ends of the branches. The white
flowers are very small; the fruits are
aggregations of reddish or yellow

berries, up to 12 in (30 cm) in diameter,
and resemble a pineapple.

#### Cultivation
Pandanus require full sun or part-shade,
and moist, well-drained soil. They can be
treated as house plants when young if
they are given ample water. Keep the
plants tidy by removing dead and
damaged leaves. Propagate from seed,
soaked for 24 hours before planting, or
by detaching rooted suckers.

### Pandanus odoratissimus
Found through the tropical Asian and
Pacific region, this species is up to 20 ft
(6 m) tall and has long slender leaves
edged with sharp spines. It has strong
aerial roots that form a stout buttress
base. Male trees have showy white flower
bracts, while female trees bear pineapple-
like fruit. The foliage is used for weaving
and thatching. Male flowers and foliage
also have culinary uses. ZONES 11–12.

### PELTOPHORUM
At home in the tropical regions of the
world, these 15 species of evergreen,
leguminous trees are grown primarily for

the dense shade they cast. In the wild some species can reach 100 ft (30 m), but in cultivation they are more usually 60 ft (18 m) tall. The fern-like leaves are deep glossy green, with individual leaflets measuring up to 1 in (25 mm) long. The impressive spikes of perfumed yellow flowers develop into long, brown pods.

### Cultivation
These trees prefer fertile, moist but well-drained soil and a sheltered, part-shaded position, although they can tolerate full sun if well watered. Propagate from pre-soaked or scarified seed or cuttings taken during the wet season.

### *Peltophorum pterocarpum*
**Rusty-shield tree, yellow flame tree, yellow poinciana**
syns *Peltophorum ferrugineum, P. inerme*
Growing to 60 ft (18 m) tall with a crown up to 25 ft (8 m) wide, this species is a good shade tree for tropical gardens. Clusters of heavily perfumed flowers with unusual crinkled petals open from vivid rust-red buds. The abundance of rust-red, flattened seed pods that follow persist on the tree until the next flowering. ZONES 11–12.

*Peltophorum pterocarpum*

## PHYLLANTHUS
This large genus of some 650 species of evergreen or deciduous herbs, shrubs and trees, comes from the tropical and subtropical regions of the world. The stalkless leaves, often red tinted when young, are arranged in two flattened ranks along the branches giving the impression of pinnate foliage. It bears small, red or yellow-green petal-less flowers. Some species have cladophylls rather than true leaves and these become fringed with small flowers, creating an unusual effect as if the leaves are flowering. Although the small pea-sized fruits of most species are inedible, a few produce gooseberry-like fruits that are palatable if cooked.

### Cultivation
Plant in rich, sandy, well-drained soil with ample water. They are good seaside plants in hot climates. Propagate from seed or cuttings.

### *Phyllanthus acidus*
**Star gooseberry, Otaheite gooseberry, Malay gooseberry**
From India and Madagascar, this is the only widely cultivated species. It quickly reaches its mature height of 30 ft (9 m) with a spread of 10 ft (3 m), and has pale green, almost stalkless leaves. It bears dense clusters of tiny red flowers; these are followed by tight bunches of ribbed, bright yellow fruit, 1 in (25 mm) long. ZONES 11–12.

## PISONIA
syn. *Heimerliodendron*
These 35 species of fast-growing, evergreen shrubs, small trees and climbers occur naturally in tropical and subtropical areas, particularly in the Americas, northern Australia and the Malaysian region. They have large, oval leaves somewhat like those of the rubber

tree *(Ficus elastica)*; variegated foliage cultivars are often grown. The small greenish flowers, though borne in panicles, are not showy but are followed by the extremely sticky fruits for which the genus is best known. These often trap insects and even small birds, although why they do this is unknown.

### Cultivation
They require rich, well-drained soil in a sunny or part-shaded site. They will grow in containers and are sometimes used as house plants. The species may be raised from seed or cuttings; the variegated foliage forms are grown from cuttings.

### Pisonia umbellifera
**Bird-catcher tree**
Native to the western Pacific region, this erect, branching shrub grows to 15 ft (4.5 m) with a spread of 10 ft (3 m). It has large, elliptical, glossy green leaves and insignificant flowers and bears very sticky, purplish fruit all year round. Trees from temperate east Australia and New Zealand are now usually separated as *Pisonia brunoniana* (syn. *Heimerliodendron brunonianum*). 'Variegata' has oval leaves 12–15 in (30–38 cm) long and beautifully patterned in tones of pale to dark green and creamy white, and small, greenish flowers. ZONES 10–12.

## PLUMERIA
**Frangipani, temple tree**
*Plumeria* commemorates Charles Plumier, a seventeenth-century French botanist who described several tropical species. The genus contains 8 species of mainly deciduous shrubs and trees, originally from Central America, known for their strongly fragrant flowers. The trees can reach a height of 30 ft (9 m), though they are generally much smaller. Their fleshy branches contain a poisonous,

milky sap. In the tropics, the terminally held flowers (generally white) appear before the leaves and continue to flower for most of the year. The fruits consist of 2 leathery follicles, although the trees rarely fruit in cultivation. Most plumerias in gardens are hybrids.

*Phyllanthus acidus*

*Pisonia umbellifera 'Variegata'*

## Cultivation
They prefer full sun and moderately fertile, well-drained soil. Propagate from cuttings that have been allowed to dry out for a couple of weeks.

### Plumeria obtusa
#### White frangipani, Singapore plumeria
This small tree grows to 25 ft (8 m) high and is best suited to a tropical climate where, unlike most frangipanis, it is reliably evergreen. The broad, blunt-ended leaves are 6 in (15 cm) or more long. The scented, creamy white flowers have a bright yellow center. With its elegant, rounded flowers and soft perfume, 'Singapore White' is one of the loveliest of all plumerias. ZONES 10–12.

### Plumeria rubra
This widely cultivated, deciduous small tree, with its broadly rounded canopy, can grow to a height of 25 ft (8 m). It is distinguished by its pale pink to crimson flowers, which are used extensively for decoration. *Plumeria rubra* var. *acutifolia* is usually seen more commonly than the species and features creamy white

Plumeria obtusa 'Singapore White'

Plumeria rubra

Plumeria rubra 'Golden Kiss'

Plumeria rubra var. acutifolia

flowers, sometimes flushed pink, with a
deep yellow center. 'Golden Kiss' has
large heads of golden yellow flowers
with a soft flush of apricot along the
lower edge of each petal. ZONES 10–12.

## POLYALTHIA

This is a genus of tropical trees with
large, very glossy, elliptical to lance-
shaped leaves. Their narrow-petalled,
yellow-green flowers are reminiscent of
those of the star magnolia *(Magnolia
stellata)* and are followed by clusters of
egg-shaped fruits.

### Cultivation

Plant in moist, well-drained soil and
shade when young. They are tough and
adaptable. Propagate from seed or from
cuttings.

### Polyalthia longifolia
#### Indian mast tree

Originating from Sri Lanka, this has
become one of the most popular park
and avenue trees of tropical Asia,
thriving in monsoonal regions such as
Thailand and southern India. Growing
to about 50 ft (15 m) tall, it has a
striking narrowly conical or columnar
habit which is sometimes almost pole-
like. A curtain of long, glossy green
leaves with slightly wavy edges conceals
all but the base of the trunk. New foliage
flushes are at first yellowish then bronzy
green. Small greenish yellow flowers are
borne in the wet season but are hidden
under the foliage; the small plum-like
fruits are eaten only by animals such as
fruit-bats. ZONES 11–12.

## PTEROCARPUS

Widely distributed in the tropics and
also found in South Africa, this genus of
legumes includes some 20 species of
trees and climbers. They have large,
pinnate leaves and are usually deciduous

*Polyalthia longifolia*

*Pterocarpus rohrii*

in the dry season, the flowers opening
before the foliage develops. The flowers
are pea-like, scented, small but brightly
colored in shades of yellow and orange
and are borne in racemes. Rounded pods
follow, their edges extended into a 'wing'
in some species and not splitting to
release their seeds like pods of most
other legumes.

### Cultivation

Plant in moist, well-drained soil in full
sun. Propagate from seed or cuttings.

### Pterocarpus rohrii

This species is widespread in tropical
America, ranging from Costa Rica to

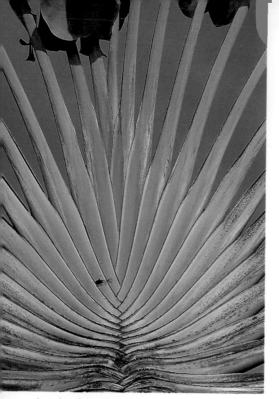

*Ravenala madagascariensis*

swaying in the breeze although they tend to fray somewhat with age.

### Cultivation
*Ravenala* needs rich, moist but well-drained soil and a sunny spot in a hot climate. Shelter from strong winds. Propagate from seed or by division of suckers.

### Ravenala madagascariensis
The bright green leaves of this species grow up to 10 ft (3 m) long, form 2 opposite rows and are held on tightly overlapped long stalks. Its trunk terminates in the sheathing bases of the leaf stalks, which lap together. The whole arrangement grows 30 ft (9 m) tall, spreading out to form a wide, flat fan of foliage. Clusters of white flowers emerge from between the leaf base. ZONES 11–12.

## SARACA
This leguminous genus consists of 71 species of small evergreen trees from tropical Southeast Asia; they occur naturally as understory trees in forests and are grown for their dense clusters of showy flowers and attractive foliage. The leaves are pinnate with paired leaflets; the new foliage is often soft and bronze red, maturing to mid-green. The flowers have no true petals but a very colorful tubular calyx opening into 4 to 5 flat sepals and long, prominent stamens, and are borne in clusters on older branches, followed by narrow oblong pods.

### Cultivation
Species of *Saraca* need a hot, humid climate, rich, moist, well-drained soil and some shade. Propagate from seed.

### Saraca indica
### Asoka, sorrowless tree
The best known species of the genus, this erect evergreen tree occurs naturally

Peru, growing in deciduous lowland rainforest. It makes a broadly spreading tree to 30 ft (9 m) or more in height with drooping outer branches and leaves with broad, deep green leaflets. Attractive sprays of pea-like flowers are followed by pods that are large for this genus, about 4 in (10 cm) across, almost circular and quite woody. ZONES 11–12.

## RAVENALA
### Traveller's palm, traveller's tree
A member of a very striking family, this genus is endemic to Madagascar but is now commonly grown throughout the tropics. It has only one species, an evergreen tree with huge, paddle-like leaves on long stalks that are similar to those of the banana (*Musa*), but spreading fan-like from the base and looking exceptionally graceful when

*Saraca indica*

*Schefflera actinophylla*

from India to the Malay Peninsula. It can grow to 30 ft (9 m) and has long, shiny, compound leaves with 3 to 6 pairs of leaflets that are soft and reddish when young. The flowers are yellow-orange to scarlet with long, showy, dark red stamens, and the pods that follow are deep reddish purple. ZONES 11–12.

## SCHEFFLERA

syns *Brassaia, Dizygotheca, Heptapleurum*
This is a vast genus of small trees, shrubs and scrambling climbers, with over 700 species occurring through most wetter tropical and subtropical regions of the world. The leaves consist of similar-sized leaflets arranged like a cartwheel at the ends of long stalks. The small flowers are arranged in branching, usually radiating spikes. The fruits are small, fleshy berries. In their native rainforests many schefleras grow as epiphytes, high on other trees or on cliffs or rock outcrops.

### Cultivation

They can be planted in the garden in a spot sheltered from wind either in the sun or part-shade. Young plants make excellent tub specimens. Grow them in well-drained soil preferably enriched with organic matter, keeping the soil moist. Propagate from fresh seed, cuttings or by air-layering.

### Schefflera actinophylla

syn. *Brassaia actinophylla*
**Queensland umbrella tree, Australian ivy palm, octopus tree**
Each leaf of this species resembles an umbrella and consists of 7 to 15 light green glossy leaflets up to 15 in (38 cm) long. From rainforests of northern Australia and New Guinea, this species reaches to 40 ft (12 m) in cultivation with multiple erect trunks and a dense canopy 20 ft (6 m) wide. Numerous clusters of flowers are arranged in spectacular radiating spikes on red stems; these appear near the top of the plant. Each ruby red flower has contrasting cream stamens and is rich in nectar. Reddish fleshy berries follow. ZONES 10–12.

## SCHINUS

The 30 species of evergreen shrubs and trees that make up this genus are indigenous to Central and South America. They are grown for their graceful habit and great resistance to very dry conditions. The leaves usually consist of many leaflets but are sometimes simple. The flowers are tiny and are arranged in clusters, male and female flowers on the same or separate trees. Female trees feature attractive round berries. They make excellent shade and street trees.

### Cultivation
Plant them in full sun in well-drained, coarse soil; they grow best in warm to hot climates. Propagate from fresh seed or cuttings.

### Schinus terebinthifolius
#### Brazilian pepper tree
A round-headed tree up to about 30 ft (9 m) high, this species has bronze-green pinnate leaves usually composed of 7 leaflets. The drooping panicles of tiny cream flowers are followed by small green berries that redden as they ripen. When trimmed it makes an excellent shade tree. In some warm, wet climates, such as in Hawaii, it has become a serious weed. ZONES 10–12.

*Schinus terebinthifolius*

## SENECIO
This large genus of vigorous leafy plants includes some 1,000 species from all over the world. Plants range from annuals, biennials and perennials to evergreen tree-like shrubs and climbers, some of the species being succulent. The daisy-like flowers, usually yellow but some-times red, orange, blue or purple, are arranged in small to large clusters at the tops of the plants. Some species contain alkaloids and are poisonous to humans and animals.

### Cultivation
Reasonably fertile, well-drained soil suits these plants, as well as a sunny location. Regular tip pruning encourages a bushy habit. Propagate shrubs from cuttings, annuals from seed and perennials by division.

### Senecio arborescens
This is a tropical species that grows to tree size, found at medium altitudes in the mountains of Costa Rica, in clearings in rainforests. It grows to 20 ft (6 m) or more tall with a thick trunk and large leaves. It bears sprays of numerous small yellow flowerheads that are strongly aromatic. ZONES 10–12.

*Senecio arborescens*

## SPATHODEA
### African tulip tree, fountain tree

This genus contains a single species of evergreen tree that occurs naturally in tropical and subtropical Africa. It is widely planted as a street tree and is ornamental all over the tropics. Its large, bell-shaped, orange or scarlet flowers are produced in dense, terminal clusters. The large pinnate leaves are deep green. The fruit are oblong capsules that split open when ripe to release the seeds. The common name fountain tree refers to the way the buds squirt moisture when they are squeezed.

### Cultivation

It prefers rich, well-drained soil, shelter from wind and a sunny position. Propagation is usually from seed, which can be variable.

### Spathodea campanulata

This spectacular, fast-growing tree grows to about 80 ft (24 m) tall. It has large, flat clusters of velvety, bronze-green buds and big, nectar-rich, orange-red flowers with yellow frilly edges. The leaves are bronze when young, maturing to deep glossy green. The fruit are 8 in (20 cm) long. ZONES 11–12.

*Spathodea campanulata*

## TABEBUIA
### Trumpet tree

The 100 or so shrubs and trees of this genus occur naturally in tropical America and the West Indies, where some are valued for their highly durable timber. They feature spectacular flowers and attractive foliage, and make excellent shade trees. Many are briefly deciduous during the tropical dry season, but some are almost evergreen. The flowers are trumpet- to bell-shaped and shades of white, yellow, pink, red or purple. They are clustered at the branch tips, usually when the leaves have fallen. Fruits are bean-like capsules. Leaves vary in shape, and may be simple or palmately compound, with 3 to 7 leaflets, their edges are often toothed.

### Cultivation

Trumpet trees need deep, humus-rich soil with good drainage. A sunny position is best, with some shelter from wind to protect the flowers. Propagate from seed or by layering or from cuttings; selected types are grafted.

### Tabebuia chrysantha

This small deciduous tree from Venezuela grows to a height of 20 ft

*Tabebuia chrysantha*

Tabebuia pallida

Tamarindus indica

(6 m) and forms an open crown of slender branches. Its leaves are composed of 5 hairy, finger-like leaflets. It bears a profusion of rich mustard-yellow, trumpet-shaped flowers about 3 in (8 cm) long. These are grouped in large heads at the ends of leafless branches. The fruit are slightly hairy. ZONES 11–12.

### Tabebuia heterophylla
#### Ipe roxo
This Brazilian species is one of the most magnificent, producing a mass of flowers on leafless branches. The blossoms hang in large, loose clusters and come in various shades of pink, from the palest eggshell to the deepest rose. Valued for its timber, this species is thought by some to be an effective treatment for syphilis. ZONES 11–12.

### Tabebuia pallida
#### Cuban pink trumpet tree
This small evergreen or briefly decidu-ous tree occurs naturally in the West Indies, Mexico and Central America. It reaches 25 ft (8 m) or so in height. This species has a straight trunk and an open, rounded crown, although it may be quite variable in its habit. The leaves consist of 1, 3 or 5 leaflets, each with a prominent yellow midrib. The flowers, borne in terminal clusters, are lilac pink paling to

white at the edges. *Tabebuia pallida* suits warm coastal areas. ZONES 11–12.

## TAMARINDUS
### Tamarind, Indian date
This legume genus consists of only one species: a tall, slow-growing evergreen tree that originated in eastern Africa, but is now naturalized in many areas of tropical Southeast Asia. Valued as an ornamental shade and street tree, it is also grown for its bean-like pods, which contain large seeds encased in an edible, sweet, fibrous pulp. This pulp, with high tartaric acid content, is cooked and strained to produce a tart-sweet syrup that is used to make a refreshing drink in Middle Eastern countries, and is an important ingredient in Asian cuisine and Worcestershire sauce.

### Cultivation
They need a sunny position if they are to thrive, but are not fussy about soil. Once established, they will tolerate drought and exposed positions. The roots can be invasive. Propagate from seed, cuttings or by air layering.

### Tamarindus indica
This handsome tree grows to 70 ft (21 m), with a broad spreading crown and dense foliage. The short trunk is covered with shaggy brown bark. The fern-like,

Terminalia brassii

Thevetia peruviana

compound, vivid green leaves are held on slender, pale brown branchlets. The small flowers, pale orange-yellow or cream with red veins, are borne in small clusters among the leaves. These are followed by the 8 in (20 cm) long pods, which ripen from green to dark brown and have brittle shells. ZONES 11–12.

## TERMINALIA
### Tropical almond
This large genus consists of around 200 species of evergreen and deciduous trees occurring in tropical and subtropical regions of Asia, Australia and southern Africa. The bark is often fissured and the branches are arranged in tiers. The leaves are generally large and leathery. The 5-petalled, greenish white flowers are small and not showy; they appear on spikes or in clusters. The fruits are yellow, dark red or black drupes, usually angled or winged and sometimes edible, though it is said that eating too many will make one drunk.

### Cultivation
They need well-drained soil and plenty of sun; some species tolerate salty winds and dry conditions. Propagate from seed.

### Terminalia brassii
This tall handsome tree has glossy mid-green ovate leaves. It makes a good

shade tree in the tropics and subtropics and is also used as a quick-growing plantation tree in the Solomon Islands, and has been trialled as a source of paper pulp. ZONES 11–12.

## THEVETIA
All 8 species of this genus of evergreen trees and shrubs have a poisonous milky sap; in fact, all parts of the plants are very poisonous. Relatives of the oleander (Nerium), they are indigenous to tropical America. They feature clusters of showy, mostly yellow, funnel-shaped flowers at the shoot tips. The fruits are berry-like. The leaves are arranged spirally on the branchlets.

### Cultivation
These grow best in a sandy, well-drained soil enriched with organic matter. They need plenty of water while in flower. The ideal location provides shelter from wind, plus full sun to part-shade. Prune the plants after flowering to maintain their dense growth. Propagate from seed or from cuttings.

### Thevetia peruviana
### Yellow oleander, lucky nut
syn. Thevetia neriifolia
This domed tree grows to 25 ft (8 m) tall. The long, shiny, rich green leaves are hard and strap-like to narrowly

lance-shaped, with barely any stalk. The yellow to soft orange, slightly perfumed flowers, each 2 in (5 cm) across, are held on long stalks. They bloom on and off for most of the year in their native habitat. The fruit are oddly shaped, fleshy drupes, rounded and with prominent ridges. They ripen from green through red to black and are regarded by some as a lucky charm, even though dangerously poisonous. ZONES 10–12.

### *Thevetia thevetioides*
#### Large-flowered yellow oleander, be-still tree, giant thevetia

This species grows to 15 ft (4.5 m) tall. Its erect but rather weak stems form an untidy crown. The leaves are narrowly lance-shaped, 4 in (10 cm) long and ½ in (12 mm) wide, with a pointed tip and prominent veins. The flowers, about 3 in (8 cm) across, are orange or pale to strong yellow, and more open than those of *Thevetia peruviana*. The fruit are green drupes. ZONES 10–12.

## TIBOUCHINA

Many of the species belonging to this genus are shrubs, and detailed information on the genus is given in the Shrubs chapter. However, *Tibouchina granulosa* is treated here as a tree.

### *Tibouchina granulosa*

Indigenous to Brazil, this fast-growing species can reach a height of 30–40 ft (9–12 m). The flower clusters are 12 in (30 cm) long and may completely hide the foliage; each bloom is rose purple to violet or pink and 2 in (5 cm) across. The branching stems are thick and woody. The leaves are lance-shaped to oblong and 6–8 in (15–20 cm) long. They are dark green and shiny on top, bright green and hairy underneath, and hairy along the edges. ZONES 10–12.

## TREVESIA

Members of the aralia family, the 12 species of shrubs and trees in this genus are found in the Himalayas, southern China and Southeast Asia. They form clumps of erect, often prickly stems clothed with large palmate leaves that are palmately lobed or dissected. Large inflorescences of small cream flowers form at the stem tips.

### Cultivation

They require a moist, humus-rich soil and reliable moisture to thrive. They are propagated from cuttings or seed and small plants can sometimes be divided.

### *Trevesia palmata*

This small evergreen tree from tropical Asia grows to a height of 20 ft (6 m)

*Thevetia thevetioides*

*Tibouchina granulosa*

with a spread of about 6 ft (1.8 m). It
has an erect, slender trunk. The large,
glossy leaves are up to 24 in (60 cm)
wide and may be either entire or lobed;
new leaves are quite prickly. The
greenish white flowers have 8 to 12
petals and are produced in clusters.
'Micholitzii' is the form commonly
grown, known as the snowflake plant on
account of the snowflake pattern of
dissection of its large leaves.
ZONES 10–12.

## TRICHILIA

This genus includes about 300 species
of tropical and subtropical trees and
shrubs, mostly from the Americas, but
with a few species found in southern
and eastern Africa. The large,
compound leaves are alternate; the
leaflets untoothed. Male and female
flowers are borne in sprays in the
leaf axils. The fruits are about 1½ in
(35 mm) across and contain several
black seeds almost covered by a
scarlet, fleshy aril. Oil derived from
the fruits have a number of uses in
traditional medicine in the trees' native
countries.

### Cultivation
*Trichilia* species prefer moist, humus-rich
soil and will not tolerate drought.
Propagate from seed cuttings.

*Trichilia emetica*
**Red ash, Natal mahogany**
This handsome evergreen shade tree is
indigenous to southern Africa and is
widely seen in warm, humid areas. It
grows to 30 ft (9 m) tall with a rounded,
spreading crown and brownish gray
bark. The leaves have 7 to 11 leaflets
and are dark green, with shiny upper
surfaces and paler undersides. Small
creamy white, fragrant, bell-shaped
flowers are borne in long sprays. The
fruit are small, creamy brown and
shaped like figs. ZONES 10–12.

## TRISTANIOPSIS

This genus of 30 species of evergreen
trees or shrubs is closely related to
*Tristania* and used to be included in that
once larger genus. Species have
obscurely veined leaves and 5-petalled
yellow to white flowers. The seeds are
usually winged. The genus contains
several species indigenous to the high-
rainfall coastal forests of eastern
Australia and others from Southeast
Asia, Papua New Guinea and New
Caledonia. These plants make excellent
screen or hedge plants.

### Cultivation
They adapt to a range of situations, but
grow best in deep, well-drained, moist
soil in shade or part-shade. Water freely

*Trevesia palmata*

*Trevesia palmata 'Micholitzii'*

Trichilia emetica

Tristaniopsis laurina

and prune to size as necessary. They should be propagated from seed.

### Tristaniopsis laurina
#### Water gum, kanuka
syn. *Tristania laurina*

A conical tree to 30–50 ft (9–15 m) high, the water gum has a smooth, creamy brown trunk attractively streaked with gray. The branches start low to the ground and form a dense canopy. The leaves are oblong to lance-shaped and 4 in (10 cm) long. Their upper surfaces are dark green and the undersides paler; in colder areas, they turn red. New leaves are pinkish. It bears clusters of small, deep yellow flowers, each blossom rich with nectar. The fruit are round capsules. ZONES 10–12.

## WEINMANNIA

This genus of about 190 species of evergreen trees and shrubs is found in Central and South America, Madagascar, the Malay Archipelago and islands of the west Pacific. They have opposite, usually pinnate leaves that may be different in juvenile and adult stages. The small white or yellow flowers in erect often showy racemes are followed by a shiny, reddish brown 2-celled capsule. They are grown for their attractive foliage, flowers and fruit and value as shade cover.

### Cultivation
They grow best in slightly acid peaty soil with good drainage. Light requirements range from part-shade to full sun. A plentiful water supply is needed during the flowering season. They will tolerate pruning. Propagate from seed or cuttings.

### Weinmannia pinnata
This small tree from Mexico to Brazil and the West Indies grows to 30 ft (10 m) tall with downy young branches and pinnate leaves to 3 in (8 cm) long. The elliptical leaflets have serrated margins. It bears small white flowers. ZONES 10–12.

## XANTHOSTEMON
The 40 or so species of evergreen trees of this genus in the myrtle family range from northeastern Australia through the Malay Archipelago and New Caledonia. The leathery oval leaves are glossy dark green, the new growth often bronze-pink. The 5-petalled flowers are white, gold or yellow with long stamens and are held in clusters at the ends of branches.

### Cultivation
These trees prefer full sun or light shade, humus-rich soil and plenty of moisture. Shelter from strong winds is beneficial. Propagate from seed or cuttings.

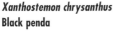
Weinmannia pinnata

Xanthostemon chrysanthus

### Xanthostemon chrysanthus
**Black penda**
Popular in tropical and subtropical
gardens in Australia, this tree reaches
25 ft (8 m) or so in cultivation, although
it is taller in its native habitat. It bears
showy heads of bright acid-yellow
flowers with masses of long stamens.
The large leaves have a pale green mid-
vein. ZONES 10–12.

## YUCCA
The 40 or so species of unusual
evergreen perennials, shrubs and trees in
this genus are found in drier regions of
North America. Often slow growing,
they form rosettes of stiff, sword-like
leaves usually tipped with a sharp spine;
as the plants mature, some species
develop an upright woody trunk, often
branched. Yuccas bear showy, tall
panicles of drooping, white or cream,
bell- to cup-shaped flowers. The fruits
are either fleshy or dry capsules, but in
most species are rarely seen away from
the plants' native lands as the flowers
must be pollinated by the yucca moth.

**Cultivation**
Yuccas do best in areas of low humidity;
they prefer full sun and sandy soil with
good drainage. Propagate from seed (if
available), cuttings or suckers.

Yucca elephantipes

### Yucca elephantipes
**Spineless yucca, giant yucca**
syn. Yucca giganteu
This yucca occurs naturally in southern
Mexico and Central America. It
develops a rough, thick trunk that often
branches and reaches a height of 30 ft
(9 m); in cultivation it is often smaller.
The leaves are 4 ft (1.2 m) long and 3 in
(8 cm) wide, shiny dark green with finely
serrated edges. White, often somewhat
drooping, bell-shaped flowers are
clustered in large panicles. ZONES 10–12.

CHAPTER 4

# Fruit &
# Nut Trees &
# Other Fruits

## ANACARDIUM
### Cashew

Only one species of this genus has been much cultivated, namely *Anacardium occidentale*, the cashew. Both branches and foliage have a very awkward, untidy aspect so the cashew tree is rarely grown for its ornamental qualities. Stiff sprays of small pinkish flowers (fragrant at night) are followed by the curious fruits, consisting of 2 parts. The 'cashew apple', actually a swollen, fleshy stalk, is colored, edible and up to 4 in (10 cm) long and 2 in (5 cm) in diameter. Sitting in its hollowed apex is the true fruit, curved like the nut, with an outer fleshy husk containing an extremely acrid, resinous sap which can badly burn the skin. The young leaves are also used as a salad vegetable in some countries but they are only sweet and edible on selected trees.

### Cultivation

Fast growing when young, cashews can be grown in the warmer subtropics as well as the tropics. Propagation is easy from fresh seed, planted directly into the ground.

*Anacardium occidentale*

### Anacardium occidentale

Growing as tall as 25 ft (8 m) but usually about half that height with a spreading, irregular crown, the cashew produces flowers early in the wet season; fruit ripen later in the wet. ZONES 11–12.

## ANANAS
### Pineapple

As well as its obvious importance as a commercial crop, this genus of 8 species of South American bromeliads includes several ornamental plants grown in subtropical and tropical gardens. They have large rosettes of narrow, tapering, tough leaves with sharply toothed or spiny edges. The flowers, which develop into the familiar compound fruit shape, are usually reddish purple, each backed by a bract and borne in a crowded head at the top of a short, stout stem that emerges from the center of the leaf rosette.

### Cultivation

Plant in full sun in fertile, well-drained soil. They are usually propagated from the basal suckers that develop on mature rosettes. Alternatively you can remove the leafy top from the fruit and treat it as a cutting, rooting either it in soil or water.

### Ananas comosus
### Pineapple

Cultivated by Central American Indians for centuries, the pineapple's wild origin is believed to be in Brazil. It was praised by early European visitors as the finest of all fruit and shipped back to the Old World. The leaf rosettes are up to 30 in (75 cm) high and 4 ft (1.2 m) wide. The sword-shaped leaves are viciously edged with tiny thorns, but recently smooth-leafed cultivars have been developed. It has an inflorescence up to 12 in (30 cm) long with yellow to red bracts and grows up to 4 ft (1.2 m) tall when in fruit. Fruit develop in the second year if conditions are suitable. 'Porteanus' has leaves with a central yellow stripe, while 'Variegatus' has leaves with cream marginal stripes and may develop red tints. ZONES 11–12.

## ARTOCARPUS

Best known in the form of one of its many species, the breadfruit of Captain Bligh of the *Bounty* fame, *Artocarpus* is actually a very large tropical Asian genus of evergreen trees. It is closely related to *Ficus*, the fig genus, and in fact many of its species are hard to tell apart from figs when not in flower or fruit. The leaves, bark and twigs exude a milky sap when damaged, and the minute, greenish, female flowers are crowded onto short, fleshy spikes which after fertilization enlarge into aggregations of fleshy fruit, very large in the case of the species mentioned below.

### Cultivation

Edible-fruited species are cultivated in the wet tropics, thriving heat in deep, fertile, well-drained soil in sheltered positions. Propagation is from seed, or more commonly from root cuttings or aerial layers (marcotts), which perpetuate desirable clones.

### Artocarpus heterophyllus
### Jackfruit, jaca

This Southeast Asian species is easily confused with its close relative the chempedak *(Artocarpus integer)*; both have similar gigantic, compound fruit and leathery, unlobed leaves, but the chempedak's fruit are sweeter. The jackfruit grows to 30 ft (9 m) tall with a single main trunk and dense, rounded crown of dark green leaves. The fruit may be up to 24 in (60 cm) long and weigh up to 40 lb (18 kg). Their outer surface is creamy brown with small conical protuberances, and the sticky

*Ananas comosus*

*Artocarpus heterophyllus*

*Averrhoa carambola*

yellow or pink flesh contains many large brown seeds which are edible, as is the sweet though malodorous flesh. ZONES 11–12.

## AVERRHOA

The genus consists of only 2 species, from Southeast Asia. They are close relatives of *Oxalis*. These are small trees with densely twiggy crowns and short pinnate leaves, some of which yellow and drop in the dry season. The slightly fragrant flowers appear in short lateral clusters from the old wood and the slow-ripening fruit hang in clusters from the branches.

### Cultivation

The trees are easily grown in full sun, making fine small shade trees. Propagation is from seed or more commonly by grafts or air-layers (marcotts) which preserve desirable clonal characteristics.

*Averrhoa carambola*
**Carambola, star fruit, five-corner**

In cultivation, this species of rather upright form normally makes a small tree about 20 ft (6 m) high. The leaflets of the compound leaves have the curious habit of folding together after being touched or at night. It flowers and fruits through much of the year, but with major flushes of flower in the middle of the wet and the middle of the dry season. The large, ornamental fruit ripen through pale yellow, when their flavor is pleasantly acid, to a deep golden orange color, when they become sweet and deliciously tangy, reminiscent of the taste of passionfruit. ZONES 11–12.

## CARICA

**Papaya, pawpaw**

Large, succulent, edible fruits characterize this genus of 22 species from Central and South America. One species, *Carica papaya*, is grown throughout the tropics for its large, sweet fruit, and two or three others with slightly smaller fruit are cultivated to a more limited extent. Although ultimately tree sized, they remain soft wooded and are short lived. The very large leaves are mostly deeply lobed in a snowflake-like pattern. Male and female flowers are normally borne on separate trees, but hermaphrodite trees have been developed in cultivation. The small, cream, male flowers are in long-stalked panicles while the larger, fleshy females are stalkless and solitary. Female flowers are followed by pointed cylindrical fruits, which usually become yellow as they ripen.

### Cultivation

Papayas can only be grown outdoors. Plant in rich, moist, well-drained soil in sun or part-shade. Propagate from seed or cuttings or by grafting.

Citrus aurantifolia

Carica papaya

## Carica papaya

This, the true papaya, is widely grown in tropical areas. It grows up to 20 ft (6 m) high with a single trunk and a palm-like head of foliage. The leaves are up to 24 in (60 cm) across and are carried on 24 in (60 cm) stems. Young plants fruit most heavily and it is wise to keep a succession of plants coming on as replacements. ZONES 10–12.

## CITRUS

The number of original wild species in this genus of evergreen small trees, originally native in the Southeast Asian region, is very uncertain as many of the cultivated forms are probably of ancient hybrid origin following their domestication, which took place mainly in China and India. While largely cultivated for their fruit, citrus plants have the bonus of looking attractive in the garden, with glossy evergreen leaves and fragrant flowers. All citrus can also be grown in pots, as long as the containers are large and the citrus are grown on dwarfing rootstocks.

### Cultivation

Very well-drained, friable, slightly acid, loam soil is best. They need full sun, regular watering and protection from wind. Citrus also need regular feeding, including large amounts of nitrogen and potassium for good fruiting. Prune only to remove dead, diseased and crossing wood. Subject to a range of virus diseases, they can be invaded by many pests including scale, leaf miner, bronze orange bug, spined citrus bug and fruit fly. They are rarely propagated by home gardeners as this is done by grafting, a specialist task.

### Citrus aurantifolia
#### Lime

The flesh and juice of this species have a stronger acidity and flavor than the lemon. It is an erect tree growing up to 15–20 ft (4.5–6 m), more irregular and less ornamental than the lemon and with spiny branches. The Tahitian lime, the variety most commonly grown, bears fruit all year round. The Mexican lime has smaller fruit with high acidity. It has a stronger flavor and is a thornier tree than the Tahitian lime. ZONES 10–12.

## LITCHI
### Lychee

This genus consists of just one evergreen tree from southern China and Southeast Asia, which is grown throughout the subtropics for its foliage and delicious fruit. The lychee is grown commercially by air layering or grafting of superior named varieties.

### Cultivation

It requires full sun and shelter from wind, and it prefers deep, moist soil and regular water. Propagate from seed or by budding. Trees raised from seed start to bear fruit after about 5 years.

### Litchi chinensis

A graceful, slim-trunked tree, the lychee reaches a height of 30 ft (9 m) and a spread of 10–15 ft (3–4.5 m). Bright green compound leaves, gold or pink when young, form a low-spreading crown. Clusters of small, petal-less,

*Litchi chinensis*

greenish yellow flowers are borne in abundance, followed by the bright red, edible fruit which enclose a brown seed. The fruit contain a sweet whitish pulp reminiscent in texture and flavor to that of grapes. ZONES 10–11.

## MACADAMIA

Consisting of 11 species, this relatively small genus from Australia, Sulawesi in Indonesia and New Caledonia is made up of small to medium evergreen rainforest trees. Their leathery, narrow leaves, usually in whorls of 3 or 4 on the twigs, have smooth or toothed edges. They bear small flowers, crowded on cylindrical spikes, and nuts that take up to 9 months to mature.

### Cultivation

They require sun, plenty of water and fertile, moist but well-drained soil. They flower and fruit year-round in the tropics, usually 5 years after planting. The best crops come from selected cultivars commonly grafted onto seedlings. Propagate from ripe seed.

### Macadamia tetraphylla
### Rough shell macadamia nut, bopple nut

Growing to about 40 ft (12 m) in height with a bushy habit when given room, this handsome tree has pink or white flowers on long, pendulous spikes. Its toothed, dark green leaves may be prickly. The young branchlets are pinkish red before darkening with age. ZONES 10–11.

## MANGIFERA

This is a genus of evergreen trees from India and Southeast Asia. Their dense, glossy leaves are drooping and tinged strongly with red when young; this feature of tropical trees is thought to protect them from sun and heavy rain. The fruits, which are drupes, consist of a big central stone usually containing 3 embryos: the first 2 result from pollination, the third arises entirely from the mother tree. If the first 2 are removed as the seed germinates, the third grows and replicates the parent. Nonetheless, it is customary to graft selected varieties.

### Cultivation

These trees tolerate subtropical conditions, but prefer tropical, monsoonal climates. Rain at flowering time can rot the blossoms and ruin the crop. Plant in full sun in deep, rich soil; they need protection from strong winds. Prune when young to encourage a single trunk. In addition to grafting, they can be propagated from ripe seed. Check for fruit fly and fungal diseases.

### *Mangifera indica*
### Mango

The mango can grow 80 ft (24 m) tall and wide, though grafted trees are normally smaller. The tiny, greenish flowers are borne in large sprays. The

*Mangifera indica*

fruit resemble enormous peaches, though the skin is smooth, ripening to orange or red. Seedling trees tend to have furry seeds, making juice extraction awkward, and their flavor is often marred by a bitter aftertaste. Selected cultivars have superior fruit, sweet to the last, with smooth pits; 'Alphonso' is universally regarded as the finest. ZONES 11–12.

## *MUSA*
### Banana, plantain

Bananas, originally native to Southeast Asia are now cultivated throughout the tropics. Nearly all the edible varieties, including red and green fruit, entirely lack seeds. The genus includes several other important species: *Musa textilis*

*Macadamia tetraphylla*

Musa × paradisiaca

## Musa acuminata
### Banana

One of the most widespread wild species in tropical Asia, *Musa acuminata* is believed to be the main parent of most edible bananas (some classified under *M.* × *paradisiaca*). It normally forms a clump of several false stems up to about 20 ft (6 m) tall, with long arching leaves and a pendulous flower spike with dull reddish bracts. The fruit are long and curved, seedless in cultivated forms. The cultivar 'Dwarf Cavendish' grows only 6–10 ft (1.8–3 m) high with short, broad leaves. ZONES 10–12.

## Musa × paradisiaca

This hybrid name covers the banana cultivars containing genes of *Musa acuminata* and *M. balbisiana*. Plants are up to 25 ft (8 m) tall, often flowering and bearing fruit 18 months or less after the shoot appears from the rootstock. 'Lady Finger', 15 ft (4.5 m) tall, is better suited to domestic gardens, being less vulnerable to bunchy top virus. ZONES 10–12.

## PASSIFLORA

Many of the species belonging to this genus are climbers, and detailed information on the genus is given in the Climbers & Creepers chapter. However, *Passiflora edulis*, the common passionfruit, is listed here.

## Passiflora edulis
### Passsionfruit

This species is valued for its glossy, bright green leaves, purple-white flowers and flavorsome fruit. It grows to 15 ft (4.5 m) and has white flowers that are green beneath. Train on a pergola or trellis and prune to prevent tangling as this encourages insect infestation. Pick fruit when the skin has turned purple

yields strong fiber known as Manila hemp; others are grown for their enormous leaves or colored flowers. The flowers are borne in large terminal spikes, erect or pendulous depending on species, the buds enclosed in large purplish bracts. Female flowers are borne at the base of the spikes, male ones further up. Though they often grow to tree size, they are really giant herbaceous perennials; each 'trunk' is composed of leaf bases and, when the flowering shoot has risen and borne fruit, it dies.

### Cultivation

Some of the smaller species can be cultivated as house plants or in greenhouses in temperate climates. Banana crops require fertile, moist soil and full sun. Protect from winds, which will cause new growth to shred. Propagate from ripe seed or by division of clumps.

*Passiflora edulis*

and is still smooth, but do not eat until the skin is wrinkled. This species is self-fertile. ZONES 10–12.

## TERMINALIA
Most of the species belonging to this genus are trees, and detailed information on the genus is given in the Trees chapter. However, *Terminalia catappa* is treated here as a nut tree.

### Terminalia catappa
#### Indian almond, sea almond, tropical almond
This attractive tree has horizontal, tiered branches and a broad, flattened canopy which is often twice as wide as its height of 60 ft (18 m). The leaves are glossy green and broadly oval with prominent veins; as they age they turn bright orange, then red, and fall at any time of year, though the tree is never completely bare. The inconspicuous but lightly fragrant white flowers are held on spikes near the ends of branches. They are followed by yellow fruit, which are tinged with red when ripe; they consist of fibrous flesh surrounding an almond-like seed of which the kernel is edible, either raw or roasted. ZONES 11–12.

*Terminalia catappa*

CHAPTER 5

*Cacti &*
*Succulents*

## AEONIUM

Native to the Canary Islands, the Mediterranean and northern Africa, this genus contains 40 species of short-lived, perennial or shrubby evergreen succulents. The plants develop either as one large (or several smaller), compact, stemless rosette, or branch into several long, thick stems terminating in leaves; some are more closely branched, with many smaller rosettes. Attractive, star-shaped, pink, red, white or yellow flowers appear in dense pyramidal sprays, from small to very large, from the center of the leaf rosettes.

### Cultivation

They prefer full sun or partial shade, light, well-drained soil. Prune off dead flower panicles after the blooms wither, although the flowering rosette will usually die and single-rosette species will die out completely. Propagate from seed or stem or leaf cuttings.

### Aeonium tabuliforme

Endemic to Tenerife in the Canary Islands, this is one of the more striking species with a single leaf rosette up to 18 in (45 cm) in diameter, and as flat as a dinner plate. Sitting on a stalk no more than 8 in (20 cm) high, it consists of

*Aeonium tabuliforme*

numerous, closely overlapping leaves. Growth is terminated by the inflorescence, about 18 in (45 cm) high, branching into sprays of yellow flowers, after which the plant dies. This is a remarkable species which needs a semi-shaded position and perfect drainage to do its best. ZONES 10–11.

## AGAVE

Occurring naturally in the Caribbean region including southern USA, Mexico and the West Indies, these perennial succulents are grown for their dramatic, sword-shaped, often sharply toothed leaves and tall flowering stems. The small species flower only after 5 to 10 years and the taller species may take up to 40 years to flower. All agaves flower only once and then the flowering shoot dies, leaving offsets (in most species) which continue the plant's growth. These plants are popular for use in Mediterranean styles of landscape design and for large rockeries and dry embankments.

### Cultivation

Plant in a well-drained, gritty soil in full sun. All are adapted to surviving very dry periods. Most species make excellent container plants. Propagate from offsets or from seed.

*Agave bracteosa*

Agave picta

Agave stricta

### Agave bracteosa

From northeastern Mexico, this species has stemless rosettes with narrow, recurving yellow-green leaves, up to 30 in (75 cm) long, that taper into a fine, soft point. It normally suckers from the base before producing a narrow, unbranched spike of pale yellow flowers that open progressively from the base over a long period. ZONES 10–12.

### Agave picta

This large agave from Mexico is similar to, and often confused with *Agave americana*. *Agave picta* is known mostly as a variegated form with cream marginal bands on the leaves. The thick, dark green, sword-shaped leaves are about 6 ft (1.8 m) long, their edges closely armed with strong, mostly hooked spines. The flowering stem is very similar to that of *A. americana* but even taller, up to 35 ft (10.5 m). ZONES 10–12.

### Agave stricta
### Hedgehog agave

This is another Mexican species with very narrow, rigid leaves, the rosettes often grow into a clump when mature. The unbranched flowering spike reaches a height of 6–10 ft (1.8–3 m). It has reddish, once-only flowers. The tapering leaves have finely toothed margins and are tipped with sharp, black spines, which may cause injury if the plant is badly positioned. One of the smaller species, it may flower when only 6–8 years old. ZONES 10–12.

### ALOE

Occurring wild in Africa, Madagascar and the Arabian Peninsula, this genus of succulent-leafed plants consists of over 300 species, including trees, shrubs and perennials. All are evergreen, mostly with distinct rosettes of sword-shaped leaves terminating the stem or branches. Leaves vary greatly between species in size, color, degree of succulence, and presence and distribution of prickles on the margins or faces. The flowers are tubular to narrowly bell-shaped, borne in long-stemmed spikes on which they open progressively from the base. These are followed by oval fruits which are ¼–2 in (0.6–5 cm) long, usually ripening from green to brown. Aloes hybridize quite freely; some attractive examples include *Aloe speciosa* × *A. ferox* and *A. splendens* × *A. speciosa*.

Aloe alooides

Aloe buhrii

## Cultivation

Nearly all aloes prefer a warm dry climate and well-drained soil. The larger species of aloes can be grown in full sun, the smaller ones in part-shade. Propagation is from offsets or stem cuttings. Infestation by mealybug can be a problem.

### Aloe alooides

From eastern Transvaal, this aloe has a short, unbranched trunk up to 6 ft (1.8 m) high, usually half-hidden by dead leaves and topped by a dense rosette of narrow, deeply channeled leaves with small teeth on their red-tinged margins. It bears yellow-green tubular flowers on 3–4 ft (1–1.2 m) tall spikes. ZONES 10–11.

### Aloe buhrii

This African evergreen has sword- or triangular-shaped leaves that grow to 16 in (40 cm). Foliage is tinged a bluish red color. It bears clusters of green-tipped, orange or red bell-shaped flowers, as well as brown seed capsules. ZONES 10–11.

### Aloe rupestris

syn. *Aloe pycnantha*
This tree-like succulent from Mozambique and Natal, South Africa, reaches a height of up to 25 ft (8 m). It bears small orange and yellow flowers. Leaves are deep green, narrow, up to 30 in (75 cm) long, with small, red-brown teeth along the pink margins. ZONES 10–11.

### Aloe sessiliflora

This species is native to Transvaal and Natal, South Africa. It has a large rosette with a central flower spike growing to 30 in (75 cm) tall. The leaves are green with red margins, the color spreading with age; it produces red flowers. ZONES 10–11.

### Aloe speciosa

This is a large aloe, reaching as high as 20 ft (6 m) with age in its native Cape Province, South Africa. Usually the trunk is unbranched and almost hidden by old dead leaves; it terminates in a dense rosette of fleshy dull green leaves 30 in (75 cm) long, with pale red margins and teeth. The short spikes of densely packed flowers are red in bud opening to greenish white. ZONES 10–11.

Aloe rupestris

Aloe sessiliflora

Aloe speciosa

Aloe spectabilis

### Aloe spectabilis
syn. *Aloe ferox var. xanthostachys*
A tree-like succulent from Natal in
South Africa, this species varies in
height from 6–12 ft (1.8–3.5 m), its blue-
green leaves have a reddish sheen and
spiny surfaces. It bears red flowers.
ZONES 10–11.

## ARIOCARPUS
### Living rock
This genus consists of about 6 species of
bizarre, slow-growing cacti from arid
hills of southern Texas and Mexico.
They have no spines and their gray or
green, overlapping tubercles are so well
developed that they almost look like little

agave leaves in some species, or like roughened pebbles in others. Some have tufts of downy hairs on the top of the plant or at the ends of the tubercles. The flowers, often quite showy, can be cream through yellow to pink or purplish.

### Cultivation

Unless your garden is in a desert, they will need to be grown under glass, in strong light and in a very open cactus mixture kept virtually dry except in the growing season. Propagate from seed.

### Ariocarpus retusus

Native to northern Mexico, this slow-growing species develops into a broad, brownish plant up to 10 in (25 cm) wide with triangular, grayish tubercles that terminate in strong, bony points. In nature the plant is usually half-buried in the soil. The smallish flowers, emerging at the plant's apex and opening only during the day, are white with pink midlines on the petals. ZONES 10–11.

### Ariocarpus trigonus

From northern Mexico this compact cactus, up to 4 in (10 cm) high and 6 in (15 cm) across, has large, pointed, 3-angled, grayish green tubercles and bears showy, apricot-tinted cream flowers 2 in (5 cm) across in a ring around the top of the plant, which is virtually bare of wood. ZONES 10–11.

*Ariocarpus retusus*

*Ariocarpus trigonus*

## ASTROPHYTUM

This popular genus contains 6 species of slow-growing cacti, all native to Mexico. They differ in size and their form varies from star-shaped—hence the Greek genus name (star-plant)—to elongated or globular. The mostly unbranched plants are divided into 5 to 10 prominent, smooth ribs, some covered in thick hair, others patterned with minute white scales. The large flowers with shiny, lemon-yellow to golden yellow petals, sometimes red at the base, appear from the top of the plant.

### Cultivation

The plants prefer porous, alkaline soil and full sun. They should be kept fairly dry except during the growing season. Propagate from seed. The tops of older plants can be grafted onto a hardier cactus, and the truncated base will then sprout new growths which can be rooted as cuttings.

### Astrophytum asterias
#### Sea urchin cactus, sand dollar cactus

Resembling a sea urchin, this grayish green, globular, spineless cactus grows to no more than 3 in (8 cm) high and 4 in (10 cm) wide. It has smooth, vertical ribs with little white areoles and is covered with fine white scales. It bears yellow flowers with orange-red centers. ZONES 10 11.

### Astrophytum myriostigma
#### Bishop's cap, bishop's miter

Also quite spineless, this odd-looking species grows up to 12 in (30 cm) high and 4 in (10 cm) wide. It has a grayish green body divided into 4 to 8 prominent ribs and typically is densely covered with tiny, white scales. It bears glossy yellow blooms. It is quite variable and a number of varieties have been named.
*Astrophytum myriostigma* var. *quadricostata*

*Astrophytum asterias*

*Astrophytum myriostigma*

*Astrophytum myriostigma* var. *quadricostata*

*Astrophytum ornatum*

*Chamaecereus silvestrii*

is distinctive for the fatness of each of its 4 ribs, separated only by shallow grooves. ZONES 10–11.

### Astrophytum ornatum
One of the most commonly grown cacti in cultivation, this cylindrically shaped species has 5 to 8 rather sharp ribs lined with yellow spines. Small white scales on the ribs are arranged in interesting patterns, varying in density. It grows to 15 in (38 cm) high and 6 in (15 cm) wide. It bears yellow flowers. ZONES 10–11.

## CHAMAECEREUS
### Peanut cactus
If recognized as distinct, this genus consists of only one species, native to northern Argentina. However, many botanists now prefer to treat the peanut cactus as just another species of the large genus *Echinopsis*. It is a clustering cactus with slender, weak stems that flop over as they elongate and become prostrate or pendulous. The small, weak spine clusters are closely spaced and give the stems a whitish appearance. It has

showy orange or red flowers that open wide in the sun.

### Cultivation
This is an easily grown cactus, popular as an indoor and balcony plant and well suited to hanging baskets as well as pots. Grow in well-drained soil in a sunny spot and watch for infestations of mealy-bug, scale insects and spider mite. Propagate from offsets or seed.

### Chamaecereus silvestrii
syns *Echinopsis chamaecereus*, *Lobivia silvestrii*
This well-known cactus is composed of clusters of initially erect, finger-sized stems that are pale green with numerous soft, white bristles. Established plants can reach a height of 6 in (15 cm) and width of 12 in (30 cm), with many crowded stems. From an early age it flowers freely indoors if conditions suit it, producing vivid orange-red blooms about 2 in (5 cm) in diameter. ZONES 10–12.

## CRASSULA
This diverse genus comprises about 300 species of annuals, perennials and ever-green shrubs, nearly all with succulent

leaves. The great majority of species, including many of extreme succulent form, are confined to southern Africa. They range in habit from tiny prostrate or clump-forming plants to erect shrubs as much as 12 ft (3.5 m) high. A fairly constant feature is the arrangement of the leaves in opposite pairs, sometimes joining at the base around the stem. Flowers are grouped in terminal clusters or panicles and are only showy in a minority of species. The genus lends its name to the large family Crassulaceae.

## Cultivation

Some of the more vigorous growers are tough, adaptable plants which will survive with almost no attention in pots, tubs or window boxes as long as soil is not waterlogged. At the other end of the scale are some of the more dwarf succulent South African species, which are grown mainly by succulent collectors willing to meet their specialized requirements. Propagate from stem or leaf cuttings, or from seed.

## *Crassula perfoliata*
### Propeller plant

Native to southeastern South Africa, this interesting species is rather variable, some of its varieties having formerly been treated as distinct species. Stems are erect, branching from the base and up to about 3 ft (1 m) high. The long, fleshy leaves are in opposite pairs. In *Crassula perfoliata* var. *perfoliata* they are green and channelled, and are 4–6 in (10–15 cm) long, arranged in alternating planes and rather drooping. In *C. p.* var. *minor* (syn. *Crassula falcata*) they are pale gray-green and shaped like curved knife blades standing on edge; their bases overlap and all the leaves are squashed into one plane. It has dense terminal panicles of quite showy deep red flowers. ZONES 10–11.

*Crassula perfoliata*

*Crassula perfoliata var. minor*

## *Crassula plegmatoides*

This species comes from Namaqualand in South Africa and extending into adjacent Namibia. It is only about 6 in (15 cm) high and has tiny blue-green, triangular leaves that are so tightly crowded they form a 4-angled column. It bears sprays of very small white flowers. ZONES 10–11.

### Crassula pruinosa

syn. *Crassula scabrella*

Native to southwestern Cape Province and reaching a height of 4 in (10 cm), this small species has green ½–1 in (12–25 mm) long leaves with a waxy whitish bloom. It has white bell-shaped flowers. ZONES 10–11.

## ECHINOPSIS
### Sea urchin cactus

syn. *Trichocereus, Lobivia*

This popular genus contains up to 120 species of cacti native to South America. Ranging from single, globe-shaped stems to readily colonizing, columnar and even tree-like plants, these cacti are mostly densely covered with spines and have pronounced ribs. Many species are valued for their funnel-shaped, brilliantly colored flowers, up to 8 in (20 cm) long. Some bloom at night and are very short lived. There are numerous hybrids.

*Echinopsis oxygona*

### Cultivation

In the garden they require full sun, a rich, well-drained soil and should be watered sparingly. In pots, use a free-draining cactus potting mix. Propagate from seed and offsets.

### Echinopsis oxygona
### Easter lily cactus, barrel cactus

syn. *Echinopsis multiplex*

Originating in Brazil, this spherical, multi-branched cactus grows to about 6 in (15 cm) in maturity and with age forms dense clumps up to 3 ft (1 m) in diameter. The stems are covered with brown, black-tipped spines; these sprout fragrant, pinkish white flowers from the tips. ZONES 10–12.

## EUPHORBIA
### Milkweed, spurge

The genus is a very large one with close to 2,000 species, among them annuals, herbaceous perennials, shrubs and numerous succulent species that at first sight look remarkably like cacti. This

*Crassula pruinosa*

variety of forms has suggested to many botanists that the genus should be divided; but the flowers of all species are almost identical in structure. They are very much reduced, consisting of only a stigma and a stamen, always green, and usually carried in small clusters. Many species have showy bracts, these are the most widely cultivated; examples include *Euphorbia cognata* and *E.* 'Excalibur'. All euphorbias have milky sap which is corrosive to sensitive areas of the skin; some can cause temporary blindness if sap contacts the eyes.

## Cultivation

Plant species of *Euphorbia* in sun or part-shade in moist, well-drained soil. Propagate from cuttings, allowing succulent species to dry and callus before placing in barely damp sand, or by division or from seed.

### Euphorbia canariensis

This erect, tree-like succulent from the Canary Islands normally grows to about 8 ft (2.4 m) tall and forms large clumps or colonies of sharply angled and spiny, bright green stems. Cup-shaped, reddish green floral bracts are produced. This makes a fascinating specimen plant for the desert garden. ZONES 10–11.

### Euphorbia cooperi

This tree-like succulent has branches that grow at right angles to the stem, then curve upwards like a candelabrum. The branches are usually 4- or 5-angled and have paired spines along the ridges. Yellowish flowers are clustered along the ridges between the spines. ZONES 9–11.

*Euphorbia canariensis*

*Euphorbia cooperi*

*Euphorbia punicea*

*Euphorbia obesa*

### Euphorbia knuthii

This species, a dwarf succulent native to Mozambique and South Africa, features gray-green stripes on its light-green, 3-angled, sinuate stems. It is thickened at its base and bears short brown thorns. ZONES 10–11.

### Euphorbia obesa
#### Gingham golf ball, baseball plant

Almost perfectly spherical at first, becoming slightly elongated with age, this unusual succulent is native to South Africa. It grows up to 8 in (20 cm) tall and 6 in (15 cm) in diameter, and is quite spineless. The pale green stem has 8 almost flat ribs and red-brown horizontal and vertical lines making a checkered pattern similar to gingham. Small, yellow-green, cup-shaped flowers appear at the apex. ZONES 10–11.

### Euphorbia punicea

This evergreen species is native to Jamaica, Cuba and the Bahamas. It has gray-green branches ascending from the stem and growing up to 18 in (45 cm). The plant's total height at maturity is 3 ft (1 m). It has red flowerheads. The foliage is green and lance-shaped, with the broadest part of the leaf above the middle. ZONES 10–12.

### Euphorbia schimperi

From southern Arabia, this shrubby succulent grows to 6 ft (1.8 m) high. Its tiny leaves are oblong. Not often found in cultivation, material sold with this name is more likely to be *Euphorbia nubica*. ZONES 10–12.

### Euphorbia tirucalli
#### Caustic bush, pencil euphorbia

This generally shrubby succulent is from eastern and southern Africa as well as the Arabian peninsula. Once used as a source of latex, it grows to a height and spread of about 15 ft (4.5 m), its twiggy stems bearing tiny, deciduous leaves. The flowers are minute and insignificant. ZONES 10–12.

*Euphorbia tirucalli*

## FURCRAEA

This genus closely allied to *Agave* consists of about 12 species of perennial succulents with terminal or basal rosettes of sword-shaped, long fleshy leaves. It bears large panicles of broad, short-tubed flowers. Bulbils are often borne between the flowers. These plants occur naturally in semi-arid regions of the West Indies and Central and South America. They are suitable for large rock gardens or desert gardens.

### Cultivation

Grow in a very well-drained soil in full sun. Propagate from seed or by division.

*Euphorbia schimperi*

*Furcraea selloa var. marginata*

### Furcraea selloa var. marginata
The leaves of this species grow to 3 ft (1 m) or more in length. They have a sharp tip and pale yellow margins with widely spaced, hooked spines. The panicles, to 20 ft (6 m) high, bear faintly scented, greenish white, bell-shaped flowers. ZONES 10–12.

## HYLOCEREUS
### Queen of the night
This genus comprises 20 species of climbing epiphytic cacti, indigenous to Mexico and parts of Central America. Some of these are commonly used as grafting stock. The broadly winged or flattened stems grow to 4 in (10 cm) across. The large flowers, which open at night, are white and funnel-shaped.

### Cultivation
Grow these cacti in sun in very well-drained, acid soil. They are most vulnerable to caterpillars, mealybug and scale insects. Propagate from seed or cuttings.

### Hylocereus polyrhizus
This species is native to Colombia and Panama in South America. Its 1½ in (35 mm) thick, reddish green stems bear long, light brown spines. This cactus

*Hylocereus polyrhizus*

produces large cream flowers opening from red buds. ZONES 11–12.

## KALANCHOE
This genus, native to subtropical and tropical Africa and Madagascar, with a scattering of species in Asia, consists of 150 species of perennial succulents, climbers or shrubs. These vary from small, leafy succulents to tree-like shrubs. They are mainly valued for their decorative foliage. Plants grow from 6 in (15 cm) to 12 ft (3.5 m) high and bear white, yellow or orange to brown, red or purple, tubular or bell-shaped flowers, followed by small seed-bearing capsules.

### Cultivation
These succulents need full sun or part-shade and well-drained soil. Propagate from stem or leaf cuttings, seed or pot up plantlets that may form along leaf margins.

### Kalanchoe blossfeldiana
### Flaming Katy
This small, shrubby African species reaches 12 in (30 cm) high and wide. Its

*Kalanchoe blossfeldiana*

multiple, upstretched branches are covered with round to rectangular, deep green leaves with red margins and notched tips. It bears thick racemes of small, deep red, cylindrical flowers; cultivated strains may be pink, yellow and also orange. It requires part-shade, and is a popular pot plant. ZONES 10–12.

### Kalanchoe grandiflora
syn. *Kalanchoe nyikae*

Originating in East Africa, this succulent grows to 3 ft (1 m) tall on an erect stem in its native habitat. The foliage is blue-green with oval-shaped leaves. It bears attractive, small, yellow, tubular flowers. ZONES 11–12.

*Kalanchoe grandiflora*

### Kalanchoe pumila

This small succulent shrub is native to central Madagascar and grows to a height of 4–8 in (10–20 cm). It has a creeping habit and its green, ovate leaves are offset by small, urn-shaped flowers

Kalanchoe pumila

Kalanchoe thyrsiflora

that are reddish violet in color. The plant prefers part-shade. ZONES 11–12.

### Kalanchoe thyrsiflora

This species is native to South Africa and grows to 24 in (60 cm) tall. Rounded whitish leaves, often with faintly red margins, are up to 6 in (15 cm) long; the young growth is bright red. *Kalanchoe thyrsiflora* dies after producing clusters of yellow, tubular flowers. ZONES 11–12.

### Kalanchoe tomentosa
#### Panda plant, pussy ears

This erect, succulent, shrubby Madagascan species grows gradually to 3 ft (1 m) tall with a spread of 8 in (20 cm). Its spoon-shaped, light gray-green leaves, covered with white felt, often have rusty brown spots along the margins. It bears yellowish green flowers tinged with

Kalanchoe tomentosa

purple on the lobes, although flowering
is rare in cultivation. ZONES 11–12.

## SANSEVIERIA
### Bowstring hemp, snake plant

Native to India, Indonesia and Africa,
these 60 species of popular and resilient
evergreen perennials are grown for
their stiff, fleshy, patterned leaves which
are 12–24 in (30–60 cm) tall. They bear
stems of greenish white, slightly fragrant
flowers. In Africa the fibers are used to
make hemp.

### Cultivation

Species of *Sansevieria* will tolerate sun or
shade and most soil types; over-watering
may cause rotting at the leaf bases and at
the roots. Propagate from leaf cuttings
or by division.

Sansevieria pearsonii

### Sansevieria pearsonii

The central fan of this species from
tropical Africa produces 3 to 5 leaves up
to 3 ft (1 m) tall. They are dark mottled
green, thinly cylindrical, and taper to a
white tip. The flowers have a wattle-like
scent. ZONES 10–12.

CHAPTER 6

*Orchids*

## ASCOCENTRUM

This genus consists of 5 species of epiphytic orchids closely allied to *Vanda*, ranging in the wild from the Himalayan foothills to the Philippines. They have short, erect stems bearing 2 rows of closely overlapping short, strap-like leaves. The flowers are rather small, clustered on short stalks but in brilliant hues ranging from yellow to red, orange and purple. More widely grown are bigeneric hybrids with vandas (× *Ascocenda*), the ascocentrums contributing red and orange coloring.

*Ascocentrum Hybrid, Kwa Geok Choo*

*Ascocentrum Hybrid, Thai Gold*

### Cultivation

These orchids require bright, indirect light. Plant them in very coarse, open, free-draining potting mix. Water and feed well during the growing and flowering season. Propagate from basal offsets.

### Ascocentrum Hybrids

This is a range of hybrids raised from some of the species of *Ascocentrum*, commonly grown in places such as Singapore for the cut flower trade. Typical examples of these hybrids are the ones pictured here, Kwa Geok Choo and Thai Gold. ZONES 11–12.

## BRASSAVOLA

This genus contains up to 20 species of epiphytic or rock-dwelling orchids. They are found in Central and South America from sea level to as high as 6,000 ft (1,800 m). Flowering stems, carrying only one or up to 7 blooms, are produced from the top of a slender pseudobulb, from which also arises the single, fleshy leaf which can be almost circular in cross-section. White, ivory or green in color, the flowers may be as wide as 6 in (15 cm). The species formerly known as *Brassavola digbyana*, which has been crossed with cattleyas to produce the many beautiful × *Brassocattleya* hybrids, is now placed in the genus *Rhyncholaelia*.

### Cultivation

Best grown in an orchid house, they need moist, humid conditions and strong light all year. Grow in baskets with a very coarse orchid mix or on a bark slab. Water when growing, applying very dilute fertilizer with every third watering. As soon as new pseudobulbs are fully expanded, withhold water for up to a month. Propagate by division when plants fill their pots.

## Brassavola nodosa
### Lady of the night

The best known member of the genus, this orchid earns its common name from its sweet fragrance, which wafts about mostly at night. *Brassavola nodosa* makes a dense clump, with cylindrical leaves that look like green extensions of the pseudobulbs. The pendent sprays of white or white and pale green flowers with large white labellum can appear at any time. ZONES 10–12.

## BRASSIA
### Spider orchid

Around 25 species belong to this genus of easily grown epiphytic orchids from Central and South America and the West Indies. The plants form large clumps of cylindrical to conical pseudo-bulbs which arise at intervals from creeping rhizomes, each pseudobulb bearing 1 to 3 large, leathery leaves. They produce long, gracefully arching sprays of spidery flowers with long narrow petals and sepals.

### Cultivation

Brassias are happy growing outdoors. They are among the easiest of orchids to grow as house plants. Brassias can be allowed to dry out a little after flowering. Propagate by division, but leave the plants undivided for years as they flower most freely when allowed to build up into sizeable clumps.

### Brassia verrucosa

The most popular member of the genus in cultivation, this species makes a clump of elongated pseudobulbs with leaves up to 18 in (45 cm) long and 2 in (5 cm) wide, above which horizontally arching flower spikes about 24 in (60 cm) long arise. The flowers are greenish white or cream with petals and sepals up to 6 in (15 cm) long, darker spotted at their

Brassia verrucosa

Brassavola nodosa

base and on the short triangular labellum. They are very fragrant, though the heavy, spicy perfume that develops as they age is not to everyone's liking. ZONES 10–12.

## CATTLEYA

The archetypal glamorous orchid flower is a cattleya, or one of its many hybrids with other orchid genera; *Cattleya* Angel Heart 'Pink Cloud' and *C.* Little Susie 'Orchid Glen' exemplify the beauty of these plants. The genus has between 40 and 60 species (depending on which botanical classification you follow) of

*Cattleya*, Bifoliate Hybrid, Chocolate Drop

*Cattleya bowringiana*

epiphytes from Central and South America, and from these countless hybrids have been bred. Just about every color but blue is available. The flower characteristically has 3 fairly narrow sepals, in front of which are 2 broader upper petals often with frilled edges, and a showy central lip or labellum with frilled margin and variously marked and spotted, its edges folded over behind to form a tube. The plants have creeping rhizomes and narrow, erect pseudobulbs: in one group of species (the bifoliate cattleyas) there are 2 broad leaves arising from the top of each pseudobulb; in the other group (the unifoliates) there is only one leaf, usually narrower and more erect. The flower sprays, 1 or 2 to as many as 10 flowers, arise from the tops of the pseudobulbs. Many cattleya hybrids in the broad sense have other related genera in their parentage—for example, × *Brassocattleya*, × *Brassolaeliocattleya*, × *Laeliocattleya*, × *Sophrolaeliocattleya*.

## Cultivation
All prefer good light but not strong sunshine and a coarse potting mix. They are propagated by division.

### *Cattleya*, Bifoliate Hybrids
### Cluster cattleya

Most of these cultivars have rather small flowers in clusters. They can be grown out of doors and can be planted to good effect on low branches of trees, if the canopy is light and open. Colors range from white through pink to magenta with some in the yellow to coral range, showing a genetic inheritance from the dainty orange-colored *Cattleya aurantiaca*. Chocolate Drop, which is an eye-catching hybrid grex between *C. aurantiaca* and *C. guttata*, is of such a deep, glossy maroon color it almost looks like chocolate. It has a small flower and grows to 18 in (45 cm) in height. It was raised in the 1960s. Fascination, which is a hybrid grex between *Cattleya intermedia* and *C. Irma*, was also raised in the 1960s. The plant is about 24 in (60 cm) high and the 2½ in (6 cm) wide flowers are pale mauve in color. ZONES 10–12.

### *Cattleya bowringiana*

This delightful bifoliate cattleya from Central America is easy to grow. The pseudobulbs are up to 24 in (60 cm) long and bear sprays of up to 15 flowers that are 3 in (8 cm) wide and deep pink in color. It looks best when allowed to make a large clump, when it will bloom profusely. It is the parent of several hybrids, some of which are optimistically described as 'blue'. ZONES 10–12.

### *Cattleya deckeri*
syn. *Cattleya guatemalensis*

A bifoliate cattleya of fairly compact growth and with small flowers, *Cattleya deckeri* is widely distributed around the Caribbean from Mexico to the Guianas and on West Indian islands. Each pseudobulb bears a small number of 2 in (5 cm) wide flowers with rather narrow reddish purple petals and sepals and a deeper purple labellum. ZONES 10–12.

### *Cattleya* Queen Sirikit 'Summer Stars'

White cattleyas are favorite wedding flowers and this one is as lovely as any bride could desire. It is a purebred cattleya, with no *Laelia* or *Rhyncolaelia* blood, and grows in cooler temperatures than many hybrid cattleyas usually require. ZONES 10–12.

*Cattleya deckeri*

*Cattleya* Queen Sirikit 'Summer Stars'

### Cattleya skinneri
### Flower of San Sebastian

This beautiful cattleya is the national flower of Costa Rica, though its range in the wild is more extensive: from southern Mexico to Venezuela. It is a bifoliate species, with thick pseudobulbs up to 15 in (30 cm) high and a spike of up to 12 flowers to 3 in (8 cm) wide. Color is normally rose-pink to purple, sometimes with a white or cream labellum with orange in the throat; white forms are also grown. It can be grown into a large clump. ZONES 10–12.

*Cattleya skinneri*

*Coelogyne cristata*

# COELOGYNE

This genus of epiphytic orchids, allied to *Cymbidium*, from tropical Asia and the Pacific Islands consists of over 100 species, though relatively few are in general cultivation. They have short, fat pseudobulbs, sometimes very smooth and cylindrical, closely to widely spaced on a creeping rhizome. Each pseudobulb bears one or two leathery leaves. Flowering stems come from bases of pseudobulbs and are usually arching or pendulous, though sometimes with a single flower only. The flowers come in many shapes and sizes, mostly in shades of green, cream, brown and dull purple, sometimes pure white, often with orange markings on the labellum (lip).

### Cultivation

Many of the coelogynes will grow into large, bulky plants, producing numerous sprays of blooms. They like a fairly coarse, soil-free compost and plenty of water while they are in active growth. However, they demand dormant rest if they are to flower freely. Propagation is by division after they have flowered.

### Coelogyne cristata
### Angel orchid

From the Himalayan hills, the angel orchid is the most popular member of the genus, and is one of the loveliest of all orchids. It makes a fine specimen plant with dozens of short sprays of scented white flowers touched with gold on the lip, among glossy deep green leaves. Cool growing, it likes shade and is one of the easiest orchids to grow as a house plant. ZONES 10–11.

### Coelogyne pandurata
### Black orchid

The purple-black is only on the labellum; otherwise the scented, spidery flowers are pale green or yellowish green. They

*Coelogyne pandurata*

*Dendrobium densiflorum*

are borne on short arching sprays of a few blooms, among large leaves which spring from egg-shaped pseudobulbs. From Borneo and the Malay Peninsula, it prefers intermediate conditions. *Coelogyne mayeriana* is the same in most respects to *C. pandurata* except for its slightly broader labellum. ZONES 10–11.

## DENDROBIUM

This is one of the largest genera of orchids with about 1,200 species occurring in Australia, New Zealand, Fiji, Papua New Guinea, India and across China to southern Japan. They grow from hot steamy tropical lowlands to altitudes of 10,000 ft (3,000 m) and in semi-arid conditions. They grow epiphytically, on rocks and even in swampy ground, so it is difficult to generalize about cultivation. Clump formers make fat pseudobulbs; those with long, stem-like pseudobulbs often carry their flowers in sprays in the axils of the fallen leaves. These latter dendro-biums are divided into 'hard' (upright) and 'soft-caned' (floppy) types, but the

distinctions are not very consistent. There are innumerable hybrids, both natural and cultivated. It is likely that the genus will be split up in the near future and many familiar names will be found under other genera.

### Cultivation

For warm-growing species the temperature should not drop below about 60°F (15°C). A very well-drained mixture of bark and charcoal, often with a little added sphagnum moss, is preferred and most species should be given a dry resting period if good flowering is required. Dendrobiums resent disturbance. Most species should be repotted when the new shoots appear. Plants may be divided at this time; cuttings may also be taken. Watch for attack by spider mite, aphid and mealybug.

### Dendrobium densiflorum

This spectacular epiphytic orchid is native to the Himalayas, Burma, Vietnam and Thailand. It forms dense clumps of erect, 4-angled pseudobulbs up to 20 in (50 cm) long with 3 to 5 narrowly elliptic leaves near the top. Pendent racemes to 10 in (25 cm) long bear many yellow flowers with fringed golden orange centers. It prefers partly shaded conditions with plenty of water in the wet season and a dry rest period. ZONES 10–11.

### Dendrobium formosum

From the Himalayas and Burma, this epiphytic orchid has erect cylindrical pseudobulbs up to 18 in (45 cm) long with leathery leaves about 5 in (12 cm) long. The large white flowers with an orange-yellow lip, up to 5 in (12 cm) across, are borne in small racemes. It is one of the parents of many lovely hybrids including 'Fire Coral' which has waxy white petals with a bright orange-red patch on the lower half of the lip. ZONES 10–11.

### Dendrobium lawesii

A native of New Guinea, this orchid has pendent pseudobulbs to 18 in (45 cm) long bearing thin-textured oval leaves to 2½ in (6 cm) long. The white, red, orange, yellow or mauve flowers are produced on short racemes throughout the year. ZONES 11–12.

### Dendrobium lindleyi
syn. Dendrobium aggregatum

This is a small-growing species of wide distribution in mountains of Southeast Asia. The pseudobulbs are tightly crowded, small, spindle-shaped to 3 in (8 cm) long with a single, leathery leaf up to 6 in (15 cm) long. The inflorescences are 4–12 in (10–30 cm) long and pendulous with 5 to 15 flowers, each about 2 in (5 cm) across, fragrant and lasting more than a week. It requires

*Dendrobium formosum 'Fire Coral'*

strong light and is best grown on a slab of wood or cork. ZONES 10–11.

### Dendrobium rhodostictum
This orchid from Papua New Guinea and the Solomon Islands may be terrestrial or epiphytic. It has club-shaped pseudobulbs to 10 in (25 cm) long with 2 or 4 lance-shaped leaves near the top. Racemes, arising near the apex, carry slightly pendent white flowers with purple spots or markings on the edges of the lip. ZONES 11–12.

Dendrobium lawesii

Dendrobium lindleyi

Dendrobium rhodostictum

Dendrobium signatum

Dendrobium taurinum

### Dendrobium signatum
syn. *Dendrobium hildebrandii*
This is a medium-sized orchid from mainland Southeast Asia with long, slender and pendulous pseudobulbs. The inflorescences are borne on the leafless stems with 2 or 3 flowers about 3 in (8 cm) across on each short stalk. The plants require intermediate to warm conditions with heavy watering during the growing season, but this should be greatly reduced in the dry season. ZONES 10–11.

### Dendrobium taurinum
This large epiphyte occurs in the Philippines where it grows on low trees in mangrove forests. The pseudobulbs are crowded, cane-like and up to 3 ft (1 m) or more long and 1 in (25 mm) in diameter. The leaves are about 3 in (8 cm) long by 2 in (5 cm) wide. The inflorescences are up to 24 in (60 cm) long with numerous purple-pink, white and greenish colored flowers, each about 2½ in (6 cm) long. *Dendrobium taurinum*

should be kept warm and moist through-out the year. ZONES 11–12.

### Dendrobium, Yamamoto Hybrids
These soft-caned dendrobiums have undergone a great deal of development in recent years by Japanese gardeners. The general name, Yamamoto hybrids, has been given to their creations, which are distinctive for their elegant shape and clear, brilliant colors. ZONES 10–11.

## DENDROCHILUM
### Rice orchid, golden chain orchid
There are around 150 species in this genus, which occurs from Thailand to Papua New Guinea with the Philippines and Borneo being particularly rich. Most are epiphytes and most grow in the cloud forests of mountains. Dendrochilums generally have long pendulous inflorescences with many small fragrant star-shaped, usually yellow flowers. The inflorescences arise from the apex of the pseudobulbs, which are crowded and squat with 1 or 2 long and broad leaves.

## Cultivation

These orchids will grow outdoors. They grow best in a small pot or basket. Use a free-draining epiphytic orchid compost mix. Care should be taken not to disturb the roots during repotting. Keep the plants moist throughout the year. Liquid fertilize once every 2 to 3 weeks in the growing season and not at all in the rest period. During this time ensure the plants get good light and water sparingly. Propagate by division.

### Dendrochilum longifolium

Occurring naturally from Malaysia to Papua New Guinea, this epiphytic orchid has a short narrow pseudobulb to 3 in (8 cm) long, topped with a large, usually solitary elliptical leaf up to 15 in (40 cm) in length. The pendent raceme of flowers, up to 15 in (38 cm) long, is densely clustered with greenish yellow, chocolate-tipped flowers. ZONES 11–12.

## DISA

This is a terrestrial genus of about 125 species of orchids from southern and eastern Africa and Madagascar. The plants arise from tuberous roots and consist of a leafy stem and a single terminal inflorescence. The 6 species from western and southwestern Cape Province in South Africa have been successfully cultivated. The species from other habitats have proved extremely difficult to grow. These plants are noted for their often large, colorful flowers in shades of red, pink, yellow and white.

## Cultivation

*Disa* once had a reputation for being difficult to grow, but the 6 commonly grown species and their hybrids are readily cultivated if care is taken. The growing mixture, coarse sand or a mixture of peat and perlite, should be well drained, but it should not be

Dendrobium, Yamamoto Hybrid

Dendrochilum longifolium

allowed to dry out. High humidity levels, along with good air circulation, are required. Regular watering with water with a pH of 4.5 to 6 is best and salts must not be allowed to build up. Broken shade is best and cool to warm conditions are required, with as little fluctuation in temperature as possible. Watch for thrips. Propagate by division.

### Disa Diores

This grex name is used for hybrids between *Disa* Veitchii and *D. uniflora*. *D.* Veitchii is itself the cross between *D. racemosa* and *D. uniflora*. *D.* Diores dates to 1898. There are up to 10 long-lasting flowers about 4 in (10 cm) across, in shades of pink to red, occasionally with some yellow. It is popular for cut flowers and has been used in making more complex hybrids. ZONES 10–11.

### Disa Hybrids

The 6 cultivated species have been used to create over 80 hybrids which are now well established in many collections. The species used are *Disa cardinalis*, *D. caulescens*, *D. racemosa*, *D. tripetaloides*, *D. uniflora* and *D. venosa*. The colorful and long-lasting flowers are suitable for the cut-flower industry. 'Inca Princess' bears racemes of pink and cream flowers with faint purple veining. ZONES 10–11.

### LAELIA

These orchids are closely allied to the cattleyas and rather resemble them, both in growth and in the shape and colors of their flowers. They are an attractive group of epiphytes in their own right and many of the 50 species and their hybrids are well worth growing. They interbreed easily with the cattleyas, bringing to the hybrids their richly colored labellum and also a neater flower shape—some of the larger cattleya species have distinctly floppy petals. Most bear their flowers in short sprays, although one group (formerly treated as *Schomburgkia*) has sprays of blooms up to 3 ft (1 m) long. They are spectacular for a large greenhouse.

### Cultivation

Grow in strong light in a very open orchid compost in a small pot or, for some creeping species, establish the plant on a slab. A dry resting period during dormancy is essential for many species. Propagate by division when the first roots appear on the new shoots.

### Laelia gouldiana

The 4 in (10 cm) pinkish mauve flowers of *Laelia gouldiana* look marvellous when brought indoors for a splash of seasonal color. The species, which comes from Mexico, grows to a height of 3 ft (1 m). Some authorities regard *L. gouldiana* as a natural hybrid between *L. anceps* and *L. autumnalis*. ZONES 11–12.

*Disa* Diores

*Disa* Hybrid 'Inca Princess'

## × *LAELIOCATTLEYA*

The laelias have been much crossed with the cattleyas, giving rise to this hybrid genus of evergreen orchids with over 2,000 names registered. The name applies to any cross between any member of each genus, plus all backcrosses and later generation seedlings. They vary from cool to intermediate growing, and can have dainty, almost miniature flowers or enormous ruffled ones in the full range of cattleya colors. The pseudobulbs bear only one leaf; it is lance-shaped and leathery.

### Cultivation

They should be grown in a very open orchid compost in bright, filtered light. Water well in the growing period, less so at other times. Propagate by division and watch for aphids, spider mites and mealybugs.

### × *Laeliocattleya* **Hybrids**

These colorful hybrids cover a wide range of plant size and flower color. Many have a large labellum (lip) that is often frilled and contrasts in color with

*Laelia gouldiana*

× *Laeliocattleya* Hybrid 'Chic Bonnet'

× *Laeliocattleya* Hybrid

the rest of the flower. The blooms are long lasting and make good cut flowers. Among the wealth of hybrids are 'Chic Bonnet', a bright pink flower with a magenta to crimson lip; and 'Orange Crush', an overall orange flower with relatively narrow petals. ZONES 11–12.

## MILTONIOPSIS

This genus was created for the pansy orchids still commonly called miltonias. There are about 5 species, from South America, but the hybrids are more commonly grown. With their flat, almost circular flowers and vivid markings, they resemble pansies, but are much larger — up to 6 in (15 cm) across — and come in stronger colors than pansies usually do: bright yellow, white, red and pink, often with gold, purple or brown flashes. Many are sweetly scented. Low-growing, clumping plants, they have round pseudobulbs and pale green, strap-like leaves. The flowers are borne in small clusters and they can appear at any time. Many plants flower twice a year.

### Cultivation

The plants like open compost and light shade. They can grow outdoors in tropical and subtropical climates. Unlike most orchids, they do not take a periodic rest. Propagate by division after flowering.

### Miltoniopsis Hybrids

Numerous complex intergeneric hybrids have been made using *Miltonia, Miltoniopsis, Odontoglossum, Oncidium, Cochlioda* and *Brassia*. Most members of the tribe Oncidiinae are interfertile. These hybrids go by names such as *Miltonidium, Odontonia, Miltonioda* and *Miltassia*. Among the multitude of forms and color resulting have been the so-called pansy orchids, which are derived from *Miltoniopsis phalaenopsis* and other species. Most of these are cool-growing species requiring shady, moist conditions. Hybrids include: Anjou 'Red Mask', deep red with a golden yellow center and dark markings; Bel Royal, crimson with a white picotee edge; Charlotte's Delight, white with a large lower lip and crimson markings; Grouville, deep purplish pink with a fine white edge, darker markings and a golden center; Hudson Bay 'Judith', deep pink with a white-edged red center; Sao Paulo, relatively narrow, soft-pink petals with a large deep-pink lip and a dark center; and Rozel, small red petals with a large red-veined and pink-edged lip. Typical of the *Miltonia × Brassia* hybrids, × *Miltassia* Anne Warne 'Alii' has strap-like leaves and differs from the *Miltoniopsis* hybrids in having relatively narrow petals and a prominent lower lip. The magenta flower has a darker throat and yellow markings. ZONES 10–11.

### ODONTOGLOSSUM

The most widely grown plants of this genus of 200 species from Central and South America are epiphytes, although terrestrial species are known. They are admired for their usually ruffled flowers borne in long sprays, and the wonderful variety of colors and markings displayed thereon. They produce egg-shaped pseudobulbs, from the bases of which

*Miltoniopsis* Hybrid, Anjou 'Red Mask'

the flower stems appear; flowering time depends on variety. The genus is closely related to *Oncidium*, and some botanists consider that they cannot be separated. Some well-known *Odontoglossum* species are now separated off into the genera *Lemboglossum* and *Rossioglossum*.

## Cultivation

Few odontoglossums are difficult to grow: most are cool growing, and need only the usual orchid cultivation of coarse compost, plenty of water in the growing period and light shade. They do not need as definite a rest as cattleyas, but do not over-water them. They can be divided after flowering.

### *Odontoglossum crispum*

This high-altitude epiphyte from Colombia is a variable species with many named forms, very popular in cultivation and with hybridists. The pseudobulbs are compressed, about 3 in (8 cm) long with 2 strap-like leaves to 15 in (38 cm) long and 1½ in (35 mm) wide. The

*Odontoglossum* Hybrid 'Samares'

inflorescence is arching or pendulous, with 8 to 25 showy flowers each about 2½–4 in (6–10 cm) across. ZONES 10–11.

### *Odontoglossum* Hybrids

Thousands of colorful hybrids have been developed suitable for greenhouse culture using *Odontoglossum*. Many other genera have also been utilized in the production of hybrids including those with *Cochlioda* (× *Odontioda*), *Oncidium* (× *Odontocidium*) and *Miltonia* (× *Odontonia*). Virtually all these are cool-growing species with similar requirements to the genus. 'La Houge Bie' is notable for its very broad, overlapping petals giving the bloom a full, rounded look. Extravagant 'Samares' is another fine example. Its pure white petals are wavy and frilly-

*Oncidium varicosum*

*Paphiopedilum callosum*

edged and each petal is decorated with a blood-red spot. ZONES 10–12.

## ONCIDIUM

This is a huge and varied genus of orchids (more than 450 species) from Central and South America, allied to *Odontoglossum* and *Miltonia* (although different in appearance) and able to be crossed with them to give odontocidiums and such multi-generic hybrids as *Wilsonara*. The species usually grown are epiphytes, and vary in their temperature requirements according to species (or parentage); they can be cool, intermediate or warm growing.

### Cultivation

They all like light shade and only a short rest, an open, coarse potting mix and high humidity; most species intensely dislike being over-watered. In the wild, many have a tendency to climb up their host tree, and are best potted with a slab of tree fern trunk to which it can cling. In humid subtropical regions, some species are easily established outdoors on trunks and branches of corky barked trees such as jacarandas. They can be propagated by division.

### Oncidium varicosum

This species from Brazil is typical of a large group that bears small flowers in large, branched sprays which dance in the slightest breeze. The most prominent feature of each flower is the brilliant yellow labellum, the other parts being small and brownish. The flowers are popular with florists, as the airy sprays last for weeks in water. ZONES 10–11.

## PAPHIOPEDILUM
### Slipper orchid, lady's slipper

This orchid genus extends from India through Southeast Asia. The plants grow mostly at moderate altitudes in dense shade on the rainforest floor or in leaf mold on rock faces and occasionally as epiphytes. They are usually compact, consisting of fleshy roots, a short stem and a few large, often mottled leaves with a terminal inflorescence of one or a few large flowers with a characteristic pouched lip. There are about 60 species, although some authorities recognize many variations as species.

### Cultivation

Cultivation depends on the origin of the plants, but most are best grown in intermediate temperatures and part-shade. They should be kept evenly moist throughout the year with well-drained potting mixture. Difficult to grow from seed, many species are threatened by over-collecting from the wild. They are propagated by division; mericlonal propagation does not suit them, and so selected clones and hybrids remain expensive.

### *Paphiopedilum callosum*

This attractive species grows to about 18 in (45 cm) tall and occurs at low altitudes in Thailand, peninsular Malaysia, Laos and Cambodia. The 3 to 5 leaves are about 4–8 in (10–20 cm) by 1–2 in (2.5–5 cm), lightly mottled on the upper surface. The inflorescence has a single showy flower, 3–4 in (8–10 cm) across and long lasting. In cultivation, this species requires warm conditions. ZONES 11–12.

### *Paphiopedilum* Hybrids

Thousands of hybrids have been produced, many in an attempt to achieve a more rounded flower shape, increased vigor and flower size, and interesting color combinations. Many will bloom several times a year. More hybrids have been registered in *Paphiopedilum* than in any other orchid genus. Unfortunately many attempts have not resulted in improvements over the original species, although there are some outstanding exceptions. Most of the hybrids come from about 25 species. King Arthur

*Paphiopedilum* Hybrid Grande Jersey

*Paphiopedilum* Hybrid 'Broadwoodwidger' × 'Momag'

'Burgoyne', a typical hybrid, shows a strong influence of *P. insigne*. *P.* Hybrid 'Broadwoodwidger' × 'Momag' is also a popular choice with gardeners. Grande

Jersey is a hybrid grex of a quite different kind, bred from the small group of species with very elongated, twisted petals; some of these have more than one flower per stem, a feature also apparent in this hybrid. ZONES 10–12.

*Paphiopedilum lawrenceanum*

*Paphiopedilum insigne*

### Paphiopedilum insigne
This species occurs in Nepal and northern India at about 6,660 ft (2,000 m) in limestone soils. It is a vigorous grower, about 12–18 in (30–45 cm) tall and often forms large clumps. The few strap-like leaves are up to 15 in (38 cm) long and 1 in (25 mm) wide. The inflorescence is 12 in (30 cm) long with 1 or 2 glossy flowers 4–6 in (10–15 cm) long. This species is the basis of many modern hybrids. Named forms combine shades of green, russet, cream and white in various patterns and markings. ZONES 10–12.

### Paphiopedilum lawrenceanum
This plant grows to about 15 in (38 cm) tall and occurs at low altitudes in Borneo, in deep leaf litter in rainforests or on mossy limestone rocks. There are 5 to 6 mottled, dark green leaves up to 8 in (20 cm) long and 2 in (5 cm) wide. The inflorescence is up to 12 in (30 cm) long with a single flower up to 4 in (10 cm) across. ZONES 11–12.

### Paphiopedilum malipoense
This is one of a group of species from southwest China, having been discovered only recently growing in cracks on rocks at moderate altitudes. It has 7 or 8 mottled leaves about 4–8 in (10–20 cm) by 1–2 in (2.5–5 cm). The inflorescence is about 10–12 in (25–30 cm) tall with a single flower about 3 in (8 cm) across with a prominent pouched lip about 2 in (5 cm) long. ZONES 10–12.

Paphiopedilum malipoense

Paphiopedilum rothschildianum

### Paphiopedilum rothschildianum

This large clump-forming species occurs only in Borneo, where it grows at low altitudes terrestrially or on rock ledges. It is regarded as one of the most threatened orchid species in the world as it is known from only 2 sites. There are several leaves, strap-like and up to 24 in (60 cm) long and 2 in (5 cm) wide. The inflorescence is up to 18 in (45 cm) long with 2 to 4 flowers about 12 in (30 cm) in diameter. Cultivation is as for the genus, but higher levels of light are recommended. ZONES 11–12.

### Paphiopedilum superbiens
syn. Paphiopedilum curtisii

This species occurs on the island of Sumatra at an altitude of 3,000–4,330 ft (900–1,300 m), growing terrestrially in coniferous forests. There are 4 to 5 leaves, mottled light and dark green, 6–10 in (15–25 cm) long and 1½–2½ in (3.5–6 cm) wide. The inflorescence is up to 12 in (30 cm) tall with a single flower 2½–3 in (6–8 cm) across. ZONES 11–12.

Paphiopedilum superbiens

## PHALAENOPSIS
### Moth orchid

The pastel flowers, broad leaves and intricate petals of the nearly 50 species in this genus from tropical Asia to New Guinea and Australia look enough like fluttering butterflies to earn the common name of moth orchid. They do not make pseudobulbs; the leaves, plain green or spotted, spring directly from the rootstock and the arching flower stems rise clear above them. The stem can be 24 in (60 cm) tall, bearing as many as 20 shapely 4 in (10 cm) flowers. They are most commonly shining white, but are sometimes pale pink, and appear at almost any time of year.

## Cultivation

*Phalaenopsis* require tropical and subtropical climates and filtered light, constant moisture and a rich but open and perfectly drained compost. They are apt to send roots out over the top of the pot: these should be left undisturbed if possible. Their lives as house plants are limited unless they can be retired to a greenhouse when the flowers fade. Propagate by division.

### Phalaenopsis amabilis

This species is an attractive, small-growing epiphyte (occasionally found growing on rocks) from the humid tropical lowlands of Indonesia, Borneo, New Guinea, the Philippines and Australia. The short stem bears 2 to 5 pendulous, fleshy leaves to 15 in (38 cm) long and 4 in (10 cm) wide. The inflorescences are branched, arching to pendulous, up to 3 ft (1 m) long with 5 to 25 flowers. The flowers are variable in size; they can be up to 4 in (10 cm) across. This large-flowered species is prominent in most hybrids. ZONES 11–12.

*Phalaenopsis amabilis*

*Phalaenopsis* Hybrid Bill Smoothey

*Phalaenopsis* Hybrid Alice Gloria 'Cecil Park'

*Phalaenopsis* Hybrid 'Giant'

## Phalaenopsis gigantea

This large-growing species from Borneo derives its name from its large leaves, which are up to 18 in (45 cm) long and 8 in (20 cm) wide, fleshy and pendulous. It grows in the understory of hillside rainforests at low elevations. It is very rare in the wild and under threat from illegal collecting. The inflorescence is pendulous, up to 15 in (38 cm) long, with many fleshy flowers, each about 2 in (5 cm) across. A slow-growing species, it is best grown on a slab or in a basket. The flowers are produced throughout the year. ZONES 11–12.

## Phalaenopsis Hybrids

Thousands of hybrids have been produced from the species of this genus. Breeders have been striving to produce more floriferous plants with larger, more rounded flowers on upright flower spikes and colorful combinations such as striped flowers. Most hybrids are white or pink, and are very popular for the cut-flower industry. Some notable examples are 'Giant', a lovely white hybrid; Alice Gloria 'Cecil Park', which is pure white; Bill Smoothey, pink with white edgings; 'Carmela's Stripe', a striking hybrid with

*Phalaenopsis* Hybrid Plantation Imp 'Moonglow'

*Phalaenopsis* Hybrid 'Carmela's Stripe'

*Phalaenopsis* Hybrid Longwood Gardens

*Phalaenopsis sanderiana*

*Renanthera storiei*

pinkish orange stripes on its whitish yellow petals, and pinkish orange lips. Some hybrids originating from *P. equestris* as a parent have a multitude of smaller flowers on branched inflorescences. ZONES 11–12.

### Phalaenopsis sanderiana

syns *Phalaenopsis amabilis* var. *sanderiana,*
*P. aphrodite* var. *sanderiana*

This compact plant with large flowers has 2 or 3 leaves marked with purple beneath, up to 10 in (25 cm) long by 3 in (8 cm) wide and pendulous. The inflorescence, sometimes branched, is about 24 in (60 cm) long with several flowers each about 4 in (10 cm) across, in shades of pink or white. ZONES 11–12.

### RENANTHERA

This orchid genus is made up of about 15 species of mostly large, climbing or

light pink petals with deep red veining and red lips; Hiramatsua 'Ching Hua', with deep pink petals; Longwood Gardens, white with brownish yellow lips; and Plantation Imp 'Moonglow', with

*Renanthera monachica*

scrambling plants of low altitudes from northeast India to southern China, mostly from Southeast Asia, the Philippines and Indonesia to New Guinea. The stems have 2 ranks of leaves and the flowers are produced from the apical third of the plants. The flowers are mostly red, but some are orange or yellow; they are borne in large, branched inflorescences. The species have been used extensively in hybridizing with *Vanda, Phalaenopsis, Vandopsis* and *Euanthe*.

## Cultivation

These plants need room to scramble, a coarse, well-drained mixture, warm conditions and a fairly even climate with year-round watering and strong light. In the tropics they are often grown in raised garden beds in full sun. Propagate by division.

### Renanthera monachica

This species is more compact than most. The stems are 18–36 in (45–90 cm) long, with dark green, fleshy leaves 2½–6 in (6–15 cm) long. The inflorescences are branched and 8 in (20 cm) long; it bears numerous, long-lasting flowers about 1 in (25 mm) across. This is one of the few renantheras suited to pot culture. ZONES 11–12.

### Renanthera storiei

This large, scrambling species is terrestrial or epiphytic, growing at low altitudes in sun and shade. The leafy stems are up to 15 ft (4.5 m) tall, with the fleshy leaves being 4–6 in (10–15 cm) long. The branched inflorescence is held horizontally and is up to 3 ft (1 m) long with numerous, long-lasting flowers 2–3 in (5–8 cm) long. This species has been widely used in hybridizing. ZONES 11–12.

CHAPTER 7

*Ferns, Palms*
*& Cycads*

*Adiantium peruvianum*

## ADIANTUM
### Maidenhair fern

These are among the best known ferns. They have billowy fronds of many delicate, membranous, almost circular fresh green leaflets, each connected by a very fine blackish stalk to a repeatedly branched main stalk which is also smooth and black. Spore-cases appear as tiny indentations with curled-over 'lips' around the edges of leaflets.

### Cultivation

Grow indoors in pots or hanging baskets, with strong light but not direct sun, and high humidity—the bathroom is a popular site. Plant in a humus-rich indoor mix in a container that is not too large for the roots, which do not like too much wetness. Remove old fronds. Propagate from spores; division of rhizomes is possible but failures are common.

### Adiantum peruvianum
#### Silver dollar fern

Valued for its silvery pink, slightly metallic looking new fronds, this fern comes from Ecuador, Peru and Bolivia. It has a stout rootstock and the fronds may ultimately reach up to 3 ft (1 m) in length. The diamond-shaped segments are fewer and larger than in most maidenhairs, up to 2 in (5 cm) long. It likes humidity and prefers a brightly lit situation with good air movement and neutral to alkaline soils. ZONES 11–12.

## ARECA

This palm genus consists of about 60 species, distributed through wetter regions of southern Asia and the Malay Archipelago, best known in the form of one of its species, the betel palm *(Areca catechu)*, from which betelnuts are obtained—chewed by many people in Asia and the Pacific as a mild narcotic. The species vary in growth habit and leaf type: from single-trunked to densely clumping, from tall and robust to almost stemless, and the fronds from long and regularly pinnate to small and almost undivided. The stem or trunk usually terminates in a 'crownshaft' of furled frond bases, with the flowering panicles emerging just below this. Flowers are not showy but the oval fruit can be brightly colored, usually red, orange or yellow.

### Cultivation

These palms prefer sheltered conditions and moist soil. Propagate from seed, which germinates readily if sown fresh.

### Areca catechu
#### Betel palm, pinang

This is a forest palm up to about 40 ft (12 m) tall with a single smooth, green trunk 4–6 in (10–15 cm) thick; its long feather-like fronds are rather erect but flop untidily with age. The yellow, orange or red fruit are egg-sized and may be borne at any time of year. The large white-fleshed seed is sliced and chewed together with lime and leaves of the betel pepper *(Piper betel)*. The wild origin of this species is not exactly known. ZONES 11–12.

## ASPLENIUM
### Spleenwort

This genus of some 700 species of mainly evergreen ferns is distributed widely

*Areca catechu*

*Asplenium australasicum*

*Asplenium daucifolium*

through most of the world. Very diverse in growth form, they include terrestrial and epiphytic species as well as many that grow on rocks. Some make dense tufts of fronds or rosettes, others creep across the surface with thick, scaly rhizomes. Most have feathery pinnate or bipinnate fronds but in some they are large and undivided: the 'bird's nest ferns' are one such striking group. The fronds of many species develop small plantlets along the ribs. The spore-bodies are typically arranged in parallel or radiating lines on the undersides of the fronds.

### Cultivation
The preferred growing environment varies greatly with the species. Most prefer woodland conditions with cool, moist, humus-rich soil and dappled shade. A few species, however, need sunnier locations and are reasonably tolerant of dry conditions. Propagate by spores, by division of established clumps, removing rooted pieces of rhizomes, or by growing on the frond-borne plantlets.

### Asplenium australasicum
**Bird's nest fern**
Found in Australia and the South Pacific, this species has leathery, undivided fronds, somewhat V-shaped in cross-section and up to 5 ft (1.5 m) long by 8 in (20 cm) wide forming a dramatic large 'nest' or funnel. In the wild it grows on tree trunks or rocks. It requires warm, humid conditions to thrive. *Asplenium nidus* is a very similar species widespread in the tropics. ZONES 10–12.

### Asplenium daucifolium
**Mauritius spleenwort**
Similar to *Asplenium bulbiferum*, this species from Madagascar and Mauritius has dark green, arching fronds up to 3 ft (1 m) long divided into very narrow segments, giving a delicate lacy effect. Numerous plantlets develop on the fronds and may be removed and grown on. ZONES 10–12.

### Asplenium nidus
#### Bird's nest fern

This pantropical, epiphytic fern colonizes trees, rock faces and boulders in humid, tropical rainforests. The glossy green, thin, tongue-like fronds have wavy margins and a prominent, almost black midrib. They arise from a densely hairy crown in a radial fashion, somewhat resembling a bird's nest. It requires warmth and ample humidity. ZONES 11–12.

## CALAMUS
#### Rattan, rotang

The stems of this palm genus of 350-odd species are the source of the world's cane, or rattan, from which cane furniture is constructed. Most species are from tropical Asia and the Malay Archipelago, with a smaller number found in Africa, Australia and the Pacific Islands. They are graceful feather-leafed palms, usually multi-stemmed from the base. The frond mid-rib may be extended into a whip-like, grappling appendage, or this may arise from the rim of the sheathing base of the frond. Similar whip-like panicles bear the tiny flowers, which are followed by small fruits with overlapping scales.

#### Cultivation

Many *Calamus* species adapt to cultivation in warm, wet climates and in their juvenile state can make attractive container plants, best grown in part-shade in moist, well-drained soil. Propagation is only possible from fresh seed.

### Calamus australis

This Australian species grows in dense rainforest in north Queensland. It is multi-stemmed with high-scrambling canes, and fronds about 6 ft (1.8 m) long. The long grappling appendages are armed with recurved hooks. The stalks and sheathing bases of the fronds also have spines. The juvenile, clumping phase is less ferocious and can be maintained for years in a pot. ZONES 10–12.

## CARYOTA
#### Fishtail palm

Very unusual palms with bipinnate fronds make up this genus of 12 species from tropical Asia and Australasia. They include both solitary-trunked palms, mostly large, and smaller multi-stemmed palms that sucker from the base. Flowering panicles first appear at the

*Asplenium nidus*

*Calamus australis*

top of the trunk and continue opening successively lower down; after the last one sets fruit, the whole stem dies. Marble-sized fruits, usually ripening dark red, are formed on the female flowers. The fruits contain 1 to 3 black seeds in a fibrous flesh that is quite irritating to the skin.

### Cultivation
Fishtail palms originate in very moist tropical rainforests and require sheltered, humid environments, but most will tolerate a surprising degree of cold as well as poorly drained soils. They are easily propagated from seed.

### Caryota mitis
#### Clustered fishtail palm
This rainforest understory palm from Southeast Asia has a number of closely crowded stems up to about 30 ft (9 m) tall and 3–4 in (8–10 cm) in diameter, nearly always with a thicket of sucker growths at the base. The fronds are rather erect, up to about 8 ft (2.4 m) long, with widely separated leaflets. The flowers and fruit appear in succession throughout the year. It is the most widely grown species for ornament. ZONES 10–12.

*Caryota mitis*

### Caryota urens
#### Toddy palm, wine palm
This handsome, single-stemmed species is commonly grown for the drink toddy in its native India, Burma and Malaysia. Toddy is obtained by cutting off the young flower clusters and collecting the sugary, vitamin-rich sap that flows from the wound. The tree grows to about 40 ft (12 m) and is widely planted, though it is relatively short lived, with a life span of about 30 years. ZONES 10–12.

## CHAMAEDOREA
This genus consists of over 100 species of small to very small palms. They include many very ornamental species with smooth, green, bamboo-like stems which can grow singly or in clusters; some species are virtually stemless. The fronds are mostly few to each crown and consist of thin segments arranged pinnately (in feather fashion), or in some species undivided apart from a shallow to deep notch at the apex. Flowering stems are mostly branched, appearing among or below the fronds, the tiny male and female flowers carried on different plants; females in particular often have

*Caryota urens*

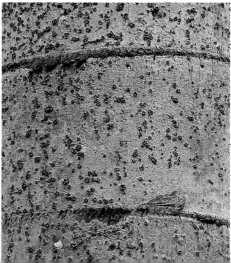

*Chamaedorea cataractarum*

stems that are bright red, orange or yellow, often contrasting with the color of the developing fruits, which are small berries.

### Cultivation
They make first-class indoor plants, tolerating low humidity and dry soil better than many other palms and surviving for years in small containers. Plant in a humus-rich soil and keep in good light but out of strong sun. Outdoors, plant in humus-rich soil, in full sun or part-shade. Propagate from seed.

### *Chamaedorea cataractarum*
### Cascade palm
This species from southern Mexico is found growing along banks of fast-flowing streams, sometimes half-submerged. Its stems are prostrate and branching, like thick green rhizomes, and each oblique shoot has only 4 to 5 dark green pinnate fronds up to 6 ft (1.8 m) long. The short green inflorescences are half-hidden beneath the leaves and bear small yellow flowers followed by reddish fruit about ¼ in (6 mm) in diameter on female plants. It is easily cultivated in a moist, sheltered spot, forming large clumps with age. ZONES 10–12.

## CHRYSALIDOCARPUS
These feather palms from Madagascar are very graceful plants that are most at home in tropical and subtropical areas. Although there are 22 species, only *Chrysalidocarpus lutescens* is widely grown, though other species are equally attractive. The flowers and fruit are unremarkable—simple yellow flowers in branched sprays followed by small yellow fruit—but the foliage is very luxuriant.

### Cultivation
Plant in moist, well-drained soil in sun or light shade. Water freely. Propagate from seed, which can take up to 5 months to germinate.

### *Chrysalidocarpus lutescens*
syns *Areca lutescens, Dypsis lutescens*
### Butterfly palm, golden cane palm
This species is one of the most widely cultivated palms. It is a clump-forming feather palm with fairly short fronds that arch elegantly from cane-like stems 10–20 ft (3–6 m) high. The basal sheaths and frond stalks are yellow and the fronds themselves are yellowish in sun but when grown in shade are a beautiful light green. It responds well to container cultivation and can be grown as a house plant. ZONES 10–12.

### *Chrysalidocarpus madagascariensis*
This Madagascan species may be either single-trunked or branch into several trunks from the base, the ringed trunks up to 30 ft (9 m) or more tall and 4–6 in (10–15 cm) in diameter. The large, plume-like fronds are arranged in 3 vertical rows at the top of the trunk, their broad, overlapping basal sheaths covered in gray scurf. The much-branched inflorescence bears tiny yellow flowers and the fruits, ½ in (12 mm) long, are also yellowish. ZONES 10–12.

## COCCOTHRINAX
This genus of slender fan palms is distributed widely through the

Chrysalidocarpus lutescens

Chrysalidocarpus madagascariensis

Caribbean region, but most of them are native to Cuba. Most are single-trunked, the upper trunk covered with fibrous remains of old leaf sheaths, sometimes forming interesting patterns. The fan-like fronds are smallish with blades divided to about midway into many pointed segments and are often coated with silvery scales on the underside. The inflorescences are mostly shorter than the fronds and moderately branched, with masses of fragrant white or cream flowers followed by small purple-black single-seeded fruits.

## Cultivation
These plants make attractive ornamental palms for tropical gardens and parks, looking particularly effective when planted in groups. They tolerate poor soil and often boggy conditions, but need shelter in the early stages of their growth. Propagation is from seed, which will usually germinate within 2 months.

## Coccothrinax alta
This species makes a medium-sized, slow growing palm of up to 30 ft (9 m)

Coccothrinax alta

with pale brown trunk about 4 in (10 cm) thick. It has graceful, drooping fan leaves that are glossy green on the upper surface, silvery underneath. The flowers are white and are followed by brownish to black shiny fruit. ZONES 11–12.

## COCOS
### Coconut

The only species in this genus of tropical feather palms is the coconut *(Cocos nucifera)*. The genus is distinguished from its relatives, which share the hard blackish inner fruit shell with 3 pores or 'eyes', by the large size of the seed and the fact that its endosperm, or stored food material, is partly liquid (the 'coconut milk').

### Cultivation

It does best in full sun in deep, porous soil with ample moisture but will of

*Cocos nucifera*

*Corypha taliera*

course tolerate coastal conditions. It is raised from seed, which germinate in a few months if the whole unhusked nut is laid on its side on moist sand.

### Cocos nucifera
#### Coconut palm

The coconut has now become distributed through most tropical lowland regions both through human agency and because its nut can survive for a month or so floating in the ocean. It is characterized by its slender, often curved trunk, up to as much as 100 ft (30 m) high, topped with a head of long, gracefully drooping fronds. It bears continuously large panicles of small creamy yellow flowers, a few of which develop into the familiar yellow-green fruit that dries and browns as it ripens. There are many selected strains, including 'Malay Dwarf' with much shorter trunk and abundant golden yellow nuts. ZONE 12.

## CORYPHA

This genus of 6 to 8 species includes some of the most massive of all palms, with huge, fan-shaped fronds. The growth of a mature palm, perhaps 30 to 40 years old, is terminated by a giant panicle of millions of small flowers, towering above the crown of fronds. The flowers are followed by an equally impressive crop of marble-sized fruit and after these ripen the whole palm dies, leaving the seeds to perpetuate the species.

### Cultivation

These are strictly tropical palms, growing normally in full sun in alluvial soil near rivers and swamps. They are usually seen in cultivation only in large parks and botanical gardens. Seed is easily germinated but even under the best growing conditions it takes 10 years at least before a trunk starts to elongate.

*Cyathea cooperi*

### *Corypha taliera*

This palm has a stout trunk up to 30 ft (9 m) tall, usually covered with old frond bases. The stiff green fronds are very large, up to 15 ft (4.5 m) in length. The terminal panicle of flowers rises above the leaves, with crowded masses of white flowers on drooping lateral branches. ZONES 11–12.

### *CYATHEA*
#### Tree fern

Apart from *Asplenium* this is the largest genus of ferns, with over 600 species. *Cyathea* species vary greatly in size, but most are single-stemmed with a trunk up to 50 ft (15 m) tall and an umbrella-like crown of very large fronds. The frond bases are usually covered in hairs or chaff-like scales which may be quite prickly. They often persist on the trunk but even after decaying, their scars make an interesting pattern on the trunk.

#### Cultivation

Few plants create such dramatic effects as these tree ferns, some of which are quite fast growing under ideal conditions. They prefer a humid atmosphere, part-shade, and a moist, humus-rich soil. They need plentiful watering and may need frequent mist-spraying during hot dry spells. When young many species make attractive indoor plants in a suitably humid environment. Propagate by spores. Transplant established plants with care.

### *Cyathea cooperi*
syn. *Sphaeropteris cooperi*
#### Straw tree fern, scaly tree fern, Australian tree fern

Also from eastern Australia, this is one of the fastest-growing tree ferns outside the wet tropics, sometimes reaching 20 ft (6 m) in less than 15 years if moisture and nutrients are abundant. It has a crown of similar size to *Cyathea australis* but the frond bases are thicker and

Cycas armstrongii

Cycas revoluta

covered densely in chaff-like scales that are pale brown to straw-colored. The foliage is fairly tolerant of sun but is easily shrivelled by drying winds. ZONES 10–12.

## CYCAS
### Sago palm

This geologically ancient genus of cycads has about 60 species. They are palm-like plants with pinnate fronds spreading from the top of a thick trunk that is packed with starchy tissue; male and female organs are on different plants, the male in long, narrow cones terminating the stem, the female on the margins of furry, leaf-like organs that ring the trunk apex and may eventually hang in a 'skirt' below the trunk apex, as the hard, egg-like seeds mature. Trunk growth is normally very slow, so large specimens are prized and fetch high prices.

### Cultivation

They like sunny positions but with some shade when young, and deep, well-drained soil. Propagation is from seed, detached offsets, or by cutting off a whole trunk and plunging the base in a trench filled with gravel and organic matter.

### Cycas armstrongii

This species from Australia occurs in flat, sandy country in open eucalypt wood-land. It is usually unbranched, with a straight, slender trunk 6–15 ft (1.8–4.5 m) tall, from the top of which emerges a circle of delicate, new, pale green fronds at the beginning of each wet season; during the long dry season they gradu-ally shrivel and droop, hanging in a brown 'skirt'. Plants in moister positions may retain fronds for longer. Female trees mostly sport another 'skirt' of seed-bearing organs, each with 2 to 4 large, orange-brown seeds. ZONES 11–12.

### Cycas revoluta
### Japanese sago palm

This palm-like species grows slowly with short, single or multiple trunks to 10 ft (3 m) with a compact crown of stiff pinnate leaves that have closely crowded, narrow, spine-tipped leaflets. It is the most widely cultivated cycad in the world and is valued as a landscape subject, es-pecially suited to courtyards and plazas. Slow growing, it is capable of living for 50 to 100 years or even more and is readily transplanted. ZONES 9–12.

## ELAEIS
### Oil palm
This is a tropical genus of 2 species of palms with narrow, straight trunks topped with long, drooping fronds. The individual leaflets also droop, which creates a soft, graceful effect. Small yellow flowers in large inflorescences are followed by the oil-bearing fruits.

### Cultivation
Plant in rich, moist soil in full sun. Propagate from seed.

### Elaeis guineensis
### African oil palm
The fruit and seeds from this species yield palm oil. Planted by the millions in tropical countries to satisfy commercial demand, it is sometimes seen as a threat by conservationists because it is replacing rainforests. It grows to 70 ft (21 m) high with fronds up to 15 ft (4.5 m) long. The all-important fruit occur in large, tightly packed bunches and change from red to black when ripe. ZONES 11–12.

## ENCEPHALARTOS
The 60 or more species of slow-growing cycads in this genus come mostly from southern Africa with a minority scattered through tropical Africa. They are commonly found on rocky outcrops, among coastal dunes or on mountainsides. They appear as large tufts of spiky fronds for many years before eventually developing a stout trunk, up to 10–12 ft (3–3.5 m) high. The stiff, palm-like leaves are pinnate, with leaflets that are spine tipped and often toothed. As with all cycads, there are both male and female plants; the latter produce spectacular cones either singly or in groups of up to 5 from the center of the crown.

### Cultivation
These plants do best in subtropical areas with full sun and plenty of moisture; they can withstand strong winds. Propagate from seed, which germinates easily, although seedlings take many years to develop.

### Encephalartos altensteinii
### Prickly cycad, bread tree
This cycad from moist coastal areas of South Africa is very slow growing. The rigid, palm-like fronds are about 6 ft (1.8 m) long, and have numerous stiff,

Elaeis guineensis

Encephalartos altensteinii

spiny-toothed leaflets. A female specimen may produce cones resembling giant, elongated pineapples 18 in (45 cm) long. ZONES 10–11.

### Encephalartos arenarius

This rare species from South Africa's eastern Cape Province has an erect stem to 3 ft (1 m) tall. The arching fronds, to 5 ft (1.5 m) in length, have lobed, blue-green leaflets. Mature specimens of *Encephalartos arenarius* bear solitary green cones with red glossy seeds. ZONES 10–11.

## LICUALA

There are around 100 species in this genus of fan palms from the wet tropics of Southeast Asia and Australasia, varying greatly in stature. Their fronds are very distinctive, from circular to fan-shaped in outline with regularly radiating ribs and toothed around the perimeter; in most species they are divided by splits into pie-wedge segments, often of unequal widths and with few to many ribs each. Slender flowering panicles arise from the frond axils, bearing numerous tiny yellowish flowers followed by small red or orange berries.

### Cultivation

They prefer part-shade and sandy, well-drained soil. Propagate from seed or suckers.

### Licuala spinosa

This is a Southeast Asian evergreen species reaching 20 ft (6 m) with a 10 ft (3 m) spread. It has clumps of slender stems and frond segments like the spokes of a wheel, 3 ft (1 m) across, and fruit of bright orange berries carried on an arching inflorescence up to 8 ft (2.4 m) long. ZONES 10–12.

## LIVISTONA

This is a genus of about 30 species of medium to tall fan palms, about half of them endemic to Australia, the remainder scattered through the Malay Archipelago and southern Asia. Most feature large, almost circular, pleated fronds up to 5 ft (1.5 m) across forming a dense crown from which dead fronds may remain hanging for some time. The frond stalks are usually long and are edged with sharp prickles. These palms are widely used for outdoor landscaping; their clusters of blue, black or rarely

*Encephalartos arenarius*

*Licuala spinosa*

Livistona rotundifolia

Livistona saribus

reddish fruits and tapering frond segments are shown to great effect.

### Cultivation
Slow growing, they prefer deep, sandy soil and, while they tolerate full sun, they produce more vigorous, deeper green foliage in dappled shade. They make excellent indoor or outdoor container plants. Propagate from seed.

### Livistona rotundifolia
This attractive fan palm from the Philippines and Indonesia grows to 80 ft (24 m). It has spherical scarlet fruit that eventually ripen black and will grow in moist soil in the tropics. The seed remains viable for a longer period than most palms, and the plant can be grown from seed in a deep container. ZONES 11–12.

### Livistona saribus
syn. Livistona cochinchinensis
This fan palm from tropical Asia and the Malay Archipelago grows to 80 ft (24 m) tall. It has quite large blue fruit like those of *Livistona chinensis* and small clusters of yellow flowers. It is distinctive for the frond stalks of younger trees being wickedly armed with very large, curved prickles. ZONES 11–12.

## LODOICEA
### Seychelles nut, coco-de-mer, double coconut
This remarkable palm genus consists of a single species, the famous 'double coconut', found only on the small islands of Praslin and Curieuse in the Indian Ocean Seychelles group. Despite the common name, it is not closely related to the feather-leafed coconut palm but is a close ally of the African doum palms (*Hyphaene*) and like them has massive fan-like fronds that radiate from the top of a tall trunk, unbranched in the case of *Lodoicea*. It is famous for having the largest single-seeded fruit of any plant, with a curious 2-lobed shape resembling large buttocks. Germination of the seeds is a remarkable process, with a cotyledon the thickness of a human arm and up to 12 ft (3.5 m) long emerging

Lodoicea maldivica

Macrozamia miquelii

over a period of months and finally producing roots and shoots from its tip.

### Cultivation
Grow in full sun in deep, moist, fertile loam. Propagate from seed, for which special provision needs to be made on account of its mode of germination. It requires warmth and high humidity.

### Lodoicea maldivica
This palm, healthy specimens of which can be seen in a number of tropical botanical gardens, grows to 100 ft (30 m) tall and has large 18 in (45 cm) fruit that resemble a wooden heart and weigh up to 40 lb (18 kg). The main source of seed is wild stands of palms in the Seychelles, the islands' government selling them to tourists at high prices. ZONE 12.

## MACROZAMIA
This genus consists of about 24 species of cycads from Australia. Their stems vary from cylindrical to almost globose, above or below ground level, and are topped with palm like fronds of ever-green foliage reaching up to 8 ft (2.4 m) long. The trunks are clothed in persistent dead frond bases. They produce large light green, pineapple-shaped, male and female cones, the individual cone scales tipped with a sharp spine; the mature female cones contain bright orange, red or yellow seeds. The starchy kernels were eaten by the Australian Aborigines after lengthy preparation that removed toxic substances. They cannot be eaten fresh.

### Cultivation
They like an open, well-drained soil in part-shade. Propagate from fresh seed, which can take 18 months to germinate.

### Macrozamia miquelii
### Zamia
This cycad's trunk reaches 24 in (60 cm) high; the dark green, 5 ft (1.5 m) long fronds have many crowded leaflets, 10–15 in (25–38 cm) long, with white or reddish bases. The barrel-shaped female cones, 15 in (38 cm) long, contain oblong red or orange seeds. Male cones are the same length, but banana-shaped. ZONES 10–12.

## NEPHROLEPIS
### Sword fern
Commonly found in the tropics and subtropics on edges of rainforests or in

Nephrolepis cordifolia

Phoenix reclinata

open forests, this genus of 30 species of evergreen or semi-evergreen ferns has fishbone-shaped fronds. These may be erect, spreading or pendent and with short, upright rhizomes.

### Cultivation
For ferns, they are extremely tolerant of dry conditions and are fast growing, provided they are given enough room to spread out and have well-composted, moist soil. These ferns are ideal for indoors, but be sure to provide lots of water in warm conditions. Propagate from spores or tissue culture, or by division.

### *Nephrolepis cordifolia*
### Fishbone fern, southern sword fern
Naturally found among rocks at the edges of rainforests, this fast-growing fern can survive in fairly dry and dark positions as well as in full sun. It is one of the toughest species in cultivation and a very easily grown plant—so much so that it can become a pest. Fronds grow to 3 ft (1 m). 'Plumosa' is a slow-growing cultivar with lobed pinnae. ZONES 10–12.

## PHOENIX
These evergreen feather palms are native to subtropical and tropical parts of Asia, Africa and the Canary Islands. There are 17 very different species; some are an important source of food (dates and palm sugar derived from dates), others are popular as house plants or avenue trees. *Phoenix* includes species with a single trunk as well as some that form clumps of stems. The long fronds have stiff, sharp spines at the base and form a dense crown. The small yellow flowers grow in clusters and are followed by the fruits. *Phoenix* is the ancient Greek name given to the date palm.

### Cultivation
Male and female plants are needed to ensure pollination. The plants prefer full sun, although they will tolerate part-shade, hot winds and poor soil if given good drainage. Hybrids between species are common. Trim off dead fronds. Propagate from seed.

### *Phoenix reclinata*
### Senegal date palm
This African species is smaller than *Phoenix canariensis* and *P. dactylifera*, reaching only 20–30 ft (6–9 m) in height. It is distinctive for its multiple trunks, each gracefully curving out from the center of the clump. The small fruit are yellow to red. ZONES 10–11.

Phoenix roebelenii

Phoenix rupicola

### *Phoenix roebelenii*
#### Dwarf date palm
From Laos, this palm is suitable for a hot-climate garden or for use as a potted specimen indoors. Growing to 10 ft (3 m) tall with a similar spread, its dark green, arching fronds give it an elegant, lacy effect. The short, slender stem is rough because the bases of the old leaves persist. The fruit are small, black, egg-shaped drupes. ZONES 10–12.

### *Phoenix rupicola*
#### Cliff date, Indian date palm
From northern India, this species has a slender 25 ft (8 m) tall trunk topped with a head of gracefully arching, rather glossy fronds up to 8 ft (2.4 m) long. Panicles of yellow flowers are followed by small, dark red fruit. Although the relatively quick growth and size of this species mean it is best grown outdoors, it is suitable for greenhouse cultivation. ZONES 10–12.

## PLATYCERIUM
The 15 species are epiphytic ferns with hanging, spore-bearing divided fronds up to 8 ft (2.4 m) long. They are valued for their dramatic appearance.

#### Cultivation
These ferns can be grown as epiphytes by tying them onto boards that are then attached to a post or tree, or grown in baskets. The sterile nest leaves catch leaf litter and other vegetable matter so that the roots eventually grow into the debris and are protected from wind. The base of the plants should be kept moist. Fertilize the plants with dilute liquid manure. Propagate by division. Check for beetle and moth larvae.

### *Platycerium superbum*
syn. *Platycerium grande*
#### Staghorn fern
In the wild, clinging to a rainforest tree, this epiphyte can reach up to 6 ft (1.8 m) in height and spread, and its sheer weight can make it fall to the ground. It does well in a fernery or garden, where it grows to about half its natural size. ZONES 10–12.

*Platycerium superbum*

## PRITCHARDIA
### Loulu palm

This is a genus of some 37 species of tropical fan palms. Found naturally in Fiji, Hawaii and other Pacific islands, they grow as tall as 70 ft (21 m) and have very large, flat fronds that are divided only about halfway to the midrib. The trunk is straight and smooth for its lower two-thirds; the upper third is often covered with old frond bases and thatch. Branched inflorescences of small cream to orange flowers develop at the base of the crown and are followed by small black fruits.

### Cultivation

These tropical palms demand a warm, humid climate. They prefer moist, humus-rich, well-drained soil and light shade when young. Propagate from seed.

*Pritchardia pacifica*

### Pritchardia pacifica
### Fiji fan palm

There is some doubt that this handsome fan palm is truly native to Fiji, though that is where it first became known to science, and some palm botanists have suggested that it was introduced from

Tonga. It is impressive for the crown of luxuriant foliage, consisting of huge, pleated fronds each up to 5 ft (1.5 m) across and only shallowly divided into segments. The flowering branches are shorter than those of many other pritchardias, not extending beyond the fronds and bearing dense clusters of yellow flowers at their ends; the fruit are small, black and round. This palm is easily cultivated and makes rapid growth. ZONES 10–12.

## RHAPIS
### Lady palm

*Rhapis* is a small genus of about 12 species of low-growing palms ranging from southern China to Thailand. They form clumps of slender, bamboo-like stems carrying small, deeply divided, fan-shaped fronds. New stem growth is covered with interwoven fibers arising from the base of each frond. The yellow male and female flowers occur on separate plants. The fruits are small berries containing a single seed.

### Cultivation

These palms are often grown in tubs, as ornamental clumps, or as hedges outdoors in warm, humid climates. They require some shade and rich, moist soil. They are usually propagated by dividing a clump but can be reproduced from seed.

### Rhapis excelsa
### Miniature fan palm

The many stems of this palm form a dense clump up to 15 ft (4.5 m) tall. The fronds, light to rich green, divide into 5 to 8 stiff, finger-like segments. The tiny, bowl-shaped, creamy flowers appear in small panicles among the frond. It will grow outside in warm climates, but slowly; its leaves may burn in full sun. ZONES 10–12.

*Rhapis excelsa*

*Roystonea elata*

## ROYSTONEA
### Royal palm

This genus of about 10 species of very tall palms comes from the Caribbean region. Capable of reaching 120 ft (36 m) tall, though usually rather less, they have single, erect, pale brown trunks. Their fronds can grow 20 ft (6 m) long and 6 ft (1.8 m) wide. Broom-like panicles of small white flowers are followed by deep purple berries. These palms are often seen planted along avenues or in parks. The genus name honors General Roy Stone, veteran of the US Civil War.

### Cultivation

They demand full sun and moist, rich, well-drained soil. Propagate from seed. If grown indoors they may be prone to attack from spider mites and scale insects.

### Roystonea elata

Very similar to *Roystonea regia*, this native of southern Florida differs visibly only in that the veining of the leaflets is inconspicuous. ZONES 11–12.

### Roystonea regia
### Cuban royal palm

When mature, this palm grows 100 ft (30 m) tall and 30 ft (9 m) wide. Its straight trunk often thickens in the middle, and the 20 ft (6 m) fronds are composed of numerous narrow, deep green leaflets. It bears small white flower clusters in pendulous spikes up to 3 ft (1 m) long, and deep purple berries 1 in (25 mm) in diameter. ZONES 11–12.

## SALVINIA

There are about 10 species of these floating annual ferns. They have no true roots, but a group of divided leaves under the water take on this function and also produce the fruiting spores. When mature the spores sink and grow just as ferns do.

*Roystonea regia*

Veitchia merrillii

Salvinia auriculata

## Cultivation

Species of *Salvinia* are easily grown as floating ferns; new plants appear in warm weather from dropped spores. They prefer full sun and still water. Propagate by separating stems.

### Salvinia auriculata

This species comes from around the Gulf of Mexico to northern Argentina. The heart-shaped leaves, to ¾ in (18 mm) long, are dark green, folded upwards, and have rows of knobs alongside longitudinal veins. They are crowded onto the slender stems. ZONES 10–12.

## VEITCHIA

The elegant, feather-leafed palms of this genus occur naturally in tropical forests of Fiji, Vanuatu and the Philippines. The 15 or so species range in height from 20–100 ft (6–30 m) and most have a slender, pale gray, smooth or lightly ringed trunk. The bright green, gently arching fronds form an umbrella-like crown. Bunches of insignificant flowers are followed by dense clusters of bright red or orange berries.

## Cultivation

They need protection from wind and moist, well-drained soil; they do best in full sun or part-shade. Mature trees make attractive lawn and landscape specimens, while young plants grow well in tubs, even indoors in well lit conditions. Propagation from seed is slow.

### Veitchia merrillii
#### Manila palm

Native to the Philippines, this is an attractive, small palm widely grown in tropical gardens. Maturing to 20 ft (6 m) tall, it has a slender trunk marked with rings. The feathery, bright green leaves, springing from a short crownshaft, form a compact crown. The bright red fruit, about 1½ in (35 mm) long, hang in clusters below the crown. This species is often seen planted in the shelter of buildings where its delicate fronds are protected from wind damage. ZONES 11–12.

## WASHINGTONIA
### Washingtonia palm

This genus is made up of 2 species of fan-leafed palms from arid parts of western Mexico, southern California and Arizona. Their stately appearance makes them ideal specimen or avenue trees. They have an upright, single trunk, and are sometimes called petticoat palms because the dead fronds hang down in a mass around the trunk, almost to the ground. The large fronds have many long, tapering segments and spiny stalks. The small white flowers cluster at intervals on long flowering branches that arch out well beyond the fronds. The fruits are small dark drupes.

### Cultivation
These palms enjoy warm to hot climates, full sun, well-drained soil and an open position. Propagate from seed.

### Washingtonia robusta
#### Mexican washingtonia palm, Mexican fan palm
This species, taller and more slender than *Washingtonia filifera* and with a more tapering trunk, occurs naturally in northwestern Mexico. It grows to 80 ft (24 m) and its crown is 10 ft (3 m) across. The shiny, bright green fronds, almost circular, are less deeply seg mented than those of *W. filifera*. The fruit are tiny dark brown berries. ZONES 10–11.

### ZAMIA
This is the largest and most diverse of the American genera of cycads. There are thought to be 60 or more species, and they include some of the most diminutive cycads. They usually have a short subterranean or above-ground stem, and arching fronds divided into few or many leaflets. The leaflets are mostly smooth, often with toothed or serrated margins. Male and female cones are borne on different plants and vary in shape. The stems in some species have been used as a source of edible starch.

*Washingtonia robusta*

### Cultivation
Grow in part-shade in well-drained soil; water liberally during growth and sparingly at other times. They make excellent container plants. Propagate from fresh seed after removing the fleshy outer covering.

### Zamia pumila
#### Coontie, Florida arrowroot
A native of the grasslands and open forests of the whole Caribbean region, this small cycad grows from freely branching, under-ground stems. The dark green, leathery, fern-like leaves are erect to spreading and are less than 3 ft (1 m) long. The male cones are cylindrical, while the female cones are ovoid; both are rusty red. Best grown in full sun, this species makes an attractive addition to a border or as a container specimen. ZONES 10–12.

CHAPTER 8

# Climbers & Creepers

## AESCHYNANTHUS

Over 100 species of mostly epiphytic creepers and subshrubs in the African violet family make up this genus, ranging through rainforests of Southeast Asia and the Malay Archipelago. Some have become popular as indoor plants, suited to hanging baskets and flowering freely for months on end. The stems are tough and wiry, sometimes clinging by roots. Leaves are fleshy and pointed, arranged in opposite pairs, and the flowers, clustered at the ends of branches are trumpet-shaped but curved, often with the base enclosed in a conspicuous calyx.

### Cultivation

They prefer a position in part-shade and are most at home in a hanging basket or established in the crotch of a large tree. Pot in a coarse indoor plant mix and water freely in the growing period. Propagate from cuttings.

Aeschynanthus javanicus

Aeschynanthus speciosus

### Aeschynanthus javanicus
#### Lipstick vine

Native to Java and other islands of the Malay Archipelago, this species bears flowers shorter than in most other species but of the most brilliant red or orange color, the cup-like calyx usually darker than the broadly lobed corolla and both covered in bristly hairs. Stems and flowers are both pendent, and a stunningwell-grown specimen in a basket can make a cascade of red and green. ZONES 11–12.

### Aeschynanthus speciosus

Native to Borneo, this species bears large clusters of tubular, 4 in (10 cm) long orange flowers with yellow throats. With a somewhat trailing habit, it reaches a height and spread of 12–24 in (30–60 cm). Stems are slender and arching and the dark green, lance-shaped leaves are carried in pairs or whorls with a terminal rosette surrounding a cluster of flowers. ZONES 11–12.

## ALLAMANDA

A dozen or so species of twining climbers and shrubs belong to this tropical American genus, a few of them widely planted in warm climates for their colorful trumpet flowers, mostly bright yellow. Glossy leaves are in whorls of 3 to 6 on the smooth stems, which bleed

*Allamanda cathartica* 'Hendersonii'

*Antigonon leptopus*

milky sap if cut. The climbing species are among the most popular ornamentals in the tropics, ideal for growing over fences or against walls. They produce a succession of flowers for much of the year

### Cultivation
Grow outdoors in a sunny, sheltered position in rich soil, watering freely. Prune periodically to maintain shape and encourage flowering. Propagate from cuttings and watch for mites which disfigure the leaves.

### *Allamanda cathartica*
### Golden trumpet vine
This vigorous climber, fast-growing to 15 ft (4.5 m), bears large, yellow, trumpet-shaped flowers to 6 in (15 cm) across. It has whorls of lance-shaped leaves and makes a luxuriant cover for walls and strong fences. The flowers of 'Hendersonii' are yellow with white spotted throats. ZONES 11–12.

## *ANTIGONON*
### Coral vine
This Mexican and Central American genus is made up of species of tendril climber, only one of which is widely cultivated for its display of delicate coral-pink blossom. The leaves are dark green and heart-shaped with wavy edges. The dense foliage canopy is decked with trailing sprays of clustered racemes of small flowers, appearing over a long season. Only the heart-shaped sepals, tightly pressed together, provide the color, which ranges from the deepest coral to quite pale pink or even white.

### Cultivation
These climbers require ample moisture. Propagate from seed, cuttings or by division of the rootstock.

### *Antigonon leptopus*
### Coral vine, chain of love
This is a fast-growing, showy creeper that may grow to 25 ft (8 m) or more. It bears masses of deep pink, heart-shaped flowers, and is ideal for trellises, pergolas and arbors where a light cover is desirable. ZONES 9–11.

Aristolochia grandiflora

Beaumontia grandiflora

## ARISTOLOCHIA
### Dutchman's pipe, birthwort

This large genus of over 500 species comprises evergreen and deciduous, twining climbers and some herbaceous perennials. The climbers are most often cultivated, chosen for their heart-shaped leaves and unusually shaped tubular flowers, which have a swelling at the base and a hood above, usually with the tube between sharply bent. Insects are attracted into the mouth of the flowers by a strong scent, and pollen is scattered over their bodies. The fruit are also curiously shaped, dangling from slender stalks and splitting at maturity to spill fine seed as they rock in the breeze.

### Cultivation
The plants require well-drained, humus-rich soil in a sunny position with some shade and support for their climbing habit. Prune growth to 2 to 3 nodes periodically. Propagate from seed or from cuttings. Watch out for spider mites.

### Aristolochia grandiflora
### Pelican flower
The curiously shaped flower buds of this Central American species resemble the neck of a pelican. The purple and green flowers, which at 6 in (15 cm) or more across are among the largest in the genus, emit an odor that is attractive to pollinating flies, but not so appealing to humans. The vine grows very quickly from seed and can be treated as an annual in temperate climates. ZONES 10–12.

## BEAUMONTIA

This is a genus of 9 species of woody, evergreen, twining vines from the lower Himalayas and Indo-Malayan region. They have large, leathery, glossy leaves, arranged in opposite pairs on the stems, that bleed sticky sap when cut. The flowers are trumpet-shaped, quite large, mostly white and fragrantly scented, opening progressively from loose clusters that terminate leafy lateral branches.

### Cultivation
They like a moist, humus-rich, well-drained soil in a sheltered position in full sun or light shade. The plants can be

trained on a strong trellis or over a stump, or allowed to mound without support, trimming back longer growths. Prune immediately after flowering. Propagation is normally from cuttings.

### Beaumontia grandiflora
#### Herald's trumpet
This beautiful, large, woody climber will climb to 20 ft (6 m) or more but needs strong support for its thick twining stems. It is valued for its large, fragrant, white trumpet flowers, 4–6 in (10–15 cm) long, and its handsome, deep green leaves, prominently veined and up to 10 in (25 cm) long. ZONES 9–12.

## BOUGAINVILLEA
The genus consists of 14 species ranging through tropical and subtropical South America, but only 3 or 4 have been grown as ornamentals. The numerous cultivars include many different kinds and colors. They are evergreen in the wet tropics, but may be deciduous where there is a severe dry season. Their finest display is in the dry season though they may flower on and off all year. The true flowers are tubular and rather insignificant, but the surrounding bracts are brilliantly colored, often changing color or shade as they age. The simple, broad leaves are soft and usually covered with fine hairs.

### Cultivation
All species do best in full sun. Only water when needed and do not over-fertilize, particularly with nitrogen, as this will produce luxuriant leaf growth but very little in the way of colorful bracts. Bougainvilleas need strong support for their vigorous growth, but can be controlled by pruning after flowering, when rampant plants can be ruthlessly cut back without harm. Flowers appear on the new wood. With

regular heavy pruning, all bougainvilleas can be grown in large containers and kept to a height and width of about 3 ft (1 m) if desired. Propagate from cuttings.

### Bougainvillea × buttiana
This hybrid is a cross between *Bougainvillea glabra* and *B. peruviana* and includes many cultivars. They are large, woody, vigorous growers with dark green leaves and spines. The bracts vary in color from white to orange-pink and deep red. 'Mrs Butt' with purplish red bracts was the original of this popular group, discovered by a Mrs Butt in a

*Bougainvillea × buttiana 'Louis Wathen'*

*Bougainvillea × buttiana 'Mrs Butt'*

*Bougainvillea glabra*

*Bougainvillea glabra 'Alba'*

garden in Trinidad some time around 1900. 'Louis Wathen' (syn. 'Orange King') has rounded orange bracts that change to a bright rose pink. 'Golden Glow' (syn. 'Hawaiian Gold') has bracts that are a magnificent shade of orange-gold, turning more pinkish as they age. ZONES 10–12.

### Bougainvillea glabra

A native of Brazil, this is one of the two common species that have been long established in gardens around the world. It includes many cultivars and is also one parent of the hybrid *Bougainvillea* × *buttiana*, which includes many more. It is a vigorous shrubby vine, growing to 30 ft (9 m), with masses of bright purple or white bracts. It has thin, curved spines and the leaves have tiny hairs. 'Alba' (syns 'Snow White', 'Key West White') has white bracts with prominent green veins and smallish pale green leaves; it is not as vigorous as most other cultivars. 'Magnifica' (syn. 'Magnifica Traillii') is the familiar bright magenta bougain-

*Bougainvillea 'Scarlett O'Hara'*

*Bougainvillea 'Temple Fire'*

villea, blooming over a long season, with glossy, dark green leaves. ZONES 10–12.

### Bougainvillea 'Scarlett O'Hara'
syns 'Hawaiian Scarlet', 'San Diego Red'
This popular free-flowering hybrid cultivar of uncertain origin is a large, vigorous grower, the new growths dark red with many thorns. The leaves are large, dark green, rather rounded, and the almost circular crimson bracts are very large, orange-tinted before they mature and often appearing before the leaves. ZONES 10–12.

### Bougainvillea 'Temple Fire'
syn. *Bougainvillea* 'Helen Johnson'
Of hybrid origin, this is one of the smallest bougainvilleas, growing to about 3 ft (1 m). It has small leaves and short thorns. The bracts are a reddish purple color with a hint of copper before they are fully expanded. This cultivar is well suited to growing in a tub. ZONES 10–12.

### CARDIOSPERMUM
This is a genus of 14 species of vigorous, fast-growing, evergreen climbers from tropical and South America, one of them naturalized in all warm regions of the world. They climb by tendrils and need support. They have soft green foliage consisting of coarsely serrated leaflets and small white flowers, but it is the inflated, balloon-like seed pods that are their most distinctive feature—the pods split at maturity into 3 delicate segments, each with a hard black seed attached; the seeds float to the earth with a spinning motion. One species is valued as a folk medicine in tropical Asia. In some warm regions they can become troublesome weeds, smothering native trees and other vegetation.

#### Cultivation
These vines self-sow and regenerate from very small sections of root. They need well-drained, fertile soil and a

reasonably long dry season to enable the seed cases to develop and dry to their attractive straw color.

### Cardiospermum halicacabum
### Balloon vine

Occurring widely throughout the world's tropics, this fast-growing vine climbs by tendrils. It has hairy, pale green leaves with oblong, 3-lobed leaflets that are pointed and toothed. It has clusters of inconspicuous white flowers. These are followed by papery, inflated, straw-colored fruit enclosing black seeds. The balloon vine is used in Indian traditional medicine. ZONES 10–12.

*Cardiospermum halicacabum*

*Clitoria ternatea*

## CLITORIA

Eighteenth-century botanists such as Linnaeus (who named this genus) were less bothered than those of the present day at the thought of naming plants for their resemblance to intimate parts of the human anatomy, and *Clitoria* is one such case. There are some 70 species of evergreen leguminous climbers, perennials and shrubs in this genus, occurring in most tropical regions but predominantly in the Americas. They have pinnate leaves and the flowers are borne singly or in small clusters. Although their basic floral structure is of the pea-flower type, the flowers are presented upside down — the 'keel' petal appears on the top rather than the underside and so insects are dusted with pollen on their backs instead of their bellies.

### Cultivation

They need full sun, fertile, moist but well-drained, loamy soil. Provide good support for twining stems and thin out growth with pruning. Propagate from seed.

### Clitoria ternatea
### Butterfly pea

This is a lovely evergreen, twining up to 12 ft (3.5 m) with slender stems and fresh green leaves divided into 3 or 5 oval leaflets. Flowers are quite large, about 2 in (5 cm) long, pale lilac with yellow centers; they are followed by flat pods. There is also a double-flowered form. The specific name refers not to the commonly ternate arrangement of the leaflets, but to the Indonesian island of Ternate, where this species was first recorded. It occurs widely in tropical Asia. ZONES 10–12.

## EPIPREMNUM

This is a genus of 8 species of evergreen climbing plants from tropical areas of

Southeast Asia and the western Pacific. Cultivated for their attractive foliage, they climb by using adhesive aerial roots and can reach great heights in forests. In the home they are easily pruned at any time to control growth. The foliage goes through both juvenile and adult forms and adult leaves of some species can be up to 24 in (60 cm) long. They are usually somewhat heart-shaped. These climbers rarely flower until they produce adult foliage.

### Cultivation

Most species are easy to grow indoors in bright, indirect light. Grow in a good, moisture-retentive potting mix. Water regularly. Provide the support of a moss pole, and to encourage branching pinch out shoot tips. Propagate from cuttings or by layering.

### Epipremnum pinnatum

syn. *Raphidophora pinnata*

Up to 60 ft (18 m) tall in its native forests from Southeast Asia to tropical Australia, this species can be kept to a manageable size in cultivation. The juvenile leaves are usually entire, although they are sometimes perforated or lobed. The perforated, adult leaves are up to 3 ft (1 m) long by 18 in (45 cm) wide and often have translucent spots along the midrib. 'Aureum' (syns *Epipremnum aureum*, *Pothos aureus*, *Rhaphidophora aurea*, *Scindapsus aureus*), devil's ivy or pothos, has apple-green, heart-shaped leaves marbled with creamy white or gold. ZONES 10–12.

### FICUS

Many of the species belonging to this genus are trees, and detailed information on the genus is given in the Trees chapter. However, *Ficus pumila* is treated here as a climber.

### Ficus pumila

syn. *Ficus repens*

### Climbing fig, creeping fig

From Japan, Vietnam and China, this vigorous evergreen climber clings by aerial roots along the stems. It has attractive small, bright green, heart-shaped juvenile leaves that turn bronze. Remove any mature woody branches that stand out strongly from the support to retain juvenile leaves. 'Minima' has much smaller, daintier foliage and is less rampant; 'Quercifolia' has lobed leaves; 'Variegata' is more vigorous with leaves mottled white to cream. ZONES 8–11.

Epipremnum pinnatum 'Aureum'

Ficus pumila

*Holmskioldia sanguinea*

*Hoya carnosa 'Compacta'*

## HOLMSKIOLDIA

This genus of 10 species of evergreen, sprawling shrubs or scrambling climbers is indigenous to warm-climate coastal regions from southeastern Africa and Madagascar to India. They are fast growing and generally suit tropical or subtropical gardens, but their range can be extended slightly by planting near a sheltering wall. The flowers are usually trumpet-shaped with a coral-red calyx.

### Cultivation

Full sun and well-drained, fertile soil suit them best, and ideally some type of support that allows their attractive and unusual flowers to be viewed from below. They are propagated from cuttings or from seed. In cooler climates, they grow in greenhouse conditions.

*Holmskioldia sanguinea*
**Chinese hat plant, parasol flower**

Its unique flowers are the main interest of this scrambling shrub: each is a narrow, orange-scarlet tube backed by a broad, circular calyx, appearing in dense terminal clusters. The mid-green leaves are pointed, oval and slightly serrated. Its long, trailing canes make it ideal for espaliering. Contain rampant growth by pruning after flowering and remove old canes. There are also yellow- and bronze-flowered forms. ZONES 10–11.

## HOYA
### Wax flower

Twiners or root climbers (sometimes both) with waxy foliage native to Southeast Asia, New Guinea and tropical Australia, hoyas all bear clusters of scented, star-shaped flowers. They are waxy and resemble cake ornaments, one star sitting atop a larger one. If plants are supported on a frame and are also slightly potbound they are more likely to flower, but may not do so for several years. There are about 200 species.

### Cultivation

Plant in any potting soil that drains well in bright to very bright light, with moderate temperatures and humidity. Allow the soil surface to become quite dry between waterings. As the new flowers come from the same spurs as the old ones, it is best not to prune or pick. Propagate from semi-ripe cuttings. Be careful where you place the plant as sticky nectar drips from the flowers. Check for mealybugs under glass.

## Hoya carnosa
### Wax plant
Native to eastern India, southern China and Burma, this twining plant can be grown against a small framework. It has dark green, glossy, oval leaves and bears scented, star-shaped flowers, white to pink in color and with dark pink centers. 'Compacta' has twisted, upward-folded leaves that give the plant a curious rope-like appearance. ZONES 10–11.

*Hoya lanceolata* subsp. *bella*

### Hoya lanceolata subsp. *bella*
syn. *Hoya bella*
### Beautiful honey plant, miniature wax plant
This compact Himalayan species has arching stems and bright green, narrow, lance-shaped leaves. It looks best when grown in a hanging pot or basket where flowers can be admired. Star-shaped white flowers, with red or purplish pink centers, hang in clusters. ZONES 10–11.

*Hoya santos* × *cumingiana*

### Hoya santos × cumingiana
This lovely hybrid has flowerheads that look like a cluster of sugared shooting stars. Each bloom has a small, reddish star attached to backward-pointing creamy beige petals. ZONES 10–11.

### Hoya serpens
The flowers of some hoyas are covered with minute hairs to give a soft downy effect. Such is the case with *Hoya serpens*, a rather rare species from the Indian state of Sikkim. It bears flowers about ½ in (12 mm) wide. ZONES 10–11.

*Hoya serpens*

## IPOMOEA
syns *Calonyction, Mina, Pharbitis, Quamoclit*
### Morning glory
This large genus of some 300 mostly climbing, evergreen shrubs, perennials and annuals is widespread throughout the tropics and warm-temperate regions of the world. It includes sweet potato and some of the loveliest of the tropical flowering vines. Most species have a twining habit and masses of funnel-shaped flowers which in many species

wither by midday. The flowers are usually short lived, lasting only one day (or night), but blooming prolifically and in succession. They are useful for covering sheds, fences, trellises and banks, and may also be grown in containers.

### Cultivation
They prefer moderately fertile, well-drained soil and a sunny position. Care should be taken when choosing species, as some can become extremely invasive. Propagate from seed which has been gently filed and pre-soaked to aid germination, or from cuttings (for perennial species).

### *Ipomoea alba*
### Moon flower
syns *Calonyction aculeatum, Ipomoea bona-nox*
From tropical America, this fast-growing, soft-stemmed, evergreen perennial vine grows to 20 ft (6 m) or more. It is cultivated for its large, fragrant, pure white flowers, which open at night.
ZONES 10–12.

### *Ipomoea horsfalliae*
### Cardinal creeper
Native to the West Indies and other tropical regions, this beautiful evergreen

flowering vine grows up to 10 ft (3 m). It bears stalked clusters of long, tubular, deep rose-pink or rose-purple flowers, which give it its common name.
ZONES 11–12.

### *Ipomoea pes-caprae*
syn. *Ipomoea biloba*
### Beach morning glory, railroad vine
A prostrate or climbing perennial, *Ipomoea pes-caprae* has 2 in (5 cm) wide flowers that can be pink to light purple with a dark throat. This species is found in tropical beaches around the world, its stems rooting at the nodes. The plant's distinctive leaf shape, with 2 rounded lobes, is referred to in the name *pes-caprae*, which means goat's foot.
ZONES 10–12.

## *JASMINUM*
### Jasmine
The name jasmine is synonymous with sweet fragrance, although among this large genus of some 200 deciduous, semi-evergreen and evergreen shrubs and vines, mostly from Asia and Africa, there are many that offer nothing to the nose. The leaves are usually compound, the flowers white, yellow or more rarely

*Ipomoea alba*

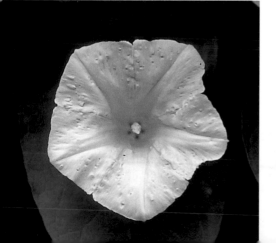

*Ipomoea horsfalliae*

reddish pink. Most of the species cultivated for their fragrance are climbing
plants.

### Cultivation
Plant in full sun in fertile, moist but
well-drained soil. Prune as required after
flowering. Propagate from cuttings.

### Jasminum nitidum
#### Angel wing jasmine
The star-shaped, white flowers of this
species are large, about 2 in (5 cm)
across, and, like many jasmines, sweetly
scented. They are borne in small sprays.
A strong-growing climber, it has glossy,
oval leaves and reaches a height of
10–20 ft (3–6 m). ZONES 10–11.

### Jasminum sambac
#### Arabian jasmine
This rather weak evergreen climber
grows to only 10 ft (3 m). It has large,
glossy green leaves and bears sweetly
perfumed white flowers. In China the
flowers are used for perfuming tea,
while in India they are made into
garlands. 'Grand Duke of Tuscany' is a
double-flowered form, rather less
vigorous. Often confused with *Jasminum
sambac* is *J. multiflorum*, with denser
flower clusters and downy stems.
ZONES 10–11.

*Jasminum nitidum*

## LONICERA
### Honeysuckle, woodbine
This diverse genus, of wide occurrence
in the northern hemisphere, consists of
around 180 species of shrubs and woody
twining climbers, both evergreen and
deciduous. They have leaves in opposite
pairs and mostly smooth-edged, and
flowers that are 2-lipped with a short to
long tube, usually sweetly scented and
yielding nectar to visiting bees or birds.
Many honeysuckle species and their
hybrids are valued garden plants, hardy,
long lived and disease free though often
becoming straggly unless pruned
annually. The shrub species are excellent
for borders, while the climbers can be
used to cover trellises, walls or fences.

*Ipomoea pes-caprae*

*Lonicera hildebrandiana*

*Lonicera japonica*

## Cultivation

They are easily grown in sun or light shade and are not fussy about soil. They benefit from regular pruning to keep them from becoming hopeless tangles. Propagate from seed or from cuttings. Watch for aphids.

### *Lonicera hildebrandiana*
### Giant honeysuckle, Burmese honeysuckle

This evergreen or semi-evergreen climber from southern China and Southeast Asia, reaches up to at least 30 ft (9 m), with vigorously twining branches and large glossy leaves. It has the longest flowers in the genus, about 4 in (10 cm) long with a curved tube and recurving lips, cream at first but soon aging to orange; they are only faintly scented and are followed by green fruit. It needs strong support. ZONES 9–11.

### *Lonicera japonica*
### Japanese honeysuckle

This vigorous climber from eastern Asia, growing to 30 ft (9 m), has glossy, dark green leaves. Pairs of fragrant white flowers, ageing yellow or sometimes purple tinged, are followed by black berries. This species can become an invasive weed, although it is very useful as a ground cover or to quickly hide fences and posts. 'Aurea-reticulata'

has attractive, gold-veined leaves but bears only a few flowers; 'Halliana' with bright green oval leaves and perfumed, small white flowers that age to yellow, has been used in Chinese medicine since the Tang dynasty in 659 AD. ZONES 4–10.

## MANDEVILLA
syn. *Dipladenia*

Native to Central and South America, many of these fast-growing, woody stemmed climbers come from the Organ Mountains forests near Rio de Janeiro, home of many exotic plants admired worldwide. They bear profuse pink or white trumpet-shaped flowers, fragrant in some species. They were named after British diplomat and gardener Henry Mandeville (1773–1861).

### Cultivation

Mandevillas like part-shade and deep, rich, well-drained soil. Provide ample water on hot days. Propagate from seed or cuttings.

### *Mandevilla* × *amoena* 'Alice du Pont'
syns *Mandevilla* × *amabilis* 'Alice du Pont', *Dipladenia* 'Alice du Pont'

Growing up to 20–30 ft (6–9 m) tall (much less in containers), this twining climber produces handsome, oval, glossy leaves and clusters of large, deep pink, scentless flowers over a long period. The

*Mandevilla × amoena 'Alice du Pont'*

*Mandevilla sanderi 'My Fair Lady'*

plant needs a warm, protected position with midday shade. ZONES 10–11.

### Mandevilla sanderi
syn. *Dipladenia sanderi*
**Brazilian jasmine**
This vine climbs by twining around its support up to 15 ft (4.5 m) in warm climates. Its foliage is rich glossy green and up to 2½ in (6 cm) long. In the wild form, the flowers are usually rose pink and 3 in (8 cm) wide. Several named cultivars have recently been released, including 'My Fair Lady', which is pink in bud opening white with pink shadings; 'Red Riding Hood' with rich bright pink flowers; and 'Scarlet Pimpernel' which flowers throughout the year and is the darkest form so far discovered with rich scarlet flowers with a yellow throat. ZONES 10–11.

### Mandevilla splendens
syn. *Dipladenia splendens*
One of the showiest species of its genus, this evergreen twining climber, native to Brazil, reaches 10 ft (3 m) in height. Its lustrous green leaves are wide and elliptical to rectangular, and 8 in (20 cm) long. It bears pink flowers with yellow centers. ZONES 10–12.

*Mandevilla splendens*

## MONSTERA
This is a genus of 25 species of often very large-growing evergreen tropical climbers, usually with long aerial roots and often epiphytic or becoming so as they clamber up forest trees. The foliage has both juvenile and adult forms: juvenile leaves are usually much smaller and entire, often growing flat to the trunk of the host plant; adult leaves are much larger and often perforated. The flower spikes are enclosed in a spathe to 18 in (45 cm) long that is sometimes shed and is usually white or greenish cream. The fruits, which often mature to white, are edible in some species. They are native to tropical America and the West Indies.

## Cultivation

Species of *Monstera* are usually grown as indoor plants in all but tropical countries, where they can climb trees to 70 ft (21 m) or more. They can be controlled by pruning. They prefer part-shade and humus-rich, moist but well-drained soil. Propagate from ripe seed or cuttings or by layering.

*Monstera deliciosa*

*Mucuna bennettii*

### *Monstera deliciosa*
#### Fruit salad plant, Swiss cheese plant, split-leaf philodendron

A close relative of *Philodendron* and native to the West Indies and tropical America, the huge, broad, glossy, perforated and deeply cut leaves of *Monstera deliciosa* grow from thick stems with aerial roots. Mature plants bear thick, cream-colored spathes followed by sweet-smelling cones of edible fruit that take about a year to ripen and usually only outdoors. This is an easy plant to grow, and adjusts to all but the coldest indoor conditions. ZONES 10–12.

## MUCUNA

There are some 100 species in this legume genus of herbaceous and woody stemmed, evergreen, twining climbers and shrubs, occurring throughout the tropics and subtropics of both hemispheres. Mucunas belong to the bean tribe and have rather showy pea-flowers in pendent sprays, and thin-walled pods that may be clothed in irritant hairs. Only one species is outstanding as an ornamental.

### Cultivation

Mucunas grow rampantly in the tropics, but languish in cooler climates except in large heated greenhouses. They like their roots kept cool and shaded, and prefer well-drained soil rich in humus. Propagate from seed or by layering.

### *Mucuna bennettii*
#### New Guinea creeper

The leaves of this strong, fast-growing climber divide into 3 oval leaflets, and it bears large, pendent clusters of pea-like, brilliant orange-scarlet flowers. It will grow only in climates like those of its native Papua New Guinea and needs abundant water during growth. It requires a well-supported, large area for climbing. Crowded stems may be thinned out. ZONES 11–12.

## PASSIFLORA

syn. *Tacsonia*

### Passion flower, granadilla

This genus contains over 400 species of mostly evergreen or semi-evergreen, tendril-climbing vines, primarily native to tropical South America. They are grown for their ornamental blossoms and their pulpy fruit, notably the passionfruit. Flowers range from pale pink to purple-red and fruits from pale yellow through to purple-black, depending on the species. Two examples of beautiful hybrids are 'Coral Seas', which is a deep red, and 'Lilac Lady' (syn. 'Lavender Lady'), with its delicate light lilac petals fading to white at their tips.

### Cultivation

Plant in rich, well-drained soil in full sun and provide support. Water regularly. Prune congested or overgrown plants. Propagate from seed or from cuttings or by layering. They are susceptible to nematodes.

### Passiflora coccinea
### Red granadilla, red passion flower

This robust, evergreen, woody stemmed climber reaches 12 ft (3.5 m) in height. It is grown for the brilliant, large, scarlet flowers with red, pink and white crowns it bears, set among large, dark green, crinkly leaves. It needs protection from hot winds. ZONES 10–12.

### Passiflora × exoniensis

A hybrid between *Passiflora antioquiensis* and *P. mollissima*, this has wide, 3-lobed, hairy leaves and pendulous flowers up to 6 in (15 cm) wide. The flowers are red on the outside with a pink interior and violet-tinted petals. ZONES 10–12.

## PETREA

This genus of some 30 species of deciduous or semi-evergreen vines, shrubs and small trees is from Mexico and tropical America. The foliage is variable, but usually broadly elliptical, 6–8 in (15–20 cm) long, deep green with toothed edges and sometimes sticky or covered with fine hairs. The 6–24 in (15–60 cm) long inflorescences smother the plant. Most species have blue or purple flowers, although mauve and white are also common. The flowers are followed by small drupes.

*Passiflora coccinea*

*Passiflora × exoniensis*

Petrea volubilis

Philodendron erubescens

### Cultivation

They are best grown in light, well-drained soil in full sun. Propagate from seed or more commonly from cuttings.

### Petrea volubilis
#### Purple wreath, sandpaper, queen's wreath

Native to Central America and the West Indies, this bushy, evergreen woody stemmed climber is grown for its clusters of delightful, star-like, violet flowers. They are set among simple, elliptic, rough-textured leaves. It grows to a height of 20 ft (6 m) or more and needs support to maintain its climbing habit. ZONES 10–12.

### PHILODENDRON

This genus of up to 500 species includes many well-known house plants as well as some shrubs and small trees. Native to tropical America and the West Indies, they are mainly epiphytic, evergreen vines and creepers with aerial roots, some dainty but others quite robust. They are known for their lush foliage, often with a dramatic outline or deep lobes, mostly green but sometimes attractively marked with white, pink or red. The petal-less flowers are inconspicuous. All parts of the plants are poisonous.

### Cultivation

All species need plenty of moisture to be cultivated outdoors. They need a sheltered, shady spot with well-drained, humus-rich soil. Water and fertilize house plants regularly. Propagate from cuttings or seed.

### Philodendron erubescens
#### Red-leaf philodendron, blushing philodendron

This climbing species from Colombia has purple-red stems and new growth. Its leaves are more than 15 in (38 cm) long, elongated heart- to arrowhead-shaped, glossy deep green above with purplish undersides. It is usually treated as a house or greenhouse plant, grown in a pot trained up a frame. *Philodendron erubescens* 'Burgundy' has 12 in (30 cm) red-flushed leaves with red veins and deep purple-red stems. ZONES 11–12.

## PIPER
### Pepper
This genus of over 1,000 species of shrubs, climbers and trees is found throughout the tropics. As might be expected of such a large genus, there is little to be said that applies to all of them. The source of pepper and kava, they are often aromatic plants and their leaves are smooth-edged, usually deep green and often heart- or lance-shaped. The flowers are minute, cream or green and are borne on short yellowish spikes that form in the leaf axils. Small green fruits that ripen to red follow.

### Cultivation
All species prefer moist, humus-rich soil. They will grow in sun or shade and in the right conditions can be vigorous. Propagate from seed or cuttings or by division or layering depending on the plant type.

### Piper betle
### Betel
Found from India to the Malay peninsula, this 15 ft (4.5 m) tall plant climbs using adventitious roots. Its leaves are heart-shaped, 4–6 in (10–15 cm) long by 3 in (8 cm) wide and are chewed by native peoples along with the nut of the betel palm (*Areca catechu*). The floral spike is up to 6 in (15 cm) long and becomes a red mass as the fruit develop. ZONES 10–12.

## QUISQUALIS
This is a genus of about 16 species of evergreen shrubs and twining climbers. They bear panicles or racemes of small, tubular, 5-lobed flowers and have simple leaves produced in opposite pairs. The translation of the genus name is 'Which? What?'—an expression of amazement at

*Piper betle*

*Quisqualis indica*

the variable growth pattern of these natives of Africa and tropical Asia.

### Cultivation
Grow in humus-rich, moist but well-drained soil in full sun or part-shade. The stems may need support; pinch out overgrowth. Propagate from seed or cuttings or by layering.

### Quisqualis indica
### Rangoon creeper, red jasmine
This strong-growing, evergreen creeper can reach 70 ft (21 m) in tropical areas. The flowers are strongly fragrant, especially at night, opening white and deepening to pink and then red. It needs a sturdy support and is useful for

*Solandra maxima*

*Solanum crispum*

covering fences, walls and pergolas. Cut back old stems and remove spent flowers. ZONES 10–12.

## SOLANDRA
### Chalice vine

This genus of 8 species of evergreen, woody stemmed, scrambling climbers was named in honor of the Swedish botanist Daniel Carlsson Solander (1736–82), a pupil of Linnaeus. Natives of tropical America, they are grown for their large, fragrant, trumpet-shaped flowers and shiny, leathery foliage.

### Cultivation

Plant outdoors in full sun in fertile, well-drained soil and water freely during the growing season. Thin out crowded stems after flowering. Propagate from cuttings.

### Solandra maxima
syn. *Solandra nitida*
**Cup of gold, Hawaiian lily, golden chalice vine**

A giant climber from Mexico to Colombia and Venezuela valued for its huge flowers and ability to cover very large areas, this is a rampant, woody vine growing to 30 ft (9 m) or more, requiring plenty of space and a sturdy support. It bears yellow flowers, to 10 in (25 cm) across and with a purplish

stripe down the center of each petal. It tolerates wind, dry conditions and salt spray, so it is an excellent plant for seaside gardens. ZONES 10–12.

## SOLANUM
syn. *Lycianthes*

There are over 1,400 species in this genus including trees, shrubs, annuals, biennials, perennials and climbers from a range of habitats worldwide. The genus includes important food plants like the potato and eggplant (aubergine), though many species are dangerously poisonous. Ornamental species are grown for their flowers and fruits. The leaves are arranged alternately, while the showy flowers are solitary or in clusters, star-shaped to bell-shaped, ranging in color from white and yellow to blue and purple. The fruits are berries that contain many seeds.

### Cultivation

Most prefer full sun and rich, well-drained soil. They are commonly grown from seed or cuttings. They are prone to attack by spider mite, white fly and aphids.

### Solanum crispum
**Chilean potato tree**

This is an evergreen or semi-evergreen scrambling climber to 20 ft (6 m) from

*Solanum wendlandii*

*Stephanotis floribunda*

Chile, with undulating oval or heart-shaped leaves up to 4 in (10 cm) long that are finely hairy. The heads of lilac-blue flowers are fragrant and are followed by white ¼ in (6 mm) fruit. 'Glasnevin' is a vigorous form with deep blue flowers. ZONES 8–11.

### Solanum seaforthianum
#### St Vincent lilac, glydine, Brazilian nightshade
This is a showy, evergreen, slender-stemmed vine growing to 20 ft (6 m) and bearing large nodding clusters of violet-blue flowers with yellow stamens. These are followed by small scarlet berries. ZONES 10–12.

### Solanum wendlandii
#### Potato vine, paradise flower, giant potato creeper
This robust evergreen or semi-evergreen vine to 20 ft (6 m) has a few hooked spines. The 8 in (20 cm) leaves are very variable, simple or divided. The hanging flowerheads of lilac flowers are up to 6 in (15 cm) across. It is native to Costa Rica. ZONES 10–12.

## STEPHANOTIS
This genus of 5 to 15 species of twining woody stemmed climbers is found in the tropical and subtropical regions of Africa, Madagascar and Asia. Growing 10–20 ft (3–6 m) tall, they have wiry stems clothed with pairs of 4–6 in

(10–15 cm) long, waxy, deep green leaves. The foliage is attractive but the primary appeal is the fragrant flowers. Opening from clusters of around 4 blooms, they are pure white, pendulous, tubular with widely flared lobes, and up to 2½ in (6 cm) long.

### Cultivation
Plant in moderately fertile, humus-rich, moist but well-drained soil in filtered sunlight as full sun will burn the flowers. The stems should be supported and shortened if they become overcrowded. Propagate from seed or cuttings.

### Stephanotis floribunda
#### Wax flower, bridal wreath, Madagascar jasmine
This evergreen climber from Mada-gascar can grow to a height and spread of 10 ft (3 m). It is grown for its pleasant fragrance and attractive foliage of paired, waxy, deep green leaves. The pure white flowers appear in clusters of about 4 blooms. ZONES 10–12.

## STRONGYLODON
This genus consists of 20 species of vigorous evergreen shrubs or woody stemmed vines that bear long racemes of pea-flowers. The flowers can be blue-green, blue, red or orange. The tripalmate leaves have lance-shaped or rounded leaflets.

## Cultivation

They prefer full sun or part-shade and fertile, humus-rich soil. Propagate from seed, by rooting stem sections or by air layering.

### Strongylodon macrobotrys
#### Jade vine, emerald creeper

A large, twining climber up to 70 ft (21 m) tall, this species is valued for its spectacular, 18 in (45 cm) long, pendulous sprays of blue-green flowers. It is native to the Philippines. Grow over a pergola or large arch where the long racemes of flowers can hang down. ZONES 11–12.

*Syngonium podophyllum*

## SYNGONIUM

There are about 33 species of these robust evergreen epiphytic or terrestrial climbing vines from tropical America. The long-stemmed and lobed leaves carry a milky sap. They are usually produced as potted climbing plants or in hanging baskets, when the juvenile simple or basal-lobed leaves are all that is seen. The flowers are seldom seen in cultivation; they may be red, orange, green or white.

### Cultivation

They need rich soil and protection from direct sun. Allow the medium to dry out between waterings. Tip pruning encourages compact growth. Propagate from cuttings.

### Syngonium podophyllum
syn. *Nephthytis triphylla* of gardens
#### Arrowhead vine, goosefoot

This plant closely resembles its relative the climbing *Philodendron*, with its handsome climbing or trailing foliage. It has an unusual feature of changing leaf shape with maturity. The young, arrowhead-shaped leaves on the ends of erect stalks become, with age, lobed with 7 to 9 glossy leaflets growing to 12 in (30 cm) long. There are several varieties with variegated leaves in cream or pink. ZONES 10–12.

*Thunbergia battiscombei*

*Thunbergia grandiflora*

*Thunbergia mysorensis*

## THUNBERGIA

This genus of 90 to 100 species of mainly twining climbers and evergreen, clump-forming shrubs, was named after the eighteenth-century Swedish botanist Dr Carl Peter Thunberg, who collected in Africa and Japan. Native to Africa, Asia and Madagascar, their leaves are entire or lobed, and the mostly trumpet-shaped blooms are borne individually from the leaf axils or in trusses.

### Cultivation

They will grow in any reasonably rich soil with adequate drainage. They prefer a position in part-shade and liberal water should be provided. Support the stems and prune densely packed foliage. Propagate from seed and cuttings.

### Thunbergia battiscombei

This species from tropical Africa is a scrambler with 4 in (10 cm) elliptical leaves and racemes of yellow-throated purple trumpet flowers. ZONES 11–12.

### Thunbergia grandiflora
**Blue trumpet vine, sky flower**

This fast-growing, vigorous, evergreen climber grows to around 15 ft (4.5 m) high. It is grown for its drooping clusters of large, sky blue to deep violet trumpet-shaped flowers. It has large-toothed, heart-shaped leaves up to 8 in (20 cm) long and looks best when grown on a trellis, fence or pergola. It requires protection from dry winds. ZONES 10–12.

### Thunbergia mysorensis

This evergreen, woody stemmed climber comes from tropical mountains in southern India and thrives in conditions similar to that of its homeland. It reaches 20 ft (6 m) and has narrow green leaves. The pendent flower spikes are a cheerful combination of brownish red and yellow. ZONES 10–11.

# Reference Table

The following table provides information about the tropical plants described in this book. It covers some of the various uses you can make of the tropical plants you choose. The table also provides information on how tall the plants may grow, so you can plan your garden knowing the requirements of each plant. However, variations in geographic locations and climate will mean differences in growth habits, especially size. Refer to the entries in this book before deciding on the plants that will best suit your locality.

| Name | Kind | Maximum height | Uses |
|------|------|----------------|------|
| *Acacia auriculiformis* | tree | 30 ft (9 m) | decorative flowers |
| *Acacia farnesiana* | shrub | 15 ft (4.5 m) | perfume, hedge, screen |
| *Achasma macrocheilos* | perennial | 20 ft (6 m) | garden tree |
| *Acalypha hispida* | shrub | 6 ft (1.8 m) | decorative flowers |
| *Acalypha wilkesiana* | shrub | 10 ft (3 m) | decorative foliage |
| *Adenium obesum* | shrub | 5 ft (1.5 m) | decorative flowers |
| *Adiantum peruvianum* | fern | 3 ft (1 m) | decorative foliage |
| *Aechmea chantii* | epiphyte | 24 in (60 cm) | decorative plant |
| *Aechmea fasciata* | epiphyte | 18 in (45 cm) | decorative plant |
| *Aechmea nidularioides* | epiphyte | 24 in (60 cm) | decorative plant |
| *Aechmea pineliana* | epiphyte | 15 in (38 cm) | decorative plant |
| *Aechmea* 'Royal Wine' | epiphyte | 18 in (45 cm) | decorative plant |
| *Aechmea* 'Shining Light' | epiphyte | 24 in (60 cm) | decorative plant |
| *Aeonium tabuliforme* | succulent | 8 in (20 cm) | ornamental plant |
| *Aeschynanthus javanicus* | creeper | 5 ft (1.5 m) | hanging basket, indoor, decorative flowers |
| *Aeschynanthus speciosus* | creeper | 24 in (60 cm) | decorative flowers, hanging basket |
| *Agapetes incurvata* | shrub | 3 ft (1 m) | decorative flowers |
| *Agave bracteosa* | succulent | 30 in (75 cm) | decorative foliage |
| *Agave picta* | succulent | 35 ft (10.5 m) | decorative foliage |
| *Agave stricta* | succulent | 10 ft (3 m) | decorative foliage |
| *Allamanda cathartica* | climber | 15 ft (4,5 m) | decorative flowers |
| *Allamanda schottii* | shrub | 6 ft (1.8 m) | flowers |
| *Aloe alooides* | succulent | 6 ft (1.8 m) | landscape subject |
| *Aloe buhrii* | succulent | 16 in (40 cm) | decorative foliage and flowers |
| *Aloe rupestris* | succulent | 25 ft (8 m) | decorative flowers |
| *Aloe sessiliflora* | succulent | 30 in (75 cm) | decorative flowers |
| *Aloe speciosa* | succulent | 20 ft (6 m) | decorative foliage |
| *Aloe spectabilis* | succulent | 12 ft (3.5 m) | landscape subject |
| *Alpinia galanga* | perennial | 6 ft (1.8 m) | spice |
| *Alpinia purpurata* | perennial | 10 ft (3 m) | decorative plant |
| *Alpinia zerumbet* | perennial | 10 ft (3 m) | decorative plant |
| *Amherstia nobilis* | tree | 40 ft (13 m) | decorative flowers |
| *Amorphophallus paeoniifolius* | perennial | 3 ft (1 m) | decorative plant |
| *Anacardium occidentale* | tree | 25 ft (8 m) | cashew nuts |
| *Ananas comosus* | tree | 4 ft (1.2 m) | fruit |
| *Anthurium andraeanum* | epiphyte | 24 in (60 cm) | flowers |
| *Anthurium scherzerianum* | epiphyte | 30 in (75 cm) | decorative plant |
| *Antigonon leptopus* | climber | 25 ft (8 m) | decorative flowers, trellis, pergola, arbor |
| *Aphelandra squarrosa* | shrub | 6 ft (1.8 m) | indoor, decorative foliage |
| *Areca catechu* | palm | 40 ft (12 m) | source of betelnuts |
| *Ariocarpus retusus* | cactus | 10 in (25 cm) | under glass, container |
| *Ariocarpus trigonus* | cactus | 4 in (10 cm) | under glass, container |
| *Ariocarpus ornatum* | cactus | 15 in (38 cm) | under glass, container |
| *Aristolochia grandiflora* | climber | 16 ft (5 m) | decorative foliage and flowers |
| *Ascocentrum hybrids* | orchid | 15 in (38 cm) | cut flowers |
| *Asplenium australasicum* | fern | 5 ft (1.5 m) | greenhouse, decorative foliage |
| *Asplenium daucifolium* | fern | 3 ft (1 m) | containers, greenhouse |

| Name | Kind | Maximum height | Uses |
|---|---|---|---|
| *Asplenium nidus* | fern | 3 ft (1 m) | greenhouse, decorative foliage |
| *Atrocarpus heterophyllus* | tree | 30 ft (9 m) | fruit |
| *Averrhoa carambola* | tree | 20 ft (6 m) | fruit, shade |
| *Bambusa multiplex* | bamboo | 30 ft (9 m) | fence, hedge |
| *Barleria cristata* | shrub | 3 ft (1 m) | bedding |
| *Barringtonia asiatica* | tree | 20 ft (6 m) | decorative flowers, fish poison |
| *Bauhinia x blakeana* | tree | 40 ft (12 m) | cut flowers |
| *Bauhinia monandra* | tree | 20 ft (6 m) | cut flowers |
| *Beaumontia grandiflora* | climber | 20 ft (6 m) | fragrant flowers |
| *Begonia* 'Cleopatra' | perennial | 24 in (60 cm) | decorative flowers |
| *Begonia* 'Erythrophylla' | perennial | 24 in (60 cm) | decorative foliage |
| *Begonia fuchsioides* | perennial | 3 ft (1 m) | decorative flowers |
| *Begonia* x *hiemalis* | perennial | 15 in (38 cm) | decorative flowers |
| *Begonia* 'Pink Shasta' | perennial | 4 ft (1.2 m) | decorative flowers |
| *Billbergia nutans* | bromeliad | 24 in (60 cm) | rockeries, containers |
| *Bixia orellana* | shrub | 10 ft (3 m) | ornamental plant |
| *Bougainvillea* x *buttiana* | climber | 10 ft (3 m) | colorful bracts |
| *Bougainvillea glabra* | climber | 30 ft (9 m) | colorful bracts |
| *Bougainvillea* 'Scarlett O'Hara' | climber | 12 ft (3.5 m) | colorful bracts |
| *Bougainvillea* 'Temple Fire' | climber | 3 ft (1 m) | colorful bracts, containers |
| *Bouvardia longiflora* | shrub | 3 ft (1 m) | cut flowers |
| *Brachychiton* | tree | 80 ft (24 m) | parks, large garden tree |
| *Brassavola nodosa* | orchid | 12 in (30 cm) | cut flowers |
| *Brassia verrucosa* | orchid | 19 in (50 cm) | cut flowers |
| *Bromelia balansae* | bromeliad | 5 ft (1.5 m) | living fence |
| *Brugmansia aurea* | shrub | 20 ft (6 m) | decorative flowers |
| *Brugmansia* x *candida* | shrub | 15 ft (4.5 m) | decorative flowers |
| *Brugmansia* 'Charles Grimaldi' | shrub | 6 ft (1.8 m) | decorative flowers |
| *Brugmansia* 'Frosty Pink' | shrub | 6 ft (1.8 m) | decorative flowers |
| *Brugmansia suaveolens* | shrub | 15 ft (4.5 m) | decorative flowers |
| *Brunfelsia pauciflora* | shrub | 5 ft (1.5 m) | decorative flowers |
| *Caesalpinia crista* | shrub | 15 ft (4.5 m) | climber, decorative flowers |
| *Caesalpinia ferrea* | tree | 40 ft (12 m) | attractive bark |
| *Caesalpinia pulcherrima* | shrub | 8 ft (2.4 m) | decorative flowers |
| *Caladium bicolor* | tuber | 24 in (60 cm) | decorative foliage |
| *Calamus australis* | palm | 6 ft (1.8 m) | cane (rattan), containers |
| *Calathea burle-marxii* | perennial | 5 ft (1.5 m) | decorative foliage |
| *Calathea veitchiana* | perennial | 3 ft (1 m) | decorative foliage |
| *Calathea zebrina* | perennial | 3 ft (1 m) | decorative foliage |
| *Calliandra californica* | shrub | 4 ft (1.2 m) | ornamental plant |
| *Calliandra emarginata* | shrub | 10 ft (3 m) | ornamental plant |
| *Calliandra haematocephala* | shrub | 12 ft (3.5 m) | ornamental plant |
| *Calliandra surinamensis* | shrub | 10 ft (3 m) | ornamental plant |
| *Callistemon formosus* | shrub | 15 ft (4.5 m) | decorative flowers, attracts birds |
| *Cananga odorata* | tree | 80 ft (24 m) | fragrant flowers, perfume |
| *Canna* × *generalis* | perennial | 6 ft (1.8 m) | decorative flowers |
| *Canna indica* | perennial | 8 ft (2.4 m) | decorative flowers, starch |

| Name | Kind | Maximum height | Uses |
|------|------|----------------|------|
| *Cardiospermum halicacabum* | climber | 6 ft (1.8 m) | pergolas, traditional medicine |
| *Carica papaya* | tree | 20 ft (6 m) | fruit |
| *Caryota mitis* | palm | 30 ft (9 m) | ornamental plant |
| *Caryota urens* | palm | 40 ft (12 m) | ornamental plant, source of 'toddy' |
| *Cassia fistula* | tree | 60 ft (18 m) | fragrant flowers |
| *Cassia javanica* | tree | 80 ft (24 m) | decorative flowers |
| *Casuarina equisetifolia* | tree | 60 ft (18 m) | seaside planting, timber, shade, firewood |
| *Cattleya*, Bifoliate hybrids | orchid | 18 in (45 cm) | cut flowers |
| *Cattleya bowringiana* | orchid | 24 in (60 cm) | cut flowers |
| *Cattleya deckeri* | orchid | 8 in (20 cm) | cut flowers |
| *C.* Queen Sirikit 'Summer Stars' | orchid | 12 in (30 cm) | cut flowers |
| *Cattleya skinneri* | orchid | 15 in (30 cm) | cut flowers |
| *Cecropia palmata* | tree | 50 ft (15 m) | large garden tree |
| *Celosia argentea* | annual | 3 ft (1 m) | cut flowers |
| *Celosia spicata* | annual | 24 in (60 cm) | dried flowers |
| *Cerbera manghas* | shrub | 20 ft (6 m) | hedge |
| *Chamaecereus silvestrii* | cactus | 6 in (15 cm) | indoor, balcony, hanging basket, containers |
| *Chamaedorea cataractarum* | palm | 6 ft (1.8 m) | indoor, containers |
| *Chlorophytum comosum* | perennial | 12 in (30 cm) | decorative foliage |
| *Chrysalidocarpus lutescens* | palm | 20 ft (6 m) | ornamental plant, indoor, container |
| *Chrysalidocarpus madagascariensis* | palm | 30 ft (9 m) | ornamental plant |
| *Citrus aurantifolia* | tree | 20 ft (6 m) | fruit, containers |
| *Clerodendrum buchananii* | shrub | 10 ft (3 m) | decorative flowers and foliage |
| *Clerodendrum paniculatum* | shrub | 8 ft (2.4 m) | decorative flowers |
| *Clerodendrum splendens* | shrub | 10 ft (3 m) | decorative flowers |
| *Clerodendrum thomsoniae* | shrub | 10 ft (3 m) | decorative flowers |
| *Clerodendrum ugandense* | shrub | 6 ft (1.8 m) | decorative flowers |
| *Clerodendrum zambeziacum* | shrub | 6 ft (1.8 m) | decorative flowers |
| *Clitoria ternatea* | climber | 12 ft (3.5 m) | decorative flowers |
| *Clivia caulescens* | perennial | 6 ft (1.8 m) | cut flowers |
| *Clivia miniata* | perennial | 18 in (45 cm) | cut flowers |
| *Clusia rosea* | tree | 30 ft (9 m) | decorative flowers |
| *Coccoloba uvifera* | tree | 30 ft (9 m) | fruit, decorative foliage and flowers |
| *Coccothrinax alta* | palm | 30 ft (9 m) | large garden tree |
| *Cochlospermum fraseri* | tree | 30 ft (9 m) | fiber |
| *Cocos nucifera* | palm | 100 ft (30 m) | fruit |
| *Codiaeum variegatum* | shrub | 8 ft (2.4 m) | decorative foliage, hedges |
| *Coelogyne cristata* | orchid | 12 in (30 cm) | cut flowers |
| *Coelogyne pandurata* | orchid | 12 in (30 cm) | cut flowers |
| *Coffea arabica* | shrub | 15 ft (4.5 m) | containers, coffee beans |
| *Colocasia esculenta* | perennial | 8 ft (2.4 m) | edible tubers, ornamental plant |
| *Colocasia gigantea* | perennial | 8 ft (2.4 m) | decorative foliage |
| *Cordia sebestina* | tree | 25 ft (8 m) | ornamental tree, fruit |
| *Cordia wallichii* | tree | 20 ft (6 m) | screen, shelter |
| *Cordyline fruticosa* | shrub | 10 ft (3 m) | containers, patio, indoor |
| *Cordyline stricta* | shrub | 8 ft (2.4 m) | indoor, patio |
| *Corypha taliera* | palm | 30 ft (9 m) | large garden tree |

| Name | Kind | Maximum height | Uses |
|---|---|---|---|
| *Costus speciosus* | perennial | 8 ft (2.4 m) | decorative foliage |
| *Couroupita guianensis* | tree | 40 ft (12 m) | fruit, decorative flowers |
| *Crassula perfoliata* | succulent | 3 ft (1 m) | container, window box |
| *Crassula plegmatoides* | succulent | 6 in (15 cm) | container, window box, decorative flowers |
| *Crassula pruinosa* | succulent | 4 in (10 cm) | containers, decorative flowers |
| *Crateva religiosa* | tree | 20 ft (6 m) | ornamental tree |
| *Crinum asiaticum* | bulb | 4 ft (1.2 m) | ornamental plant, beside ponds |
| *Crinum pedunculatum* | bulb | 4 ft (1.2 m) | ornamental plant |
| *Crossandra pungens* | perennial | 3 ft (1 m) | containers, greenhouse |
| *Ctenanthe oppenheimiana* | perennial | 18 in (45 cm) | decorative foliage, containers |
| *Cuphea ignea* | shrub | 24 in (60 cm) | decorative flowers |
| *Cyathea cooperi* | tree fern | 20 ft (6 m) | large garden plant |
| *Cycas armstrongii* | cycad | 15 ft (4.5 m) | ornamental plant |
| *Cycas revoluta* | cycad | 10 ft (3 m) | landscape subject, courtyard, plaza |
| *Cyperus papyrus* | rush | 8 ft (2.4 m) | ornamental plant, source of papyrus (paper) |
| *Delonix regia* | tree | 40 ft (12 m) | shade, decorative flowers |
| *Dendrobium densiflorum* | orchid | 12 in (30 cm) | cut flowers |
| *Dendrobium formosum* | orchid | 14 in (35 cm) | cut flowers |
| *Dendrobium lawesii* | orchid | 8 in (20 cm) | cut flowers |
| *Dendrobium lindleyi* | orchid | 4 in (10 cm) | cut flowers |
| *Dendrobium rhodosticum* | orchid | 12 in (30 cm) | cut flowers |
| *Dendrobium signatum* | orchid | 10 in (25 cm) | cut flowers |
| *Dendrobium taurinum* | orchid | 4 ft (1.2 m) | cut flowers |
| *Dendrobium*, Yamamoto hybrids | orchid | 19 in (50 cm) | cut flowers |
| *Dendrochilum longiflorum* | orchid | 15 in (40 cm) | cut flowers |
| *Dichorisandra thyrsiflora* | perennial | 8 ft (2.4 m) | decorative flowers |
| *Diffenbachia seguine* | perennial | 10 ft (3 m) | indoor plant |
| *Dillenia indica* | tree | 50 ft (15 m) | shade, decorative foliage, flowers, fruit |
| *Disa* Diores | orchid | 15 in (38 cm) | cut flowers |
| *Disa* Hybrids | orchid | 24 in (60 cm) | cut flowers |
| *Dracaean draco* | tree | 30 ft (9 m) | ornamental tree |
| *Dracaena marginata* | shrub | 20 ft (6 m) | decorative foliage, indoor |
| *Duranta erecta* | tree | 25 ft (8 m) | decorative flowers, hedge |
| *Echinopsis oxygona* | cactus | 6 in (15 cm) | decorative flowers, containers |
| *Eichhornia crassipes* | perennial | 18 in (45 cm) | pond |
| *Elaeis guineensis* | palm | 70 ft (21 m) | palm oil |
| *Encephalartos altensteinii* | cycad | 6 ft (1.8 m) | decorative cones |
| *Encephalartos arenarius* | cycad | 3 ft (1 m) | decorative cones |
| *Epipremnum pinnatum* | climber | 60 ft (18 m) | decorative foliage |
| *Episcia dianthiflora* | perennial | 6 in (15 cm) | containers, decorative flowers |
| *Eranthemum pulchellum* | shrub | 4 ft (1.2 m) | decorative flowers, decorative foliage |
| *Erythrina crista-galli* | tree | 30 ft (9 m) | ornamental tree |
| *Erythrina fusca* | tree | 80 ft (24 m) | ornamental tree |
| *Erythrina haerdii* | tree | 15 ft (4.5 m) | ornamental tree, attracts birds |
| *Erythrina livingstonia* | tree | 80 ft (24 m) | ornamental tree |
| *Erythrina variegata* | tree | 80 ft (24 m) | ornamental tree |
| *Etlingera elatior* | perennial | 20 ft (6 m) | decorative bracts |

| Name | Kind | Maximum height | Uses |
|---|---|---|---|
| *Eucalyptus grandis* | tree | 200 ft (60 m) | decorative flowers, shade |
| *Eucalyptus papuana* | tree | 50 ft (15 m) | moist areas, decorative flowers |
| *Eucalyptus tetraptera* | shrub | 6 ft (1.8 m) | decorative flowers |
| *Euphorbia canariensis* | succulent | 8 ft (2.4 m) | colorful bracts, landscape subject |
| *Euphorbia cooperi* | succulent | 3 ft (1 m) | decorative flowers |
| *Euphorbia knuthii* | succulent | 2 in (5 cm) | container |
| *Euphorbia obesa* | succulent | 8 in (20 cm) | container, rockery |
| *Euphorbia pulcherrima* | shrub | 12 ft (3.5 m) | Christmas decoration, decorative bracts |
| *Euphorbia punicea* | succulent | 18 in (45 cm) | colorful bracts |
| *Euphorbia schimperi* | succulent | 6 ft (1.8 m) | decorative foliage |
| *Euphorbia tirucalli* | succulent | 15 ft (4.5 m) | landscape subject |
| *Euphorbia viguieri* | shrub | 5 ft (1.5 m) | colorful bracts |
| *Fagraea fragrans* | tree | 70 ft (21 m) | ornamental tree, shade |
| *Ficus aspera* 'Parcellii' | tree | 10 ft (3 m) | indoor, decorative foliage |
| *Ficus aurea* | tree | 60 ft (18 m) | shade, ornamental foliage |
| *Ficus benghalensis* | tree | 70 ft (21 m) | shade |
| *Ficus benjamina* | tree | 50 ft (15 m) | indoor, container |
| *Ficus cordata* subsp. *salicifolia* | tree | 10 ft (3 m) | food source for animals |
| *Ficus dammaropsis* | tree | 30 ft (9 m) | decorative foliage |
| *Ficus elastica* | tree | 100 ft (30 m) | shade |
| *Ficus lyrata* | tree | 100 ft (30 m) | shade, indoor |
| *Ficus macrophylla* | tree | 130 ft (39 m) | shade, parks |
| *Ficus opposita* | tree | 30 ft (9 m) | fruit, shade |
| *Ficus pumila* | climber | 25 ft (8 m) | decorative foliage |
| *Ficus religiosa* | tree | 25 ft (8 m) | shade, ornamental foliage |
| *Ficus virens* | tree | 50 ft (15 m) | ornamental tree, shade |
| *Fittonia verschaffeltii* | perennial | 6 in (15 cm) | containers, indoor, conservatory, ground cover |
| *Furcraea selloa* var. *marginata* | succulent | 3 ft (1 m) | rockery, container |
| *Garcinia xanthochymus* | tree | 40 ft (12 m) | fruit, pigment |
| *Gardenia augusta* | shrub | 3 ft (1 m) | cut flowers |
| *Gerbera jamesonii* | perennial | 18 in (45 cm) | cut flowers |
| *Gloriosa superba* | tuber | 8 ft (2.4 m) | decorative flowers |
| *Graptophyllum pictum* | shrub | 5 ft (1.5 m) | indoor, decorative foliage |
| *Guzmania lingulata* | bromeliad | 18 in (45 cm) | decorative bracts, greenhouse |
| *Guzmania* 'Squarrosa' | epiphyte | 3 ft (1 m) | greenhouse |
| *Hakea nitida* | shrub | 8 ft (2.4 m) | informal hedge |
| *Hamelia patens* | shrub | 10 ft (3 m) | decorative flowers |
| *Hedychium coronarium* | perennial | 5 ft (1.5 m) | cut flowers |
| *Hedychium gardnerianum* | perennial | 8 ft (2.4 m) | decorative flowers |
| *Heliamphora heterodoxa* | insectivorous perennial | 15 in (38 cm) | novelty ornamentals, insect control |
| *Heliamphora nutans* | insectivorous perennial | 8 in (20 cm) | novelty ornamentals, insect control |
| *Heliconia bihai* | perennial | 5 ft (1.5 m) | colorful bracts |
| *Heliconia caribaea* | perennial | 8 ft (2.4 m) | colorful bracts |
| *Heliconia collinsiana* | perennial | 12 ft (3.5 m) | colorful bracts |
| *Heliconia psittacorum* | perennial | 5 ft (1.5 m) | colorful bracts, mass planting |
| *Heliconia rostrata* | perennial | 20 ft (6 m) | colorful bracts |
| *Heliconia wagneriana* | perennial | 12 ft (3.5 m) | colorful bracts |

| Name | Kind | Maximum height | Uses |
|---|---|---|---|
| *Hevea brasiliensis* | tree | 120 ft (36 m) | rubber, parks |
| *Hibiscus calyphyllus* | shrub | 6 ft (1.8 m) | decorative flowers |
| *Hibiscus cisplatinus* | shrub | 10 ft (3 m) | decorative flowers |
| *Hibiscus insularis* | shrub | 12 ft (3.5 m) | decorative flowers |
| *Hibiscus mutabilis* | shrub | 12 ft (3.5 m) | decorative flowers |
| *Hibiscus rosa-sinensis* | shrub | 15 ft (4.5 m) | decorative flowers |
| *Hibiscus schizopetalus* | shrub | 12 ft (3.5 m) | decorative flowers |
| *Hibiscus syriacus* | shrub | 12 ft (3.5 m) | decorative flowers |
| *Hibiscus tiliaceus* | tree | 30 ft (9 m) | decorative flowers |
| *Holmskiolda sanguinea* | climber | 8 ft (2.4 m) | decorative flowers, espalier |
| *Hoya carnosa* | climber | 20 ft (6 m) | decorative flowers, containers |
| *Hoya lanceolata* subsp. *bella* | climber | 12 in (30 cm) | decorative flowers, hanging baskets |
| *Hoya santos* x *cumingiana* | climber | 3 ft (1 m) | decorative flowers, containers |
| *Hoya serpens* | climber | 4 ft (1.2 m) | decorative flowers, containers |
| *Hylocereus polyrhizus* | cactus | 8 ft (2.4 m) | decorative flowers |
| *Hymenocallis caribaea* | bulb | 24 in (60 cm) | indoor plant |
| *Impatiens*, New Guinea hybrids | perennial | 18 in (45 cm) | bedding, patio, indoor |
| *Impatiens pseudoviola* | perennial | 6 in (15 cm) | bedding, patio, indoor |
| *Impatiens repens* | perennial | 2 in (5 cm) | hanging basket |
| *Impatiens zombensis* | perennial | 3 ft (1 m) | bedding, containers, patio |
| *Ipomoea alba* | creeper | 20 ft (6 m) | decorative flowers, trellis, bank, covering fences |
| *Ipomoea horsfalliae* | creeper | 10 ft (3 m) | decorative flowers, trellis, bank, covering fences |
| *Ipomoea pes-caprae* | creeper | 133 ft (40 m) | decorative flowers, trellis, bank, covering fences |
| *Ixora chinensis* | shrub | 4 ft (1.2 m) | massed bedding, hedges, screens, containers |
| *Ixora coccinea* | shrub | 3 ft (1 m) | massed bedding, hedges, screens, containers |
| *Ixora javanica* | shrub | 5 ft (1.5 m) | massed bedding, hedges, screens, containers |
| *Jacaranda mimosifolia* | tree | 40 ft (12 m) | ornamental tree, timber |
| *Jasminum nitidum* | climber | 20 ft (6 m) | fragrant, decorative flowers |
| *Jasminum sambac* | climber | 10 ft (3 m) | fragrant, decorative flowers, tea |
| *Jatropha multifida* | shrub | 6 ft (1.8 m) | decorative foliage and flowers |
| *Justicia carnea* | shrub | 5 ft (1.5 m) | containers |
| *Justicia spicigera* | shrub | 6 ft (1.8 m) | hedge, evergreen filler |
| *Kalanchoe blossfeldiana* | succulent | 12 in (30 cm) | decorative flowers |
| *Kalanchoe grandiflora* | succulent | 3 ft (1 m) | dcorative foliage |
| *Kalanchoe pumila* | succulent | 8 in (20 cm) | decorative foliage and flowers |
| *Kalanchoe thyrsifolia* | succulent | 24 in (60 cm) | decorative foliage |
| *Kalanchoe tomentosa* | succulent | 3 ft (1 m) | decorative foliage |
| *Kigelia africana* | tree | 40 ft (12 m) | decorative flowers |
| *Laelia gouldiana* | orchid | 3 ft (1 m) | cut flowers |
| × *Laeliocattleya* Hybrids | orchid | various, depending on cultivar | cut flowers |
| *Lantana camara* | shrub | 6 ft (1.8 m) | ground cover, hedge, ornamental plant |
| *Lagerstroemia speciosa* | tree | 80 ft (24 m) | decorative flowers |
| *Lantana montevidensis* | shrub | 3 ft (1 m) | ground cover, hedge |
| *Licuala spinosa* | palm | 20 ft (6 m) | ornamental plant |
| *Liriope muscari* | perennial | 24 in (60 cm) | ground cover, path edging |
| *Litchi chinensis* | tree | 30 ft (9 m) | fruit |
| *Livistona rotundifolia* | palm | 80 ft (24 m) | large garden tree, landscape subject |

| Name | Kind | Maximum height | Uses |
|---|---|---|---|
| *Livistona saribus* | palm | 80 ft (24 m) | landscape subject |
| *Lodoicea maldivica* | palm | 100 ft (30 m) | fruit |
| *Lonicera hildebrandiana* | climber | 30 ft (9 m) | fragrant, decorative, trellis, walls, covering fences |
| *Lonicera japonica* | climber | 30 ft (9 m) | fragrant, decorative, covering fences, trellis, Chinese medicine |
| *Macadamia tetraphylla* | tree | 40 ft (12 m) | nuts |
| *Macrozamia miquelii* | cycad | 5 ft (1.5 m) | decorative cones |
| *Malpighia coccigera* | shrub | 30 in (75 cm) | decorative foliage, formal hedge |
| *Mandevilla* × *amoena* 'Alice du Pont' | climber | 30 ft (9 m) | decorative flowers, containers |
| *Mandevilla sanderi* | climber | 15 ft (4.5 m) | decorative flowers |
| *Mandevilla splendens* | climber | 10 ft (3 m) | decorative flowers |
| *Mangifera indica* | tree | 80 ft (24 m) | fruit |
| *Maranta leuconeura* | perennial | 12 in (30 cm) | decorative foliage |
| *Megakepasma erythrochlamys* | shrub | 12 in (30 cm) | decorative flowers |
| *Melia azedarach* | tree | 30 ft (9 m) | avenues, attracts birds |
| *Michelia champaca* | tree | 100 ft (30 m) | fragrant flowers |
| *Miltoniopsis* Hybrids | orchid | 12 in (30 cm) | cut flowers |
| *Monstera deliciosa* | climber | 25 ft (8 m) | decorative foliage, fruit |
| *Mucuna bennettii* | climber | ?25 ft (8 m) | decorative flowers |
| *Murraya koenigii* | shrub | 10 ft (3 m) | aromatic foliage |
| *Murraya paniculata* | shrub | 10 ft (3 m) | aromatic foliage and flowers |
| *Musa acuminata* | tree | 20 ft (6 m) | fruit |
| *Musa* × *paradisiaca* | tree | 25 ft (8 m) | fruit |
| *Musa velutina* | perennial | 6 ft (1.8 m) | fruit, decorative flowers |
| *Mussaenda* 'Aurorae' | shrub | 10 ft (3 m) | ornamental plant |
| *Mussaenda erythrophylla* | shrub | 6 ft (1.8 m) | colorful bracts |
| *Mussaenda philippica* | shrub | 14 ft (4 m) | ornamental plant |
| *Neoregelia carolinae* | bromeliad | 19 in (50 cm) | decorative foliage |
| *Neoregelia chlorostica* | bromeliad | 14 in (35 cm) | decorative foliage |
| *Neoregelia concentrica* | bromeliad | 15 in (40 cm) | decorative foliage |
| *Nepenthes* × *coccinea* | climber | 14 ft (4 m) | insect control |
| *Nepenthes maxima* | climber | 6 ft (1.8 m) | insect control |
| *Nepenthes rafflesiana* | climber | 30 ft (9 m) | insect control |
| *Nephrolepis cordifolia* | fern | 3 ft (1 m) | borders, indoor, greenhouse |
| *Nerium oleander* | shrub | 12 ft (3.5 m) | decorative flowers, hedge |
| *Nymphaea gigantea* | aquatic perennial | flat to water's surface | ponds |
| *Nymphaea nouchali* | aquatic perennial | flat to water's surface | perfume, ponds |
| *Nymphaea*, TDH | aquatic perennial | flat to water's surface | ponds |
| *Nymphaea*, TNH | aquatic perennial | flat to water's surface | ponds |
| *Nymphoides indica* | aquatic perennial | flat to water's surface | ponds |
| *Ochna serrulata* | shrub | 8 ft (2.4 m) | decorative flowers and fruit |
| *Ocimum basilicum* | annual | 18 in (45 cm) | aromatic leaves, culinary uses |
| *Odontoglossum crispum* | orchid | 19 in (50 cm) | cut flowers |
| *Odontoglossum* Hybrids | orchid | 19 in (50 cm) | cut flowers |
| *Oncidium varicosum* | orchid | 5 ft (1.5 m) | cut flowers |
| *Ophiopogon japonicus* | perennial | 8 in (20 cm) | ground cover |

| Name | Kind | Maximum height | Uses |
|------|------|----------------|------|
| *O. planiscapus* 'Nigrescens' | perennial | 10 in (25 cm) | decorative foliage |
| *Pachystachys lutea* | perennial | 3 ft (1 m) | indoor, greenhouse |
| *Pandanus odoratissimus* | tree | 20 ft (6 m) | ornamental tree, culinary uses |
| *Paphiopedilum callosum* | orchid | 18 in (45 cm) | cut flowers |
| *Paphiopedilum* Hybrids | orchid | flower stem height is plant height | cut flowers |
| *Paphiopedilum insigne* | orchid | 18 in (45 cm) | cut flowers |
| *Paphiopedilum lawrenceanum* | orchid | 15 in (38 cm) | cut flowers |
| *Paphiopedilum malipoense* | orchid | 12 in (30 cm) | cut flowers |
| *Paphiopedilum rothschildianum* | orchid | 19 in (50 cm) | cut flowers |
| *Paphiopedilum superbiens* | orchid | 12 in (30 cm) | cut flowers |
| *Passiflora coccinea* | climber | 12 ft (3.5 m) | ornamental plant, fruit |
| *Passiflora edulis* | climber | 15 ft (4.5 m) | fruit |
| *Passiflora × exoniensis* | climber | 10 ft (3 m) | decorative flowers |
| *Peltophorum pterocarpum* | tree | 60 ft (18 m) | shade, fragrant flowers |
| *Pentas lanceolata* | shrub | 3 ft (1 m) | decorative flowers |
| *Peperomia argyreia* | perennial | 10 in (25 cm) | terrarium, dish garden |
| *Peperomia caperata* | perennial | 8 in (20 cm) | terrarium, dish garden |
| *Petrea volubis* | creeper | 20 ft (6 m) | decorative flowers |
| *Phalaenopsis amabilis* | orchid | 3 ft (1 m) | cut flowers |
| *Phalaenopsis gigantea* | orchid | 15 in (40 cm) | cut flowers |
| *Phalaenopsis* Hybrids | orchid | various, up to 3 ft (1 m) | cut flowers |
| *Phalaenopsis sanderiana* | orchid | 30 in (75 cm) | cut flowers |
| *Philodendron bipinnatifidum* | shrub | 10 ft (3 m) | decorative foliage |
| *Philodendron erubescens* | climber | 25 ft (8 m) | decorative foliage |
| *Phoenix reclinata* | palm | 30 ft (9 m) | fruit, ornamental plant |
| *Phoenix roebelenii* | palm | 10 ft (3 m) | container, indoor |
| *Phoenix rupicola* | palm | 25 ft (8 m) | greenhouse, large garden tree |
| *Phyllanthus acidus* | tree | 30 ft (9 m) | seaside planting, decorative flowers |
| *Pilea involucrata* | perennial | 12 in (30 cm) | indoor, terrarium |
| *Pilea nummulariifolia* | perennial | 2 in (5 cm) | hanging basket |
| *Piper betle* | climber | 15 ft (4.5 m) | aromatic foliage |
| *Pisonia umbellifera* | tree | 15 ft (4.5 m) | containers |
| *Pistia stratiotes* | perennial | 8 in (20 cm) | ponds |
| *Platycerium superbum* | fern | 6 ft (1.8 m) | landscape subject, fernery |
| *Plumbago indica* | shrub | 3 ft (1 m) | container, decorative flowers |
| *Plumeria obtusa* | tree | 25 ft (8 m) | fragrant flowers |
| *Plumeria rubra* | tree | 25 ft (8 m) | fragrant flowers |
| *Polyalthia longiflora* | tree | 50 ft (15 m) | avenues, parks |
| *Portulaca grandiflora* | annual | 8 in (20 cm) | decorative flowers, rockery, border |
| *Pritchardia pacifica* | palm | 5 ft (1.5 m) | decorative foliage |
| *Pterocarpus robrii* | tree | 30 ft (9 m) | shade |
| *Quisqualis indica* | climber | 70 ft (21 m) | covering fences, walls, pergolas |
| *Ravenala madagascariensis* | tree | 10 ft (3 m) | ornamental tree |
| *Renanthera monachica* | orchid | 3 ft (1 m) | cut flowers |
| *Renanthera storiei* | orchid | 10 ft (3 m) | cut flowers |

| Name | Kind | Maximum height | Uses |
|------|------|----------------|------|
| *Rhapis excelsa* | palm | 15 ft (4.5 m) | container, hedges |
| *Rhododendron aurigeranum* | shrub | 8 ft (2.4 m) | decorative flowers |
| *Rhododendron brookeanum* | shrub | 15 ft (4.5 m) | decorative flowers |
| *Rhododendron jasminiflorum* | shrub | 8 ft (2.4 m) | decorative flowers |
| *Rhododendron javanicum* | shrub | 12 ft (3.5 m) | decorative flowers |
| *Rhododendron laetum* | shrub | 5 ft (1.5 m) | decorative flowers |
| *Rhododendron zoelleri* | shrub | 6 ft (1.8 m) | decorative flowers |
| *Roystonea elata* | palm | 80 ft (24 m) | large garden tree, parks |
| *Roystonea regia* | palm | 100 ft (30 m) | parks, avenues |
| *Russelia equisitiformis* | shrub | 3 ft (1 m) | seaside planting |
| *Salvia tiliifolia* | perennial | 3 ft (1 m) | culinary uses |
| *Salvinia auriculata* | fern | flat to water's surface | ponds |
| *Sanchezia speciosa* | shrub | 8 ft (2.4 m) | decorative flowers |
| *Sansevieria pearsonii* | succulent | 3 ft (1 m) | decorative foliage, hemp |
| *Saraca indica* | tree | 30 ft (9 m) | decorative foliage and flowers |
| *Scaevola crassifolia* | perennial | 3 ft (1 m) | seaside planting |
| *Scaevola taccada* | perennial | 5 ft (1.5 m) | border |
| *Schefflera actinophylla* | tree | 40 ft (12 m) | container, ornamental tree |
| *Schefflera arboricola* | shrub | 15 ft (4.5 m) | indoor, container, decorative foliage |
| *Schinus terebinthifolius* | tree | 30 ft (9 m) | shade, avenues |
| *Senecio arborescens* | tree | 20 ft (6 m) | decorative flowers |
| *Solandra maxima* | climber | 30 ft (9 m) | decorative flowers, seaside planting |
| *Solanum crispum* | climber | 20 ft (6 m) | ornamental plant |
| *Solanum mauritianum* | shrub | 15 ft (4.5 m) | decorative foliage and flowers |
| *Solanum pyracanthum* | perennial | 5 ft (1.5 m) | decorative flowers |
| *Solanum seaforthianum* | creeper | 20 ft (6 m) | decorative flowers |
| *Solanum wendlandii* | creeper | 20 ft (6 m) | decorative flowers |
| *Solenostemon amboinicus* | perennial | 12 in (30 cm) | flavoring herb |
| *Solenostemon scutellarioides* | perennial | 24 in (60 cm) | decorative foliage |
| *Spathiphyllum* 'Mauna Loa' | perennial | 15 in (40 cm) | indoor, decorative flowers |
| *Spathiphyllum* 'Sensation' | perennial | 12 in (30 cm) | indoor, decorative flowers |
| *Spathiphyllum wallisii* | perennial | 12 in (30 cm) | decorative flowers |
| *Spathodea campanulata* | tree | 80 ft (24 m) | ornamental tree, avenues |
| *Strelitzia nicolai* | perennial | 20 ft (6 m) | decorative flowers |
| *Strelitzia reginae* | perennial | 6 ft (1.8 m) | decorative flowers |
| *Stephanotis floribunda* | climber | 10 ft (3 m) | decorative foliage, fragrance |
| *Strongylodon macrobotrys* | climber | 70 ft (21 m) | pergola, arch |
| *Syngonium podophyllum* | climber | 50 ft (15 m) | decorative foliage |
| *Tabebuia chrysantha* | tree | 20 ft (6 m) | shade, decorative foliage and flowers |
| *Tabebuia heterophylla* | tree | 30 ft (9 m) | timber, decorative foliage and flowers |
| *Tabebuia pallida* | tree | 25 ft (8 m) | shade, decorative foliage and flowers |
| *Tabernaemontana divaricata* | shrub | 6 ft (1.8 m) | informal hedge, container |
| *Tacca integrefolia* | perennial | 3 ft (1 m) | decorative flowers |
| *Tamarindus indica* | tree | 70 ft (21 m) | ornamental tree, avenues, culinary uses |
| *Tapeinochilos ananassae* | perennial | 6 ft (1.8 m) | cut flowers, colorful bracts |
| *Tecoma stans* | shrub | 20 ft (6 m) | decorative flowers |
| *Tecomaria capensis* | shrub | 25 ft (8 m) | decorative flowers |

| Name | Kind | Maximum height | Uses |
|------|------|----------------|------|
| *Terminalia brassii* | tree | 30 ft (9 m) | shade, paper pulp |
| *Terminalia catappa* | tree | 60 ft (18 m) | nuts |
| *Thevetia peruviana* | tree | 25 ft (8 m) | decorative flowers |
| *Thevetia thevetioides* | tree | 15 ft (4.5 m) | decorative flowers and fruit |
| *Thunbergia battiscombei* | climber | 10 ft (3 m) | decorative flowers |
| *Thunbergia grandiflora* | climber | 15 ft (4.5 m) | decorative flowers, trellis, fence, pergola |
| *Thunbergia mysorensis* | climber | 20 ft (6 m) | decorative flowers |
| *Thunbergia natalensis* | shrub | 3 ft (1 m) | decorative flowers |
| *Thunbergia togoensis* | shrub | 5 ft (1.5 m) | decorative flowers |
| *Tibouchina clavata* | shrub | 8 ft (2.4 m) | decorative flowers |
| *Tibouchina heteromalla* | shrub | 3 ft (1 m) | decorative flowers |
| *Tibouchina granulosa* | tree | 40 ft (12 m) | decorative flowers |
| *Tibouchina lepidota* | shrub | 12 ft (3.5 m) | decorative flowers |
| *Tillandsia argentea* | bromeliad | 6 in (15 cm) | decorative foliage, flowers |
| *Tillandsia caulescens* | bromeliad | 18 in (45 cm) | decorative foliage and flowers |
| *Tillandsia flabellata* | bromeliad | 15 in (38 cm) | decorative flowers |
| *Tillandsia lindenii* | bromeliad | 24 in (60 cm) | decorative foliage and flowers |
| *Trevesia palmata* | tree | 20 ft (6 m) | ornamental tree |
| *Trichilia emetica* | tree | 30 ft (9 m) | oil used in traditional medicine, fragrant flowers |
| *Tristaniopsis laurina* | tree | 50 ft (15 m) | screen, hedge |
| *Veitchia merrillii* | palm | 20 ft (6 m) | landscape subject, container |
| *Victoria amazonica* | aquatic perennial | flat to water's surface | large ponds |
| *Vriesia carinata* | epiphyte | 10 in (25 cm) | decorative flowers |
| *Vriesia splendens* | bromeliad | 18 in (45 cm) | decorative flowers |
| *Washingtonia robusta* | palm | 80 ft (24 m) | parks, large garden tree |
| *Wedelia trilobata* | perennial | 6 ft (1.8 m) | ground cover, hanging basket |
| *Weinmannia pinnata* | tree | 30 ft (9 m) | shade, decorative foliage, flowers and fruit |
| *Wigandia caracasana* | shrub | 10 ft (3 m) | decorative foliage |
| *Wittrockia superba* | bromeliad | 3 ft (1 m) | oranmental plant |
| *Worsleya rayneri* | bulb | 3 ft (1 m) | decorative flowers |
| *Xanthorrhoea preissii* | perennial | 20 ft (6 m) | landscape subject |
| *Xanthostemon chrysanthus* | tree | 25 ft (8 m) | shade |
| *Yucca elephantipes* | tree | 30 ft (9 m) | ornamental tree |
| *Zamia pumila* | cycad | 3 ft (1 m) | containers, borders |
| *Zingiber zerumbet* | perennial | 6 ft (1.8 m) | decorative foliage, potpourri |

# INDEX